The Prophet Amos

J. Alberto Soggin

THE PROPHET
AMOS

A translation and commentary

SCM PRESS LTD

Translated by John Bowden from the Italian
Il profeta Amos,
published by Paideia Editrice, Brescia 1982,
with additional material supplied by the author.

British Library Cataloguing in Publication Data
Soggin, J. Alberto
The prophet Amos: a translation and commentary
1. Bible. O.T. Amos — commentaries
I. Title
II. Bible. O.T. Amos. *English*. 1987
III. Il profeta Amos. *English*

224'.8077   BS1583
ISBN 0-334-00053-X

First published in English 1987
by SCM Press Ltd
26–30 Tottenham Road, London N1

Phototypeset by the Spartan Press Ltd
and printed in Great Britain by
Redwood Burn Ltd
Trowbridge, Wiltshire

UNIVERSITATI LAVSONIENSI HELVETIORVM
LAVREAM PROPTER COLLATAM
HONORIS SIBI CAVSA
AVCTOR GRATISSIMVS IPSE
VOLVMEN HOC SVVM
DAT DICAT DEDICAT

CONTENTS

CONTENTS

PREFACE

The manuscript of this commentary served as a basis for my lectures at the University of Rome, the Waldensian Faculty of Theology and the Pontifical Biblical Institute before being rearranged, revised, brought up to date, corrected and sent to the publisher. Inevitably it still retains some marks of its original purpose which distinguish it from a work written directly for publication.

A general bibliography appears at the beginning of the book, and further bibliographies appear at the beginning of each chapter; literature is also referred to in the notes. All these bibliographies are select ones. There would in fact be no point in repeating what others have already done or will do again in the context of more ambitious and therefore more complete works. Nor have I thought it necessary to enter into general questions relating to the literature of the Old Testament; the reader should consult my *Introduction to the Old Testament*, SCM Press and Westminster Press 1976, [2]1980, a third edition of which will appear in English in early 1988. That work also contains a chronological synopsis.

The commentary is divided into three: first a translation of the Hebrew text, then a philological-critical commentary which gives the reasons for the choice of the translation, and finally a historical and exegetical commentary. Whereas a philological-critical commentary presupposes at least the rudiments of Greek and Hebrew, the historical and exegetical commentary can be used even by those who do not know these languages. Of course such readers will have to accept the translation I suggest, without being able to follow the way in which it has been arrived at.

I have already translated the book of Amos once, about fifteen years ago, for the commentary by Giorgio Tourn (see the bibliography). The translation which I suggest here differs from that in some points, which is only to be expected.

The text of this English translation, made five years after the completion of the Italian manuscript, has been corrected to take account of printing errors and updated in the light of studies which have appeared in the meantime. I have also taken account of some earlier studies which were not important for the Italian text. In this work I have been helped by the suggestions and corrections of my colleague F. Luciani of the Catholic University of Milan, summarized in *RiBib* 32, 1984, 351–97; also by the review by C. Conroy, *Greg* 66, 1985, 333f. So the text of this English translation can be considered a second revised edition, corrected and updated to the end of 1986.

GENERAL BIBLIOGRAPHY

1. Commentaries (cited in the text with an asterisk)

(a) On the twelve minor prophets

J. Wellhausen, *Die kleinen Propheten mit Noten, Skizzen und Vorarbeiten* V, Berlin ³1898 and reprints

K. Marti, *Das Dodekapropheton*, KHCAT XIII, Tübingen 1904

A. van Hoonacker, *Les douze petits prophètes*, Paris 1907

S. R. Driver, *The Minor Prophets*, CB, London ²1915

W. Nowack, *Die kleinen Propheten*, HKAT III, 4, Göttingen ²1922

G. A. Smith, *The Book of the Twelve Prophets*, London ²1928

E. Sellin, *Das Zwölfprophetenbuch*, KAT XII, 1, Leipzig ²,³1929

J. A. Bewer, *The Prophets*, New York and London 1949 (on all the prophets)

G. Rinaldi, *I profeti minori* (three vols), Turin 1952–68

T. H. Robinson and F. Horst, *Die zwölf kleinen Propheten*, HAT 1,14, Tübingen ²1954

A. Weiser and K. Elliger, *Das Buch der zwölf kleinen Propheten*, ATD 24–25, Göttingen ⁷1974 and ⁶1975

(b) On Amos (and sometimes on others)

W. Harper, *Amos and Hosea*, ICC, Edinburgh 1895

R. S. Cripps, *A Critical and Exegetical Commentary on the Book of Amos*, London ²1955

H. Gressmann, *Amos*, SATA II, 1, Göttingen ²1921, 323–59

H. Guthe, *Der Prophet Amos*, HSAT II, Tübingen ⁴1923

N. H. Snaith, *Amos* (two vols), London 1945–6

H. E. W. Fosbroke, 'The Book of Amos', *IB* VI, Nashville 1956, 761–868

E. Osty, 'Amos-Osée', *BJ*, Paris ²1960

E. Jacob, C. A. Keller, A. Amsler, *Osée, Joël, Amos, Abdias, Jonas*, CAT XIa, Neuchâtel 1965, Geneva ²1982

H. W. Wolff, *Joel and Amos*, Hermeneia, Philadelphia 1977

C. Hauret, *Amos et Osée*, Verbum Salutis-AT 5, Paris 1969

BIBLIOGRAPHY

M. Bič, *Das Buch Amos*, Berlin DDR 1969
J. L. Mays, *Amos*, OTL, London and Philadelphia 1969
E. Hammershaimb, *The Book of Amos*, Oxford 1970
W. Rudolph, *Joel, Amos, Obadja, Jona*, KAT XIII, 2, Gütersloh 1971
G. Tourn, *Amos, profeta della giustizia* (text edited by J. A. Soggin), Turin 1972
K. Koch and collaborators, *Amos*, ATAO 30 (three vols), Neukirchen 1976
R. Martin-Achard, *Amos – L'homme, le message, l'influence*, Geneva 1984
– and S. P. Re'emi, *God's People in Crisis: a Commentary on the Book of Amos and a Commentary on the Book of Lamentations*, ITC, Edinburgh 1984 (which I have been unable to use)

2. Studies and monographs (cited in the text with two asterisks)

E. Balla, *Die Droh- und Scheltworte des Amos*, Leipzig 1926; the work was inserted in an abbreviated, revised and updated form into E. Balla, *Die Botschaft der Propheten*, Tübingen 1958, 73–92
I. P. Seierstad, *Die Offenbarungserlebnisse der Propheten Amos, Hosea und Jeremias*, Oslo 1946
V. Maag, *Text, Wortschatz und Begriffswelt des Buches Amos*, Leiden 1951
R. Hentschke, *Die Stellung der vorexilischen Propheten zum Kultus*, BZAW 75, Berlin 1957
J. D. W. Watts, *Vision and Prophecy in Amos*, Leiden 1958
J. L. Mays, 'Words about the Words of Amos', *Int* 13, 1959, 259–72
J. M. Ward, *Amos and Isaiah*, Nashville 1969
E. Würthwein, 'Amos-Studien', *ZAW* 62, 1950, 16–24
H. Reventlow, *Das Amt des Propheten bei Amos*, FRLANT 80, Göttingen 1962
H. Gese, 'Kleine Beiträge zum Verständnis des Amosbuches', *VT* 12, 1962, 417–38
H.-W. Wolff, *Amos the Prophet*, Philadelphia 1973
W. H. Schmidt, 'Die deuteronomistische Redaktion des Amosbuches', *ZAW* 77, 1965, 168–93
J. Vollmer, *Geschichtliche Rückblicke und Motive in der Prophetie des Amos, Hosea and Jesaja*, BZAW 119, Berlin 1971
S. Wagner, 'Überlegungen zur Beziehung des Propheten Amos zum Sudreich', *TLZ* 96, 1971, 654–70
I. Willi-Plein, *Vorformen der Schriftexegese innerhalb des Alten Testaments*, BZAW 123, Berlin 1971

W. Rudolph, 'Schwierige Amosstellen', in *Wort und Geschichte, FS Karl Elliger*, ATAO 18, Neukirchen 1973, 157–62

W. Berg, *Die sogenannten Hymnenfragmente im Amosbuch*, Berne and Frankfurt am Main 1974

L. Markert, *Struktur und Bezeichnung des Scheltwortes*, BZAW 140, Berlin 1977

K. Koch, *The Prophets*, Vol. 1, London and Philadelphia 1982, 36–75

J. Vermeylen, *Du prophète Isaïe à l'apocalyptique*, Paris I, 1977, II 1978: II, 519–69

W. Schottroff, 'Der Prophet Amos', in W. Schottroff and W. Stegemann, *Der Gott der kleinen Leute*, Munich I, 1979, 33–60

J. L. Sicre, *Los dioses olvidados*, Madrid 1979, 109–16

R. B. Coote, *Amos among the Prophets*, Philadelphia 1981

H. Gese, 'Komposition bei Amos', *SVT* 32, 1981, 74–95

L. Salcman, 'Astronomical Allusions in Amos', *JBL* 100, 1981, 53–8

A. S. van der Woude, 'Three Classical Prophets: Amos, Hosea and Micah', in *Israel's Prophetic Heritage, FS P. R. Ackroyd*, Cambridge 1982, (32–57) 34–43

A. van der Wal, *Amos – A Classified Bibliography*, Amsterdam 1983, [3]1986 – and E. Talstra, *Amos*, Amsterdam 1984

J. Blenkinsopp, *A History of Prophecy in Israel*, London 1984, 86–96

H. M. Barstad, *The Religious Polemics of Amos*, SVT 34, Leiden 1984

I have not been able to use the following works:

H. B. Huffmon, 'The Social Role of Amos' Message', in *The Quest for the Kingdom of God – Studies . . . G. E. Mendenhall*, Winona Lake, Ind. 1983, 109–16

H. Weippert, 'Amos', in H. Weippert, K. Seyboldt and M. Weippert, *Beiträge zur prophetischen Bildsprache*, OBO 64, Freiburg CH 1985, 1–29

H.-J. Zobel, 'Prophet in Israel und in Judah. Das prophetische Verständnis des Hosea und Amos', *ZTK* 82, 1985, 281–99

N. P. Lemche, *Early Israel*, SVT 37, Leiden 1985, 108–12

M. Weiss, *The Bible from Within*, Jerusalem 1986

A. G. Auld, *Amos*, Sheffield 1986

ABBREVIATIONS

'A	Translation of the Old Testament into Greek by Aquila
ABLAK	Aufsätze zur biblischen Landes- und Altertumskunde, Neukirchen (selected works by M. Noth)
AHw	B. Meissner and W. von Soden, Akkadisches Handwörterbuch (three volumes), Wiesbaden 1965–82
AJBI	Annual of the Japanese Biblical Institute, Tokyo
AnBibl	Analecta Biblica, Rome
ANEP	The Ancient Near East in Pictures, ed. J. B. Pritchard, Princeton ³1969
ANET	Ancient Near Eastern Texts, ed. J. B. Pritchard, Princeton ³1969
Antt.	Flavius Josephus, Jewish Antiquities
AO	Der Alte Orient, Leipzig
ASNSP	Annali della Scuola Normale Superiore di Pisa
ASTI	Annual of the Swedish Theological Institute, Jerusalem
ATAO	Altes Testament und Alter Orient, Neukirchen and Kevelaer
ATD	Das Alte Testament Deutsch, Göttingen
ATANT	Abhandlungen zur Theologie des Alten und Neuen Testaments, Zürich
Aug	Augustinianum, Rome
BA	The Biblical Archaeologist, Cambridge, Mass.
BASOR	Bulletin of the American Schools of Oriental Research, Cambridge, Mass.
BBB	Bonner Biblische Beiträge, Bonn
BDB	A Hebrew and English Lexicon of the Old Testament, ed. F. Brown, S. R. Driver and C. A. Briggs, Oxford 1907
BeO	Bibbia e Oriente, Genoa and Milan
BHH	Biblisch-historisches Handwörterbuch, Göttingen
BHK³	Biblia Hebraica, ed R. Kittel, Stuttgart ³1947
BHS	Biblia Hebraica Stuttgartensia, edd. K. Elliger and W. Rudolph, Stuttgart 1977 = BHK⁴
Bibl	Biblica, Rome

BiblOr	Biblica et Orientalia, Rome
BJ	*La S. Bible de Jérusalem,* Jerusalem and Paris
BJRL	*Bulletin of the John Rylands Library,* Manchester
BK	Biblischer Kommentar, Neukirchen
BL	*Bibel-Lexikon,* ed. A. v. d. Born, Einsiedeln [2]1968
BN	*Biblische Notizen,* Bamberg
BRL	*Biblisches Reallexikon,* Tübingen [2]1977
Brockelmann	C. Brockelmann, *Hebräische Syntax,* Neukirchen 1956
BWANT	Beiträge zur Wissenschaft vom Alten und Neuen Testament, Stuttgart
BZ	*Biblische Zeitschrift,* Paderborn
BZAW	Beihefte to *ZAW*
CAT	Commentaire de l'Ancien Testament, Neuchâtel
CB	The Cambridge Bible, London
CB-OTS	Coniectanea Biblica, Old Testament Series, Lund
CBQ	*Catholic Biblical Quarterly,* Washington DC
CCSL	Corpus Christianorum Series Latina
coord.	Coordinates on the 1:100,000 map by the Survey of Israel, 1975
CTA	A. Herdner, *Corpus des tablets en cunéiforme alphabétique découvertes à Ras Shamra-Ugarit de 1929 à 1939,* Paris 1963
Dtr	Deuteronomistic (History Work)
ErIs	*Ereṣ Iśrā'ēl,* Jerusalem
EstBibl	Estudios Biblicos, Madrid
ÉthR	*Études théologiques et religieuses,* Montpellier
EvTh	*Evangelische Theologie,* Munich
EVV	English Versions
ExpT	*The Expository Times,* Edinburgh
FRLANT	Forschungen zur Religion und Literatur vom Alten und Neuen Testament, Göttingen
FS	Festschrift
GA	Gesammelte Aufsätze
GesK	*Gesenius' Hebrew Grammar as edited and enlarged by the late E. Kautzsch,* second English edition by A. E. Cowley, Oxford 1910
Greg	*Gregorianum*
GS	Gesammelte Studien
HAT	Handbuch zum Alten Testament, Tübingen
HKAT	Handkommentar zum Alten Testament, Göttingen
Hen	*Henoch,* Turin
HSAT	Die Heilige Schrift des Alten Testaments, ed. E. Kautzsch and A. Bertholet, Tübingen

HTR	*Harvard Theological Review*, Cambridge, Mass.
HUCA	*Hebrew Union College Annual*, Cincinnati
IB	*The Interpreter's Bible*, New York and Nashville 1954
ICC	The International Critical Commentary, Edinburgh
IEJ	*Israel Exploration Journal*, Jerusalem
Int	*Interpretation*, Richmond, Va
ITC	International Theological Commentary, Edinburgh and Grand Rapids
JAOS	*Journal of the American Oriental Society*, New Haven, Conn.
JBL	*Journal of Biblical Literature*, New Haven, Conn.
JNES	*Journal of Near Eastern Studies*, Chicago
Joüon	P. Joüon, *Grammaire de l'Hébreu biblique*, Rome 1923
JPOS	*Journal of the Palestine Oriental Society*, Jerusalem (ended in 1948)
JSS	*Journal of Semitic Studies*, Manchester
JTS	*Journal of Theological Studies*, Oxford
KAI	*Kanaanäische und Aramäische Inschriften*, ed. H. Donner and W. Röllig, Wiesbaden ²1966–70
KAT	Kommentar zum Alten Testament, first series Leipzig; second series Gütersloh
KB	L. Köhler and W. Baumgartner, *Lexicon*, Leiden 1953, ³1967
KgAO	Kulturgeschichte des alten Orients, Munich
KHCAT	Kurzer Handcommentar zum Alten Testament, Tübingen
KS	Kleine Schriften
KuD	*Kerygma und Dogma*, Gütersloh
LXX	Translation of the Hebrew Bible into Greek, the so-called Septuagint
Meyer	R. Meyer, *Hebräische Grammatik*, Berlin I ³1966, II ²1969, III ²1972, IV ²1972
MT	Massoretic text
OA	*Oriens Antiquus*, Rome
OBO	Orbis Biblicus et Orientalis, Freiburg
OTL	Old Testament Library, London and Philadelphia
OTS	*Oudtestamentische Studien*, Leiden
OTW	M. Noth, *The Old Testament World*, Philadelphia and London 1966
OTWSA	OT Werkgemeenschap in Suid Afrika
PL	J. P. Migne, *Patrologia Latina*
RA	*Revue d'Assyriologie*, Paris
RB	*Revue Biblique*, Jerusalem and Paris
RGG	*Die Religion in Geschichte und Gegenwart*, Tübingen

ABBREVIATIONS

RHR	*Revue d'histoire des religions*, Paris
RiBib	*Rivista Biblica*
SATA	Die Schriften des Alten Testaments in Auswahl, Göttingen
SBFLA	*Studii Biblici Franciscani Liber Annuus*, Jerusalem
SBL.MS	Society of Biblical Literature, Monograph Series, New Haven, Conn.
SBT	Studies in Biblical Theology, London
SNVA	Skrifter utgift av Det Norske Videnskaps-Akademi, Oslo
SOTS.MS	The Society for Old Testament Study. Monograph Series, Cambridge
SSAW	Sitzungsberichte der Sachsichen Akademie der Wissenschaften, Berlin
STU	*Schweizerische Theologische Umschau*, Zurich and Berne
Syr	Syriac translation of the Old Testament (Peshitto)
SVT	Supplements to Vetus Testamentum
TDNT	English translation of *TWNT*, Grand Rapids, Mich.
TDOT	English translation of *TWAT*, Grand Rapids, Mich.
Tg	Targum, Aramaic translation of the Old Testament
TGI	K. Galling, *Textbuch zur Geschichte Israels*, Tübingen ²1968
TGUOS	*Transactions of the Glasgow University Oriental Society*
THAT	*Theologisches Handwörterbuch zum Alten Testament*, Munich 1971–6
TLZ	*Theologische Literaturzeitung*, Leipzig
TWAT	*Theologisches Wörterbuch zum Alten Testament*, Stuttgart 1973ff.
TWNT	*Theologisches Wörterbuch zum Neuen Testament*, Stuttgart 1933–1979
TZ	*Theologische Zeitschrift*, Basel
UF	*Ugaritforschungen*, Münster im Westfalen
UT	C. H. Gordon, *Ugaritic Textbook*, Rome 1965
Vg	Vulgate, Latin translation of the Old Testament
WMANT	Wissenschaftliche Monographien zum Alten und Neuen Testament, Neukirchen
WuD	*Wort und Dienst*, Bethel-Bielefeld
WUS	J. Aistleitner, *Wörterbuch der ugaritischen Sprache*, Berlin DDR 1963 and reprints
ZAW	*Zeitschrift für die alttestamentliche Wissenschaft*, Giessen then Berlin
ZDPV	*Zeitschrift des deutschen Palästinavereins*, Wiesbaden
Zorell	F. Zorell, *Lexicon Hebraicum et Aramaicum Veteris Testamenti*, Rome 1968

ZTK	*Zeitschrift für Theologie und Kirche*, Tübingen
Σ	Translation of the Old Testament into Greek by Symmachus
Θ	Translation of the Old Testament into Greek by Theodotion

COMMENTARY

INTRODUCTION

1. Amos and his time

J. A. Soggin, *A History of Israel*, London 1984 and Philadelphia 1985, IX.4.5–5.1, 217–19.

The book mentions Jeroboam II, king of Israel (*c.*786–46 or 787–47 BC: 1.1 and 7.10–11; cf. also 7.9) and his contemporary Uzziah, king of Judah (*c.* 783–42 or 787–36, also called Azariah: 1.1). The latter was replaced by his son Jotham (*c.*750–35 or 756–41) when he contracted leprosy after reigning for about thirty years. Jotham acted as regent until Uzziah's death (cf. II Kings 15.1–6, 32–38//II Chron. 26.1ff.). The superscription of Hosea 1.1 also in fact mentions Jotham. But since his name does not appear in the book of Amos it is probable that the last period of Uzziah's reign and therefore also that of Jeroboam need not be taken into account for the chronology of the prophet.

In the book of Amos we find some references to contemporary events which are not always easy to evaluate. We may set aside 6.1ff., according to some scholars a recollection of the occupation of Jerusalem by Joash, king of Israel and father of Jeroboam II (*c.*801–786 or 802–787: II Kings 14.13–14//II Chron. 25.17–24): this is in fact an improbable explanation of a text which poses a very diverse set of problems (cf. ad loc.). In 1.3ff., however, there is an indication of Aramaean occupation of the territory of Gilead in Transjordan, along with atrocities inflicted on the civil population, and there is an analogous note in 1.13, where similar atrocities are said to have been committed by the Ammonites, also in a war against Israel aimed at recapturing their own territory. 1.3ff. mentions Hazael and Ben/Bar Hadad (III or IV, depending on the numeration adopted), kings of Damascus. In 6.13–14 we have an apparent reference, accompanied by a play on words (cf. ad loc), to the reconquest of the region by Jeroboam II (cf. II Kings 14.25–28). With this operation Israel succeeded in establishing in Transjordan a frontier very close to the traditional frontier of the Davidic empire in the first half of the tenth century BC, as

1

is made quite clear in 6.14: 'from the "Gate of Hamath" to the "River of the *ᵃrābāh*"'. II Kings 14.28 provides us with more information here: Jeroboam II is said to have succeeded even in occupying Damascus itself. However, the text is corrupt and the information suspect. At all events, Amos mentions the reconquest of Transjordan,[1] but makes no reference to the conquest of Damascus.

The successes of Jeroboam II are set, with the limitations that we shall see shortly, in the context of increasing pressure from the Assyrians on the Aramaeans from the second half of the ninth century BC onwards. The effects of these pressures could still be felt during the first half of the eighth century. They continued although the Assyrian troops, victors in the military sphere as a result of the battle of Qarqar on the Orontes in 853 BC against a coalition made up of Aramaean rulers and Ahab of Israel (*c*.869–50 or 871–52; this is the Ahab against whom the prophets Elijah and Elisha struggled),[2] did not succeed in gaining any political advantage from their victory. The pressures reached a climax when Adad Nirari III of Assyria (*c*.810–783) occupied Damascus in the fifth year of his reign, i.e. towards 806 BC.[3] It was as a result of this campaign that the Aramaean state came to be wiped off the geographical map. During the reign of this ruler the Aramaean powers were thus reduced to virtually nothing, allowing the revival of Israel.[4]

However, on the death of Adad Nirari III the Assyrian empire was attacked from the north by the kingdom of Urartu (present-day Armenia) and its army was largely immobilized on the northern frontier. The pressure on Damascus thus ceased almost completely and the Aramaeans were able to recover. It is in fact possible that they went over to the attack and drove off the Assyrians between the first and second quarter of the eighth century, rather than being attacked, as is so

---

[1]Y. Aharoni, *The Land of the Bible*, London 1967, 313; M. Haran, 'The Rise and Decline of the Empire of Jeroboam ben Joash', *VT* 17, 1967, 266–97; J. A. Soggin, 'Amos VI: 13– 14 und 1:3 auf dem Hintergrund der Beziehungen zwischen Israel und Damaskus im 9. und 8. Jahrhundert', in *Near Eastern Studies in Honor of W. F. Albright*, Baltimore 1971, 433–41. See also the important study by G. Garbini, 'L'impero di David', *ASNSP* III, 13, 1983, 1–20; Garbini would prefer to date to this period the majority of the historically valid traditions on the empire of David and Solomon. For other details see my *History*, ad loc.

[2]Cf. *ANET*, 278b–279a, and *TGI*, 49ff. Ben/Har Hadad II appears there as *hadad 'idri*, which in Hebrew and Aramaic would be *hadad 'ezer*.

[3]*ANET*, 281; TGI, 53ff. For a history of this period see W. W. Hallo, 'From Qarqar to Carchemish', *BA* 23, 1960, 34–61.

[4]Cf. R. de Vaux, 'La chronologie de Hazaël et de Benhadad III, rois de Damas', *RB* 43, 1934, 512–18 = *Bible et Orient*, Paris 1967, 75–82; A. Dupont-Sommer, *Les Araméens*, Paris 1949, chs. III–IV; M. F. Unger, *Israel and the Aramaeans of Damascus*, London 1957, chs. V–IX; B. Mazar, 'The Aramaean Empire and its Relations to Israel', *BA* 25, 1962, 98–120. Cf. also recently K. N. Schoville, 'The Sins of Aram in Amos', in *Proceedings of the Sixth World Congress of Jewish Studies . . . Jerusalem 1973*, Jerusalem 1977, I, 363–75.

often said.[5] The Aramaean recovery succeeded in freeing the country from the Assyrians, a development which also brought about a notable economic revival in the area, now that it was freed from the burden of paying tribute to the Assyrians; that is, if this is how we are to interpret the abundance of cheap agricultural produce described in the damaged beginning of the inscription of Panammuwa I, king of Sam'al, from the first half of the eighth century BC.[6]

So the information given in Amos 1.3 probably belongs in the context of the Aramaean revival during the first half of the eighth century; it seems that the Aramaeans, freed from Assyrian pressure, invaded the Transjordan territory of Israel (Gilead) during the course of the second quarter of the century, committing the atrocities which are referred to. It is on this episode that the invective against Damascus and its rulers, past and present, is based: Hazael (c.841–06) ascended the throne following a plot in which according to II Kings 8.7 the prophet Elisha will have played an active part, and Ben/Bar Hadad III or IV (from 806 or 797 to c.773, the dates are uncertain) are both mentioned several times in the Old Testament and on the stele of Zakir (or perhaps better Zakkur, on the basis of the Assyrian transcriptions of the name), king of Hamath, from the second half of the eighth century BC.[7] The invective does not spare the capital Damascus, which is mentioned with varied and picturesque epithets in vv.4–5 (cf. ad loc.).

After a long period of relative tranquillity, then, on the northern and eastern frontiers of Israel there reappeared the spectre of the Aramaean wars which had blighted the first part of the ninth century BC (II Kings 10.32ff.). The recapture of central and southern Transjordan by the Ammonites, which is mentioned in Amos 1.13 with expressions resembling those in 1.3, seems probable in this context, even if we cannot know whether the Ammonites did this as it were in their own right or as allies of Damascus.

The victories mentioned in Amos 6.13–14 can therefore be explained as the result of an Israelite counter-attack on the occupying forces from Damascus and any possible allies. Now, since the occupation of the region by Damascus must be put in the first years of the reign of Jeroboam II, when Ben/Bar Hadad III or IV (with whom Amos 1.3 explicitly connects the matter) had need of a strategically sound southern frontier, the Israelite reconquest must have taken place in a

[5]E.g. in K. Galling, 'Damaskus', *RGG*[3] 2, 1958, 22ff.

[6]Cf. *KAI*, 214. For this reason J. L. Mays** 1959, 269, can also speak of a 'flourishing, prosperous and confident upper class' in Israel.

[7]Cf.*ANET*, 501f. For the details of what is presented in the biblical texts as a double *coup d'état*, in Israel and Damascus, see my *History*, IX.3.6 and 4.1, 210ff., 215ff.

later period of the reign of Jeroboam, under a successor of Ben/Bar Hadad whose name we do not know: however, he is certainly prior to that Rezin of uncertain chronology who reigned over Damascus during the period of the so-called 'Syro-Ephraimite' war of 734, a few years before the final fall of Damascus in 732. So it is only reasonable to put the ministry of Amos towards 760, with a *terminus ad quem* of 750 BC (Amsler*).

It is not easy, necessary or even useful in these circumstances to maintain the historicity of the note according to which Jeroboam II succeeded in taking possession of Damascus as well. First of all we must separate this from the campaign of the reconquest of Transjordan, mentioned above, as is in fact done in II Kings 14.28. It might just be put in the first years of Jeroboam, when Ben/Har Hadad was preparing for his anti-Assyrian reconquests and concentrating his forces in the north east to that end. In fact we could conjecture that Jeroboam profited from the temporary stripping of the southern frontiers of Damascus to launch his attack on the capital, and that it was as a reaction to this campaign that Ben/Bar Hadad had planned the occupation of northern Transjordan to safeguard his security in this vital region. But this incursion (because in any case that is all it can have been) remains no more than a conjecture, which any scholar can easily challenge. It is certain that the effects of the expedition against Damascus must have been very scanty to the degree that we do not find any hint of them elsewhere.[8]

So to sum up, we have the following certain or at least probable chronology:

853: Battle of Qarqar;
841: Jehu pays tribute;
806: Occupation of Damascus by Adad Nirari III;
796: Joash pays tribute;
783: Death of Adad Nirari III and the beginning of the pressure on Assyria from Urartu.

Soon after that, at a date we cannot determine, there will have been an Aramaean attack on northern Transjordan, held by Israel, and an occupation of it, followed by an attack by the Ammonites on central and southern Transjordan;
c.760 Israelite reconquest of Transjordan.

[8]For these problems see S. Cohen, 'The Political Background of the Words of Amos', *HUCA* 36, 1965, 153–60; L. M. Muntingh, 'Political and International Relations of Israel's Neighbouring Peoples according to the Oracles of Amos', in A. H. van Zyl (ed.), *Studies in the Books of Hosea and Amos*, Pretoria 1965, 134–42; J. García Trapiello, 'Situación histórica del profeta Amos', *EstBibl* 26, 1967, 247–74.

II Kings 14.28 speaks of the occupation of Damascus by Jeroboam II, probably at the beginning of his reign, i.e. around the end of the first quarter of the reign, but as we have seen, the note seems problematical.

However, the superscription, Amos 1.1, offers another date, which is clear in itself: the mention of the 'earthquake', two years before which Amos is said to have exercised his ministry in the North. The phenomenon, the epicentre of which must have been in the immediate vicinity of Jerusalem, will certainly have been quite remarkable if some centuries afterwards it could be used to describe the pangs of the last days (Zech. 14.4f.). According to the Hebrew text of this last passage, the earthquake will have produced the small valley which now divides Mount Scopus from Mount of Olives; LXX, supported by Flavius Josephus (*Antt.* 9.222–7) also mentions a great movement of earth on the Western slope of the Mount of Olives, obstructing the Kedron valley beneath. Not all the details of the description are clear, but it is sufficient illustration of the gravity of the phenomenon, which today we would rate as being of the greatest intensity on the various scales (Mercalli or Richter), serious enough to modify the topography of the region affected.[9] Flavius Josephus connects the earthquake with an act of impiety committed by Uzziah, king of Judah, in the temple of Jerusalem, which would have been seriously damaged by the earthquake, as a result of which the king is said to have been afflicted with leprosy, thus necessitating the regency of his son Jotham. So for Josephus the earthquake coincided with Uzziah's illness. Both therefore fall around 750, by the American School's dating, or 759, by that of Begrich-Jepsen.[10]

Moreover, the excavations carried out on the ruins of Hazor in Upper Galilee have provided features allowing an approximate dating of the earthquake, among the discoveries in area A, stratum VI, during the 1956 campaign.[11] This place is some distance from the epicentre of the earthquake, and that explains the diminished effects. Many walls also collapsed here, and in the view of the archaeologists, the event falls towards the end of phase VI of the place, and the corresponding phases of Megiddo and Samaria, even if those involved do not speak explicitly

[9]Cf. F. -M. Abel, *Géographie de la Palestine* I, Paris 1933; A. van den Born, *BL*[2]1968, 408.
[10]For this problem see my 'Das Erdbeben von Amos 1, 1 und die Chronologie der Könige Ussia und Jotham von Judah', *ZAW* 62, 1970, 117–21; bibliographical details can also be found there.
[11]Cf. Y. Yadin (ed.), *Hazor II*, Jerusalem 1960, 24f., 36; id., 'Ancient Judaean Weights and the Date of the Samaria Ostraka', *Scripta Hierosolymitana* 8, 1961, 9–25; 24 n. 73. Y. Yadin, *The World History of the Jewish People*, Vol. IV, 2, Jerusalem and London 1979, 193, has recently clinched the connection between the Hazor earthquake and that of Amos 1.1.

of an earthquake. The end of Hazor VI is usually dated between 765 and 760, more towards the end of the period.[12]

So it would seem reasonable to argue for a dating 'around 760' (Rudolph*).

2. Amos as an individual

In considering the personality of Amos, I would want to leave out of account any romantic, sentimental or even popular evaluation, of the kind which is sometimes offered in church circles. I am thinking of past comments like that of O. Procksch: 'Solitude with the flock made his soul meditative and solemn . . .', or E. Balla**, 35: 'What he observed in the countryside, he observed with the eyes of a shepherd who kept alive the best traditions of the time of Moses'; even now É. Osty*, 10, can write: 'The poor and invigorating life of the desert left a profound mark on Amos's soul', while C. Stuhlmueller calls Amos 'a prophet formed in the desert', where 'the bare realities of life' not only inculcated 'the great truths' into him but made him become a 'God-seeker'.[13] These are features which do not appear in any part of the book and in any case would be irrelevant, even if they could be verified.

We have in 7.10–17 a passage on the life of Amos which is important not only for evaluating his person but also because texts of this kind are very rare. It is a prose passage, the work of a third person who seems to have been well informed. In it the prophet gives some details which describe his past life. We shall be looking at the passage in more detail in the commentary (125ff.); for the moment we can derive some information from it, albeit only provisionally.

Verse 14 contains the reply of Amos to the priest who has forbidden him to continue to preach at Bethel and has asked him to leave the region and go to earn his living in his homeland. There is no verb in the sentence and its exact chronological significance can only be determined from the context. For a series of reasons this has ended up as a *crux interpretum*. A further contributory factor towards this has been that so far we have no comprehensive study of the verbless sentence in

[12]Cf. Y. Aharoni and R. Amiran, 'A New Scheme for the Sub-Divisions of the Iron Age in Palestine', *IEJ* 8, 1957, (171–84) 178ff., 183, partially corrected by the Yadin 1961 article mentioned in the previous note.
[13]O. Procksch, *Geschichtsbetrachtung und geschichtliche Überlieferung bei den vorexilischen Propheten*, Leipzig 1902, 63 (unavailable to me; quoted from Rudolph): E. Osty* and C. Stuhlmueller, 'Amos Desert-Trained Prophet', *The Bible Today*, 1962–63, 224ff.; a contrast to this kind of presentation could be found earlier in J. L. Mays** 1959, who stresses the irrelevance of the personal element, and R. Scharbert, *Il profeta contadino*, insert 16 of the popular magazine *Jesus* 3, 1981, no. 4, April, 502–5.

biblical Hebrew and how to determine tenses in it.[14] Moreover, one of the main reasons why this passage has become a *crux* is that it has become involved as a proof text in a discussion of a historical ideological kind, namely, as to whether or not Amos was a *nābī'*, the Hebrew word for prophet: a term understood here in a derogatory sense, as referring to a person who earns his living by a prophetic ministry. At the least, it is used in a consideration of what his attitude may have been towards the *nᵉbī'īm*. This may be an important problem, but it presupposes a distinction between prophet and *nᵉbī'īm* which cannot be demonstrated on either the semantic or the sociological level, and in any case its solution must not be combined with the discussion of a syntactical and grammatical problem on which it cannot, and therefore should not, have any bearing.

Until we come to the discussion of the text in question, it should be enough to point out that in Hebrew a verbless sentence followed by a sentence including a verb indicates the situation existing either at the time of the action expressed by the verbal clause in question or prior to it.[15] So in this case Amos's reply indicates simply (and solely) the occupation that he was (or was not) engaged in at the time of his calling, without any reference to his occupation at the time of his encounter with the priest. So it seems that we should translate the passage: 'I *was not* a prophet nor did I belong to a school of prophets, but YHWH seized me . . .'; LXX also has this temporal syntax, though Jerome already took the opposite view: *Non sum* . . . Nor is there any point in arguing that a verbless sentence is to be translated as present, so long as another tense is not explicitly indicated by the verb 'to be' (in this case we should then have *lo' hayītī* . . .), since an assertion of this kind does not prove anything. A passage often cited as support for this theory, Ex. 6.2–3, proves nothing, since the phrase 'I am YHWH, I have seen' belongs to the literary genre of 'self-manifestation',[16] and the diversity of the literary genre makes the apparent identity of the two syntactical constructions problematical from the start.

---

[14]The only monograph on the theme is limited to the Pentateuch, cf. F. I. Andersen, *The Hebrew Verbless Clause in the Pentateuch*, JBL MS XIV, Nashville and New York 1970, and this text is not mentioned in it.

[15]D. Michel, *Tempora und Satzstellung in den Psalmen*, Bonn 1960, 184 § 29a. By contrast, R. R. Wilson, *Prophecy and Society in Ancient Israel*, Philadelphia 1980, 289, is among those favouring a rendering in the present. For other information cf. on 7.10ff.

[16]Cf. the authoritative statements by O. Eissfeldt, *The Old Testament: An Introduction*, ET Oxford 1965, § 51.1; G. Fohrer (E. Sellin), *Introduction to the Old Testament*, ET London and Nashville 1968, 431ff.; also S. Cohen, 'Amos was a Navi', *HUCA* 43, 1961, 175–8. For the oracle of self-presentation see W. Zimmerli, 'The Word of Divine Self-manifestation (Proof-Saying): A Prophetic Genre', in *I am Yahweh*, ed. Walter Brueggemann, Atlanta 1982, 99–110 and the bibliography there.

Moreover Amos himself, again in his reply (v.15), tells the priest that he has been sent 'to prophesy' (root *nb'*), whereas the priest addresses him with the title 'seer'; furthermore throughout the book the verb *nb'* and the noun *nābī'* (the verb six times, the noun four times) never have negative connotations. So we can accept that before he was called Amos did not exercise the prophetic ministry nor did he belong to a prophetic school; in other words, he did not possess the qualifications which were normally required for exercising the profession that he exercised in the sanctuary of Bethel.

The difficulties which I have just indicated (largely, as we have seen, artificial) suggested to some scholars at the beginning of the century that Amos had ulterior motives, that he may have been something like a spy who was using his preaching with its marked theological content as a cloak for subversion. According to H. Winckler and E. Schrader,[17] two Assyriologists, Amos will have been for Ahaz (sic!) of Judah what Elisha was for Jehu of Israel. However, these theories can easily be refuted, though we have to note that the very nature of the prophetic ministry could lead someone who exercised it faithfully to positions of opposition or even to break with the policies of his ruler, either at home or abroad. There is sufficient evidence of this in the examples of Isaiah and especially of Jeremiah, as they are presented by biblical tradition.

We have no idea how old Amos was at the beginning of his ministry or how long that ministry lasted; nor do we have any information about the dates of his birth and death. Phrases thought to be 'rash', of the kind that we find in 4.1; 5.5; 6.12, have suggested to Wolff*, 90, that Amos must have been relatively young, but we have no certain knowledge in that respect. As to the duration of his ministry, it seems improbable that he made only one brief and fleeting appearance at Bethel; his words have been handed down in a fragmentary fashion, but seem fairly complex. Moreover 3.9; 4.1; 6.1 seem to suppose a good knowledge of what was happening in Samaria, while 4.4; 5.5 suggest that he must have had good knowledge of certain cultic practices in the sanctuaries. The malfunctioning of justice also seems to have been well known to Amos. These are features which suggest that he had a relatively long stay in Israel. It is certainly possible that he already travelled or had lived in the North before his calling, or that this was information in the public domain. On the other hand, there is nothing to suggest that his ministry continued after the earthquake, so that the two years before it,

---

[17]This theory was once put forward by E. Winckler, *Geschichte Israels in Einzeldarstellungen* 1, Leipzig 1894, 91, cf. E. Schrader, *Die Keilinschriften und das Alte Testament*, Berlin 1903, 267. J. Hempel, *Politische Absicht und Wirkung in biblischen Schrifttum*, AO 38.1, 1939, 28ff. produced valid arguments against it.

to which the beginning of his ministry is dated, would seem to be a *terminus ante quem.*

Again according to 1.1 Amos was a Judahite who came from Tekoa, a place located south-east of Jerusalem (coord. 170–115), and therefore already in the dry area. That Amos came from Judah is also implicitly presupposed by 7.12, where the priest of Bethel asks the prophet to return to Judah. But of these two passages the first comes from the redactor and the second, as we have seen, is the work of a third person. So we should not exclude *a priori* the possibility that the Judaean or perhaps even the Deuteronomistic redaction made Amos come from Judah with the intention of making him the standard-bearer of the legitimate cult of the Jerusalem temple and possibly of the reunion of the two kingdoms under the sovereignty and religious supremacy of the South, a theme dear to the Deuteronomistic writers and their successors.[18] (For another Tekoa in Galilee see the notes on the text.) However, Amos carried on his ministry only in Israel, and there is nothing to suggest that he continued it in the South, after he had been driven away.

The profession exercised by Amos before being called to the prophetic ministry is also a matter of controversy, as we shall see when we look at 1.1 and 7.14 in more detail. The latter text uses the term *bōqēr* and the expression *bōlēs šiqmīm*. The former in the participial form is a *hapax legomenon*, but at all events it refers to some activity connected with rearing cattle; this is the sense attached to it in the Vulgate and the minor Greek translations.[19] However, in v. 15 the prophet also claims that he was called by God 'from following the flock', where the text has *ṣō'n*, a term used exclusively for flocks of sheep or goats, never for cattle. And according to 1.1, Amos came from the *nōqᵉdīm* of Tekoa, a title

[18]On this last theme see G. H. Davies, 'Amos, the Prophet of Reunion', *ExpT* 92, 1980–81, 196–201, even if his presuppositions and conclusions differ. If the theory, to which I can only refer here in passing for lack of sound material, proved defensible, we would have a phenomenon similar to that which has recently been examined in the case of Jeremiah; see the first chapters of R. P. Carroll, *From Chaos to Covenant*, London 1981. For the revision in the South see H. Gottlieb, 'Amos und Jerusalem', *VT* 17, 1967, 430–63.

[19]M. Bič, 'Der Prophet Amos – ein Haepatoskop', *VT* 1, 1951, 293–6, cf. Bič*, ad loc., tried to explain the term as indicating that Amos will have been a cultic diviner. He bases his theory on the meaning that the root has in Ugaritic, where it appears in connection with an official working in the sphere of the temple, *WUS*, 1840; *UT*, 1694. But even in this context it is possible to think of a person employed for looking after either the animals belonging to the temple, or animals set aside for sacrifices. Moreover, for a prophet to function as a diviner, and for this to be said in such explicit terms, would be something unique in the Hebrew Bible. Against this theory cf. also A. Murtonen, 'The Prophet Amos – A Hepatoscoper?' *VT* 2, 1952, 170f.; H. J. Stoebe, 'Der Prophet Amos und sein bürgerlicher Beruf', *WuD* 5, 1957, 160–81.

which II Kings 3.4 gives to Mesha king of Moab, who is presented as a cattle-breeder on a large scale. The second expression in 7.14, which Jerome translated *vellicans sycomoros*, refers to a process applied to fruits of the plant in question so that it can serve as food and cattle fodder.[20]

The problem of the profession carried on by Amos before his calling (and hence of his economic and social status) therefore seems quite complex. We can sum up the various solutions put forward under the following four headings:

(*a*) Amos was a shepherd or watched over someone else's flocks and herds: during the dry season he used sycamore fruit to feed his animals and perhaps also himself (cf. G. Rinaldi*: '. . . someone who gathered sycamore fruit'); this was evidently extra work for him. So he worked for others, and was badly paid.[21] Amos will therefore have belonged to one of the poorest and most exploited classes, that of the manual labourers, which came into being in Israel, also, following the dissolution of the traditional tribal structures (and with it of the usufruct of land and flocks under common ownership) and the rise of a landholding class, tied to the royal palace and the city, on the existing model of the Syrian and Palestinian city states. In that case the invective of Amos against the abuses of the rich would simply have been an expression of his solidarity with the poor and dispossessed, a solidarity which was part of his own personal experience in that he too was exploited and oppressed. It is not surprising that this kind of theory has been welcomed in recent times by 'progressive' Jews and Christians. However, it is not the only possible explanation, nor even the most probable one.

(*b*) Alternatively, Amos will have bred cattle and flocks, and in addition have owned sycamores which served as fodder during the dry season. In that case he would seem to have been well-to-do, with his own, albeit modest, income,[22] and would have been a member of the so-called *'am hā'āreṣ*, an expression which before the exile denoted a quite specific social class. These were the people who had succeeded in

[20]Jerome, *PL* 25, 1077; G. Dalman, *Arbeit und Sitte in Palästina* I, 1, Gütersloh 1928, 61–3; and J. J. Glück, 'Three Notes on Amos', in A. H. van Zyl, op. cit. (n. 8), 119. Moreover the expression was already obscure in antiquity: *Σ* and Tg make Amos an owner of sycamore trees, cf. Talmud bNed. 38a, which makes the prophets, including Amos, well-to-do figures.'A has the same translation as Vg. Although conventionally translated 'sycamore', this tree (and its fruit) is different from the British sycamore, evidently bearing some kind of fig.

[21]Thus J. Feliks, 'Maulbeerfeigenbaum', *BHH* 2, 1964, 1177.

[22]Cf. H. Frehen, 'Maulbeerfeigenbaum', *BL* [2]1968, 1114; H. -W. Wolff*, 107f.; the *Introductions* of Eissfeldt, § 51.1 and Fohrer, 431; Schottroff** 1979, 41. Finally the recent noteworthy work by Wilson (n. 15), 266–70, who describes Amos as 'a member of the upper classes of Judah, even if he was not in reality a member of the political or religious establishment'!

maintaining the old tribal structures in Israel and in Judah, who sat in the tribal assembly and had usufruct of the land belonging to the tribes by rotation.[23] This is therefore a very different meaning from that indicated by the term in late Judaism or even in modern Hebrew. This group seems to have been faithful to the Davidic dynasty in the South and stands out for its Yahwistic orthodoxy.

(c) A third possibility is that suggested by H. Cazelles.[24] Amos will have been 'an official' in the service of king Uzziah of Judah who according to II Chron. 26.10 'had large quantities of animals' and embarked on many works of various kinds. 'His attack on Jeroboam and his dynasty in the vicinity of Bethel could mean that he had an unsuspected relationship with the beginnings of the political activity of Tiglath-pileser III in Syria, which would explain the alliance between Judah and Assyria against Damascus and Ephraim . . .' But the text cited, in addition to being late and very general, does not mention the prophet anywhere, so it does not seem capable of establishing a feature which does not appear in the book at any point.

(d) A fourth possibility which has recently been put forward[25] is that the whole speech should be considered rhetorical and therefore fictitious: in fact it would be merely a literary theme, as in the narratives about David (II Sam. 7.8; cf. I Sam. 16.11), intended to legitimate a ministry by means of a direct divine vocation. That would also explain the, as it were, technical difficulty that Amos is said to have bred cattle and smaller animals at the same time, a form of activity for which there is no evidence in the region.

However, 7.10ff., which stress the economic independence of the prophet in his own country, would seem to tilt the scales decisively in favour of the second of the solutions put forward here, even if the fourth one has much in its favour. Amos is presented as a person with a sound

---

[23]For this social class cf. J. L. McKenzie, 'The "People of the Land"', in *Akten des 24. Internationalen Orientalistenkongresses . . . 1957*, Wiesbaden 1959, 206–8; my 'Der judäische *'am hā'āres* und das Königtum in Juda', *VT* 13, 1963, 187–95; R. de Vaux, 'Le sens de l'expression "people du pays" dans l'Ancien Testament et le rôle politique du peuple d'Israël', *RA* 58, 1963, 167–72; S. Talmon, 'The Judaean *'am hā'āres* in Historical Perspective', in *Proceedings of the Fourth World Congress of Jewish Studies . . . 1965*, 1, Jerusalem 1967, 71–6; Ihromi, 'Die Königinmutter und der *'amm ha'arez* (sic!) im Reich Juda', *VT* 24, 1974, 421–9; T. Ishida, 'The "People of the Land" and the Political Crises in Judah', *AJBI* 1, 1975, 23–38; and finally H. Cazelles, *Le Messie de la Bible*, Paris 1978, 110 n. 3 (122).

[24]H. Cazelles, 'Mari et l'Ancien Testament', in *XVe Rencontre assyriologique international . . . 1966*, Paris 1967, (73–90) 90.

[25]Cf. H. Schult, 'Amos 7.15 und die Legitimation des Aussenseiters', in *Probleme biblischer Theologie – FS G. von Rad zum 70. Geburtstag*, Munich 1971, 462–89; cf. again in a similar direction, but undecided, R. P. Carroll, *From Chaos to Covenant*, 42ff.

11

economic standing, independent of third parties, with his own sources of income, and probably well integrated into the traditional tribal structures. An increasingly broad consensus is forming among scholars to this effect, to such a degree that there are those who would prefer to see Amos as a well-to-do person or even a member of the religious or political ruling class in Judah. Nor is there any information which would suggest that, as Jerome affirmed, Amos was a person inexperienced in speaking, if not uneducated (*imperitus sermone, sed non scientia*); the great commentator was perhaps judging by the canons of Western rhetoric in his time. Far less does Amos seem to have been a person with little learning: he knows too much about the cult, the practical functioning of justice, immorality, and the social structure in general along with its power relationships, for such suspicions to apply.

Finally, out of curiosity I would draw attention to two other features. First, according to some scholars Amos would seem to have been a contemporary of Hesiod, who was also a 'pastor' and inspired by the Muses (H. Gressmann*, cf. *Theogony*, 22f.; *Works and Days*, 658ff). However, nothing came of the pastoral activity of the ancient Greek poet: on the contrary, he seems to have become a shepherd after having first been a sailor, and the inspiration of the Muses related to poetry and music, not prophecy.[26] Secondly, Amos is said to have lacked the human warmth necessary for establishing relations on a personal level, in fact he would have had no personal piety (cf. W. Harper*, 1905, CIX, and G. A. Smith*, ²1928, 81). This accusation is claimed already to have been directed against him by his contemporaries, so that he combated it with his visions, two of them with intercessions, and his lament in 5.1ff. These are curiosities because not only do they relate to features which cannot possibly be demonstrated, but are also hardly relevant to the study of the prophet.

3. Literary genres and stylistic characteristics

All the commentaries since the Second World War discuss in one way or another the literary genres utilized by the book of Amos. However, the only ones which discuss the complex material in a complete and satisfying way are H. W. -Wolff*, 91ff., and Coote*, ch. 1, 'The Stages'. In most cases I shall be following Wolff's treatment of the material.

Despite the relative brevity of the work, a great many literary genres are represented in it; however, according to Wolff*'s analysis they can be reduced to three main ones among the roughly two dozen sections

[26]Cf. A. Lesky, *A History of Greek Literature* I, London 1966, 131ff.

whose authenticity seems reasonably certain: the 'messenger formula', the 'testimony' and the reports of the visions Amos received.

(*a*) The 'messenger formula' (German *Botenformel, Botenspruch* or *Botenrede*) stands out because it leaves little or no freedom to the messenger to give his own form to the message he bears: he is in fact also bound to the form of the text he has received, which he must transmit in its original form. The genre derives from the diplomatic correspondence of the Ancient Near East: in it the envoy communicated his message verbally, directly to the recipient, by reciting the text. When the message had been received, the text was often deposited in the temple, where the archive was. These procedures are attested in the Mesopotamian city-state of Mari (eighteenth to seventeenth centuries BC), in the Syrian city-state of Ugarit (second half of the second millennium BC), and also in the Old Testament (cf. II Kings 19.10–19).[27] The prophet, too, is sent by YHWH who speaks through him in the first person; thus he has the awareness of being the bearer of a message which is not his own, but which is endorsed by the authority of the one who sends him. So the presence of the first person, when it is a feature to be referred not to the prophet but to God, is a reasonably sure criterion for distinguishing this literary genre, even if it is not always present. At all events it is often qualified by formulae like *kōh 'āmar YHWH*, 'thus YHWH has said/says' (about eleven times).

In this context we must now examine a particular literary genre, that of the oracles against the nations, represented in 1.3–2.16. This is a variant of the 'messenger formula'. In it God pronounces the oracle, the prophet transmits it and its object is each time a different people, including Judah and Israel. There was a thorough examination of the genre at the beginning of the 1950s by A. Bentzen,[28] who sought to connect it with the Egyptian 'execration' texts. In these the name or the country of an enemy ruler was written on a jug or a pot which was then broken, clearly a symbolic magical action meant to produce the destruction of the person or nation thus specified. Obviously Bentzen did not think in terms of a derivation, however indirect, of this literary

[27]For details see my *Introduction*, 59ff.; C. Westermann, *Basic Forms of Prophetic Speech*; ET Nashville 1968, *passim*; R. Rendtorff, 'Botenformel und Botenspruch', *ZAW* 74, 1962, 165–77 = GS, Munich 1975, 243–66; L. Markert**, § 7ff.; H. Gese** 1984; also R. R. Wilson, op. cit. (n. 15), 141–6, which is also valuable for its important material on ethnology and ancient and modern history of religion relating to the prophets.

[28]G. Posener, *Princes d'Asie et de Nubie*, Brussels 1940, cf. *ANET*, 328. Thus A. Bentzen, 'The Ritual Background of Amos I 2 – II 16', *OTS* 8, 1950, 85–99; G. Fohrer, 'Prophetie und Magie', *ZAW* 78, 1966, (25–47) = *Studien zur alttestamentlichen Prophetie*, BZAW 99, Berlin 1967, (242–64): 40/257ff.; M. Haran, 'Rise and Decline' (n. 1), 272–8; J. Barton, *Amos' Oracles against the Nations*, SOTS.MS 6, Cambridge 1980.

genre from the Egyptian practice in question, but rather of an example which shed light on its basis, its background. On the other hand none of our oracles suggests any connection with practices of this sort or rituals of this nature. That is all the more relevant since such practices appear to be known and are explicitly mentioned in the Old Testament: in Jer. 19.1–11a the prophet, who is also the author of numerous oracles against the nations, acquires a pot from a potter and breaks it before witnesses after explaining that the act refers to imminent divine judgment. And following this action, the intent and implications of which are manifest to all, Jeremiah is arrested and imprisoned (20.1–6)! So the Old Testament knows practices like those attested in the execration texts, but there is no specific mention of them in the oracles against the nations, in Amos and elsewhere.

Another interesting theory is one recently put forward by Barton to explain the condemnation of atrocities which appears in some of these oracles: he thinks that at that time there must already have been something like an international code of war to which all belligerents had to subscribe.

Another expression which qualifies a text as being a message from the deity is the formula n^e'um YHWH, 'word' or 'oracle of YHWH', a verbless sentence more solemn than the previous ones with verbs in them.[29] On the other hand it does not seem possible to trace this phrase back to the prophet himself; it would seem to be the work of the redactors. One of its variants is 'āmar YHWH, 'YHWH says' or 'has said', which appears about five times. Both appear at the end of the phrase they describe in this way. The phrase appears once with Amos as subject in 7.10ff., in the message sent to Jeroboam II from Amaziah priest of Bethel, this time obviously without YHWH as subject: 'Amos says this . . .'

The oath formula nisba' YHWH b^e-X, 'YHWH has sworn by . . .' is also possible: it often serves to reinforce preceding formulae (cf. 4.2 and 8.7, cf. also 6.8). We also have the formula of the town-crier: sim^e'u . . , 'hear!'; this is also often, though not necessarily, used to introduce this genre. According to Wolff*, about twenty passages are presented as 'messenger formulae', half of them with this formula at the beginning.

(b) In Amos the 'testimony' (German Zeugenrede) is distinguished from the previous genre, not always clearly, by the liberty which is left to the prophet to formulate the content of his own message. Often the divine sender is no longer mentioned, or there may possibly be an indirect reference to him in the third person. This is a less frequent genre

[29]Cf. Baumgärtel, 'Die Formel n^e'um jahwe', ZAW 73, 1961, 227–90.

than the first one, so it is less easy to describe. It, too, can begin with the call 'Hearken!' (cf. 3.1; 4.1; 5.1). Sometimes there can be a certain interval between the beginning of the discourse and the oracle proper. It can also begin with a rhetorical question (in the sense that a reply does not seem to be expected), the aim of which is to put the hearer into a relationship of cause and effect with the imminent divine announcement. 3.3–8 is typical; it is apparently a discussion with someone who denies that the prophet is a spokesman of YHWH (cf. 5.20). The fictitious funeral lament, with its note of bitter irony, also belongs to this genre (cf. 5.18–20; 6.1, 3–6).

(c) The report of visions received appears in 7.1–8 or 9; 8.1–2; 9.1–4. This is a genre which comes closer to autobiographical narrative than the two previous ones. It is possible that it was originally intended for more intimate circles of disciples, a problem with which we shall be concerned in §5c.

(d) Among the stylistic characteristics I would mention the progressive numerical formula, well attested in Ugaritic[30] as well as in Hebrew. It is typical of Wisdom literature, but with an important difference: in Amos the numerical formulae are purely rhetorical in the sense that punishments are not listed in a quantity corresponding to the number first mentioned. In Amos these formulae are limited to the oracles against the nations.[31] We have further verbless sentences with a participle (5.18; 6.1–3, 6, 8, 14); antitheses (2.13; 5.4f. and 24); and word-plays (5.5b; 8.1–2). Finally, the recent study by H. Gese[32] has brought out the quinary character of the majority of the compositions in the book, a form also well attested elsewhere in the Hebrew Bible. This is an unequivocal sign of a redactional process.

4. Composition

The majority of the book of Amos can easily be classified under the category 'threat' and 'announcement of judgment', the German *Drohwort* and *Gerichtswort*. The threat is often accompanied by features giving reasons for the measures announced, the aim of which is to establish a causal link between transgression and punishment. These reasons are of a historical, ethical or theological kind: the one does not exclude the other. One typical feature is the construction 'al . . . 'because of . . .' with the infinitive, while the announcement itself

---

[30]CTA 17, 2.26–46, translation in C. H. Gordon, *Ugaritic Literature*, Rome 1949, 87f.
[31]For the problem in the Old Testament cf. G. Sauer, *Die Sprüche Agars*, BWANT 84, Stuttgart 1963, ch. IV.
[32]H. Gese, 'Komposition bei Amos', *SVT* 32, 1981, 74–95.

appears in the consecutive perfect. We also have the construction with *hinnēh*, 'Lo', and the participle, especially in the oracles against the nations. In 5.11 we find *ya'an*, 'since', which introduces the motivations, while the announcement proper is introduced by *lākēn*, 'therefore', cf. 3.11. The formula *'al kēn*, 'so', is similar.

Only twice do we find a genuine 'taunt' (German *Scheltwort*): in 4.4f. we have a text which adopts the tone of priestly teaching, but followed by its opposite, with harsh irony. The first words in fact make the demand correctly: 'Go . . , sacrifice . . , offer . . , proclaim . . .', while the second part shows the intention that the prophet attributes polemically to those who submit to the practices in question: 'Sin . . , sin again . . .', concluding with the manifestly provocative argument that the faithful perform these cultic acts not for the love of God but for love of themselves. Another case is 6.12: 'Do horses run on the rock? Does one plough the sea with oxen? (emended text). But you have turned the law into poison – the fruit of justice into bitterness.' Here again we have elements drawn from wisdom teaching, but used by the prophet to serve his own proclamation. The classical study on the 'taunt' is that by E. Balla**, 1926; for the second passage only see the study by L. Markert**, 1977.

Finally, we have an independent announcement of imminent judgment in which the recipient appears in the third person: 5.1ff.

5. The origins of the book

Despite its relatively small size, Amos is quite a complex work. This complexity is clearly evident from its use of different literary genres, the variety of themes treated and the imagery used, the alternation of comments in the first and the third person, and the presence (as we shall see shortly) of revisions which are either Deuteronomistic or similarly late, and are clearly intended to provide the key for reading the whole work. At any event it does not seem possible to date the completion of the work before the Babylonian exile, i.e. before the beginning of the second half of the sixth century.

The process of the formation of the book evidently began with the preaching of the prophet Amos himself, even if it is difficult, if not impossible, to recover the *ipsissima verba* of the prophet. Nor, I think, can we claim, as G. Rinaldi*, 127f., would like to, that the fall of the kingdom of Israel around 722–720 is a *terminus ante quem* for the formation of the book, on the basis of the observation that there is no mention of this in Amos: see 3.11; 5.5; 7.9, 11, which evidently affirm the contrary. However, we can recognize three earlier strata, in all probability going back to the work of the prophet himself and his disciples: the 'Words of Amos of Tekoa', the autobiographical accounts of the visions and finally the earliest texts from the school of Amos.

(*a*) The 'Words of Amos of Tekoa' are so called because of the superscription in 1.1 without the relative clause (cf. ad loc.), and to distinguish them from the various forms of the 'messenger formula' as being 'testimonies'. However, since we are dealing with a very fragmentary and often corrupt text, it is not always easy to interpret them and the authenticity of each individual passage needs to be examined according to its merits.

(*b*) The autobiographical accounts of the visions appear in the passages which we have already examined (above, §3c). Only the last one presents some problems, for which see on 9.1ff.

(*c*) For the oracles against the nations, some of which are authentic and others clearly Deuteronomistic, cf. below, section (*f*).

(*d*) According to A. Weiser* and H.-W. Wolff*, the earliest school of Amos appears in the second relative clause of 1.1 which does not use the verb *rā'āh*, 'see', as do the other reports of the visions, but *hāzāh*, 'have a vision', cf. the title with which the priest of Bethel addresses Amos, *hōzēh*, 'seer' (7.10ff.). However, it should be noted that in 1.1 the subject is the *dibrē 'āmōs*, 'the words of Amos', and that a different idiomatic expression may go with a different subject. Moreover the second relative clause can only be inserted into the text with difficulty. One of the significant difficulties at this point seems to be that the book does not allude in any way to the existence of a prophetic school with Amos as its head, even if there are those who think that the formulation of 7.10–17 in the third person could be evidence for the existence of eye-witness testimony. However, the antiquity of the passage seems to be supported by the fact that it also reports an oracle of Amos against Jeroboam in v. 11a, a prophecy which was not fulfilled, so that v. 9 had to be amplified at a secondary stage perhaps by the school (or even by the Deuteronomist) to cover the 'dynasty of Jeroboam'. And in fact Jeroboam's successor Zechariah was indeed assassinated, by Shallum (II Kings 14.29; 15.20).

(*e*) According to Wolff* the detailed mention of the altars of Bethel in 3.14b (cf. 5.5b; 9.1–4) goes back to the time of Josiah's reform, and therefore probably to an earlier Deuteronomistic reaction: the destruction of the sanctuary of Bethel by Josiah seems to have been of considerable interest to the Deuteronomistic historian; he refers to it explicitly in I Kings 13.1–3, a passage which recalls Amos 9.1ff. and in II Kings 23.15ff.

(*f*) Material from the Deuteronomistic redaction appears where intrinsically old texts of Amos were adapted to a re-reading in the exilic period. For a detailed examination see the study by W. H. Schmidt**,

17

1965, and J. Vermeylen**, II, 1978, 519–69. These include (perhaps) a mention of Tyre in 1.9–10; that of Edom (or perhaps Aram? cf. ad loc.) in 1.11f.; especially that of Judah in 2.4–5, which transforms transgressions against humanity into sins of a theological kind; the theme of the exodus in 2.10; the theme of prophetic inspiration with a problem similar to that of Deut. 18.19ff. in 3.7; and perhaps also, according to Schmidt**, the mention of the kings in 1.1.

(g) According to Wolff*, 9.11–15, the passage with a messianic flavour, in which we find a straight quotation of 5.11b in order to modify it, is post-exilic. There are many reasons for putting it so late: the judgment announced is here mitigated, something which has no parallel in Amos; the mention of the 'unsteady booth of David' seems to suggest a time after 587/6. A recent important study by F. Foresti considers the three hymnic sections 4.13; 5.8f.; 9.5f. ('participial passages') post-exilic for very interesting reasons.[33] At the relevant point we shall consider the details after examining the texts.

(h) Wisdom-type material is found every now and then in the text of Amos and some scholars conclude from its presence[34] that the prophet, or at least the redactors of the book, must have been influenced by Israelite wisdom. That possibility should not be excluded, but in the present state of research this material has not been studied enough for conclusions of this dimension to be based on it.

6. Amos's thought

On the basis of what I have just said about the authentic, redactional and inauthentic material in the book, that going back to the prophet or his school and the later material, we should now be in a position to examine the thought of the prophet, or rather, of the book which bears his name.

(a) In his function as a messenger of YHWH, the prophet was aware of being the herald of the one who had sent him. YHWH is always presented as subject and therefore as the one who holds the threads of the skein in his hands. He is clearly not defined in systematic categories, either theological or philosophical. However, anthropomorphism, such a characteristic feature of the theological language of the Old Testament, is rarely used in Amos (1.8; 9.4, 8). Moreover, polemic against paganism and syncretism, which is an important feature of the message

[33]F. Foresti, 'Funzione semantica dei brani participiali di Amos: 4, 13; 5, 8; 9, 5s.', *Bibl* 62, 1981, 168–84.

[34]For this problem see J. L. Crenshaw, *Old Testament Wisdom: An Introduction*, Atlanta and London 1981, 40f., esp. n. 21 (and the comprehensive bibliography).

of his younger contemporary Hosea, also appears very rarely (so rarely that many scholars doubt its existence; cf. 8.14. 5.26 is Deuteronomistic). In fact YHWH is also responsible for the other peoples, as is already indicated by the oracles against the nations (Wolff*, 102f.).[35] However, the sanctuaries of the northern kingdom are condemned *en bloc*. Bethel, probably the principal scene of the proclamation of Amos, was restored by Jeroboam I immediately after the schism between Israel and Judah (I Kings 12–13); Gilgal, an ancient sanctuary, goes back, traditionally, to the time of the crossing of the Jordan (Josh. 3–4), and Saul, the first king of Israel, was crowned there (I Sam. 11; cf. Amos 4.4ff.; 5.4ff.). The insertion of Beersheba is probably a Judahite gloss; in 8.14 Dan also appears in a similar context, and in 1.2 we find the mention, outside any context, of a hymn which links YHWH with Zion – there are, however, problems about how this is related to the book of Amos.[36] These are features which must have sounded extremely polemical to the ears of anyone living in the North, whereas the prophet proclaims them as though they were a matter of course. At all events, an absolute form of monotheism seems to be presupposed in Amos's preaching.

As we have seen, the prophet was very much aware of his own vocation and mission; the legitimacy of his own ministry was based on it: in 3.8 (v. 7 is, as we have seen, Deuteronomistic) he indicates the irresistibility of the divine calling; in the third-person account in 7.15 he says that YHWH has 'seized him' (verb *laqah*); in describing the visions that he has received he makes quite clear the authoritative character of the message that he is passing on, and in two of them he also appears as an intercessor, as a mediator between God and the people. However, it is the consequence rather than the origin of his role that is his main concern: the message that he has to deliver to the people (7.3,6,8; 8.2; 9.4). Moreover this is a perfect match to the literary genre which is represented most in the book, the 'messenger formula'. Phenomena of this kind are not unknown in the history of religions: the case of Mohammed would be a characteristic example.

The novelty of Amos's message consists in the fact that he essentially announces divine judgment on the people, seeming to be unaware of the possibility of a religious reform, notwithstanding the rather earlier example of Elijah and Elisha, whose movement, according to the texts,

[35]G. Pfeifer, 'Die Denkform des Propheten Amos (III 9–11)', *VT* 34, 1984, 276–81, stresses the forward perspective and the global horizon of the prophecy of Amos.

[36]So it is difficult to talk of Amos either in terms of purely cultic prophecy, as the Scandinavian school used to, or as a prophet intrinsically hostile to the cult, cf. A. S. van der Woude** 1982, and on the whole problem, recently H. M. Barstad** 1984.

directly gave rise to a military rebellion, immediately followed by a religious reform. But as Hosea was to say shortly afterwards (1.4), this development was judged severely in other prophetic circles, so that nothing of this kind is said in Amos. In Amos the existing situation, whether in the state or in the cult, is attacked from the roots up, and the result is the announcement of judgment: the people, incapable as it is of realizing in its midst structures which correspond to its vocation, is now doomed to destruction.[37] This could, however, be a statement *post eventum*, i.e. during or after the exile.

(*b*) However, Amos feels the need to give reasons for his position and to that end makes a diagnosis of the state of the nation. Israel's present can be summed up in the phrase which appears in 3.10a: 'They are incapable of acting with justice . . .', a taunt which is directed essentially against the rich, but which basically seems to have some reference to everyone. The terms *ṣĕdāqāh*, 'justice', and *mišpaṭ*, 'law', recur often throughout the book; in Israel these are trampled on, first of all in the courts, where they should triumph (5.7,24; 6.12 and elsewhere). Thus the theme of the corruption of justice seems to be one of the *Leitmotive* of the book. It is possible, though not necessary, 'that these are references to the ethics which prevailed during the ancient tribal structure of the people, which was then destroyed in favour of new forms of life associated with the monarchy, that came to be consolidated during the Aramaean wars in the ninth century. The prophet does not confine himself to general statements, but makes specific ones: honest judgment, true evidence which holds nothing back, and honest people are objects of hatred and persecution (5.10); the poor and the weak are no longer safeguarded by the law (2.7a; 5.12); because of the excessive rates of interest the poor can be sold like slaves for the smallest debts (2.6b). However, because of the absence of adequate evidence about the economy, it does not seem easy to make an analysis of the social situation, which some authors have been able to compare with that of the rise of capitalism (H. W. Wolff*, 104: *Frühkapitalismus*). The prophet tries to establish causes for the effects, turning to the life-style of the leading classes. It is distinguished by unbridled and vulgar riches (3.12b,15; 5.11a; 6.8–11), by unlimited feasts and pleasures (4.1; 6.4–6), usually at the expense of the poor. He mentions categories of the poor which are not always easy to distinguish on the semantic and sociological level: *'ebyōnīm*, 'poor'; *dallīm*, 'humble'; and *'anīyīm*, 'oppressed'; always assuming that such a distinction existed and that

---

[37]For the predominantly negative character of the message of Amos and the way in which it casts doubt on the structures of his society at a religious, political and social level cf. R. Smend, 'Das Nein des Amos', *EvTh* 23, 1963, 404–23.

the terms are not synonymous. Often these people, when they were innocent or at any rate had right on their side, were completely at the mercy of the powerful and their judgments, even in the law courts (2.7–8; 4.1b; 5.11); the powerful felt themselves completely secure (6.1.3, 13). Moreover the situation cannot have been much better in the South, if we read the invective formulated slightly later by Isaiah and Micah, and the reference in the ostrakon of Yabneh-Yam,[38] even if, as I have said, it is probable that the tribal structures were maintained for a longer period, perhaps up to the exile.

(c) Now the problem which the prophet was soon to face was the approval that such a situation seemed to receive from theology and the official cult, which went on its way without uttering any words of condemnation, or even of criticism. But the prophet discovers that the official cult is only a façade, behind which in fact there is very little: the faithful no longer seek God (5.4ff.) but what pleases them (4.5b). In fact the regularity of the cult, the zeal shown in it (the prophet notes with consternation that the faithful tend to do too much rather than not enough), formed elements of only apparent order in the real disorder which surrounded it. On the other hand the prophet, only making paradoxical affirmations, does not proclaim the need for the cult to be abolished: that would have been the first and only time in the history of ancient religions that a man of God had made a proposal of this kind.

[38]*KAI* 200, cf. my *Introduction*, 479f.; also L. Randellini, 'Ricchi e poveri nel libro del profeta Amos', *SBFLA* 2, 1951–52, 5–46; H.-J. Kraus, 'Die prophetische Botschaft gegen das soziale Unrecht Israels', *EvTh* 15, 1955, 295–307 = *Biblische-theologische Aufsätze*, Neukirchen 1972, 120–33; H. Donner, 'Die soziale Botschaft der Propheten im Lichte der Gesellschaftsordnung in Israel', *OA* 3, 1963, 229–45; G. Pettinato, 'Is. 2, 7 e il culto del Sole in Giuda nel sec. VIII a.C', *OA* 4, 1965, 1–30; K. Koch, 'Die Entstehung der sozialen Kritik bei den Propheten', in *Probleme biblischer Theologie*, FS *Gerhard von Rad*, Munich 1971, 236–57; G. Wanke, 'Zu Grundlagen und Absicht prophetischer Sozialkritik', *KuD* 18, 1972, 2–17; G. Fohrer, *Theologische Grundstrukturen des Alten Testaments*, Berlin 1972, 237ff.; M. Fendler, 'Zur Sozialethik des Amos', *EvTh* 33, 1973, 32–53; O. Loretz, 'Die prophetische Kritik des Rentenkapitalismus', *UF* 1975, 271–8; S. Holm-Nielsen, 'Die Sozialkritik der Propheten', in *Denkender Glaube*. FS *K. H. Ratschow*, Berlin 1976, 7–23; J. Ebach, 'Sozialethische Erwägungen zum alttestamentlichen Bodenrecht', *BN* 1, 1976, 31–46; M. Schwantes, *Das Recht der Armen*, Frankfurt 1977, 87–99 and *passim*; K. Koch**, 44–50; J.-L. Vesco, 'Amos de Teqoa, défenseur de l'homme', *RB* 87, 1980, 481–513. In any case we know very little about the economy of Israelite Palestine, and in the present state of research it is almost impossible to remedy our ignorance; we would have to discover archives in temples and palaces from which we could obtain the necessary information on the tithes and on the other offerings in kind or in coin. For a comparison with the rural economy of Ugarit, albeit on the basis of information from about half a millennium earlier and from a location much further north, see the basic study by M. Heltzer, *The Rural Community in Ancient Ugarit*, Wiesbaden 1976, passim. It should be noted that the only economic texts we have for Israel are the Samaria ostraca from the second half of the eighth century BC, *KAI*, 183–8; *ANET*, 321.

The people legitimates its own existence by means of the concept of divine election (3.2a; 9.7). But while accepting these premises, the prophet cannot accept the conclusions that the people seems to want to draw from them, that of being a privileged people. No, election means giving account continuously to the God who produces the election: and the exodus from Egypt on which the people based all its confession of faith comes almost to be demoted to being one of the many migrations of peoples, of which the history of the ancient Near East was full. If the people had drawn any conclusions at all, they should have drawn negative ones: they had not fulfilled the duties to which they were committed; the evident privileges which they had received were not matched by achievements which justified these favours. We find a very similar position in the New Testament, cf. the dialogue between Jesus and the disciples in Luke 12.48b.

So the prophet can only be very pessimistic about the future of Israel: the time of salvation is over and that of tribulation, of judgment is beginning. Only a funeral elegy can be intoned over the 'virgin Israel' (5.1ff.). The catastrophe is described with earthquake imagery (9.1ff.; perhaps this is the earthquake indicated in 1.1; cf. 2.13, a passage the text of which is difficult, but which is probably to be understood in this way). However, war imagery can also be used (3.11; 6.14; 7.17), a war which must end in defeat (5.3), with the death of the king (7.11) and the deportation of the survivors, their leaders at the head (6.7) along with their wives (4.2f.). The great sanctuaries will also be devastated (5.5, 27). Many will die in the country (5.2f.,16; 6.9; 7.17; 8.3; 9.10). Other peoples will be settled on the land where the deportees once lived (7.17). It is true that in a passage like 5.4f. Amos exhorts the people to 'seek YHWH' if they want to live, but this is the only possible alternative, and the prophet now does not seem to be very convinced of its practicability. Even a remnant, the salvation of whom the prophet sometimes seems to foresee, seems threatened (4.2b; 6.10; 9.10b), while the lament in 5.1ff. is for the whole people.

It is understandable that in such a negative and pessimistic context the few oracles of salvation have been looked on with suspicion as the product of later re-reading, made at a time when the judgment had already been given: on the North in 722–20, on the South in 597/86 and 587/86. Only the awareness that judgment had come, that the debt had been paid (cf. the beginning of Deutero-Isaiah, 40.1f.), could in fact restore an attitude of faith in the years to come, a certainty that the will of God for his people was not death, but conversion and life.

7. The Septuagint and the ancient versions

In this context I do not want to enter into a highly specialized discussion of the ancient versions of the book. So I shall limit myself to referring the reader to the following monographs:

W. O. E. Oesterley, *Studies in the Greek and Latin Versions of the Book of Amos*, Cambridge 1902; G. Howard, 'Some Notes on the Septuagint of Amos', *VT* 20, 1970, 108–12; id., 'Revisions toward the Hebrew in the Septuagint Text of Amos', *ErIs* 16, 1982, 125*–33*; J. de Waard, 'Translation Techniques used by the Greek Translators of Amos', *Bib* 59, 1978, 339–50.

The Superscription

(1.1)

S. Segert, 'Zur Bedeutung des Wortes *nôqēd*', in *Hebräische Wortforschung, FS W. Baumgartner*, SVT 16, 1967, 279–83; I. Willi-Plein**, 15; H. F. Fuhs, 'Amos 1, 1', in *Bausteine biblischer Theologie – FS G. J. Botterweck*, BBB 50, Bonn 1977, 271–89; M. D. Isbell, 'A Note on Amos 1.1', *JNES* 36, 1977, 213f.; J. J. Stamm, 'Der Name des Propheten Amos und sein sprächlicher Hintergrund', in *Prophecy, Essays presented to Georg Fohrer*, BZAW 150, Berlin 1980, 137–42; R. R. Wilson, *Prophecy and Society in Ancient Israel*, Philadelphia 1980, 266–70.

1 [1]Words of Amos, who was one of the (cattle) breeders in Tekoa, which he received in a vision, concerning Israel, in the time of Uzziah, king of Judah, and in the time of Jeroboam (II), son of Joash, king of Israel, two years before the earthquake.

'Words of . . .' not 'acts of . . .'; the first rendering is the only one possible because of the 'vision'. For the name 'Amos' (Hebrew *'amōs*) cf. now the study by Stamm. It is a theophorous name, the latter part of which is missing. Theophorous names with the root *'ms* are known from the texts of Mari (18th-17th century BC) and later in Phoenician and Punic. The first *ᵃšer* in the MT refers to Amos; however, the relative clause is syntactically harsh. LXX connects it with the 'words' (λόγοι . . . οἱ ἐγένοντο . . .), words which, again in the LXX understanding, will have been addressed to . . . It is possible that this is an attempt to overcome the syntactical harshness of the phrase. 'In a vision': the term determines the mode of the communication from God to the prophet; we do in fact have visions in the text, but not all the book is visionary. Thus a concept of visionary prophecy underlies the statement. An interesting suggestion to resolve the matter has recently been presented by one of my students at the Waldensian Theological Seminary in Rome, John Hobbins, in the preparatory work for his MA dissertation. He has maintained with arguments which I consider to carry a good deal of weight that where the context allows it, the root *ḥāzāh* and derivatives mean 'act' or 'speak like a *ḥōzēh*', rather than 'see' or 'have a vision'. So in this case it seems possible, albeit hypothetically, to suppose that the meaning is 'declare', so that the root is to be classified under *verba* *dicendi.* 'One of the breeders . . .': *bannōqᵉdīm*; the economic and social implications of the term are not completely clear. In II Kings 3.4 the title is given to Mesha, king of Moab, a great cattle-breeder, as is explicitly stated by II Kings 3.4 and confirmed by the tribute paid to Ahab of Israel; Amos, too, could have been in a similar position, albeit on a smaller scale (cf. 7.14ff.). The term is common to other semitic languages: it appears in Akkadian as *naqīdu*, *AHw* II, 744, in Ugaritic as *nqd*, *WUS*, 1840, and *UT*, 1964; in Syro-Palestinian Arabic as *naqqad*, '(poor) shepherd of sheep and goats'. The term also appears in the inscription of Mesha from the end of the ninth century BC, *KAI* 181, line 30, but in a doubtful context: the text is mutilated and the meaning of the term remains hypothetical. The LXX simply transliterated it and read it as a place name, while the Vulgate has *in pastoralibuś*. 'A and *Σ* read ποιμνιοτρόφοις and ποίμεσιν respectively; instead, *Θ* simply transcribed it *nocedim* (according to St Jerome). 'One of': the verb *hāyāh* always indicates situations or conditions; so Amos was a *nōqēd* by profession and not a prophet, cf. 7.14ff. Tg paraphrases: 'Who was an owner of flocks'. So Hauret*'s rendering 'owner and breeder of large flocks' would seem correct. 'Tekoa': a place usually identified with *ḫirbet teqū'*, near the village of *sa'ir*, about ten miles from Jerusalem as the crow flies (coord. 170–116), and around 2500 feet above sea level, east of the watershed and therefore already in the dry area. Note the shift, which can easily be explained by assonance, from the Hebrew *t* to the Arabic *ṭ*. However, in Talmudic literature there is also a Tekoa of Galilee, situated near Meron, probably on *ḫirbet šame'* (Koch*: coord. 265–191). So in the first understanding Amos would seem to come from the South and in the second from the North; however, in either instance he exercised his ministry in the North. 'Received in a vision . . .': in LXX this is not followed by 'concerning Israel' but by 'concerning Jerusalem' (perhaps an abbreviation ICΛ read as ICM?, Maag**); it is improbable that these are variants, since the capital is mentioned only in 1.2 and 2.5, in clearly secondary contexts; moreover Amos never exercised his ministry in Jerusalem (Maag**, Wolff**). The second *ᵃšer* should be the object of *ḫāzāh*, a verb which never appears without an object (Wolff*, against Maag**, who would render it 'Who had visions about . . .', Weiser* and Rinaldi*), at least in contexts like this one; cf. Isa. 1.1; 2.1; 13.1; Micah 1.1; Hab. 1.1, etc.; the translation of LXX and Vg is therefore correct. 'The earthquake'; cf. again Zech. 14.4–5 and Josephus, *Antt.* 9, 222–7. The phenomenon led to a landslide involving part of the Mount of Olives with the temporary obstruction of the Kidron valley, giving rise to the short depression which separates the Mount of Olives from Mount Scopus (today it is almost invisible because of the hospital built there by the *waqf* in the 1960s, at the time of Jordanian rule). At the time of the earthquake, which Josephus connects with an act of sacrilege committed by Uzziah king of Judah and which will have partially destroyed the temple, Uzziah was smitten with leprosy, which necessitated Jotham's regency. For Josephus the earthquake and the beginning of the regency thus coincided in time, and the date proposed for the two is about 750 BC according to the dating of the American Schools; around 759 or 756 according to the dating of J. Begrich and A. Jepsen.

The whole verse is often considered to be Deuteronomistic, cf. W. H. Schmidt**.

In Amos 1.1 we have the classical prophetic superscription made up of chronological and topographical information, sometimes accompanied by the patronym of the prophet (which is missing in Amos) and an indication of his profession (cf. Hos. 1.1; Isa. 1.1; Jer. 1.1; etc.). It therefore clearly stands apart from v. 2, though a number of commentators would like to connect the two verses; it is also clearly separate from the oracles against the nations (1.3ff.). It is written in prose, another feature which marks it out, this time stylistically. As we have seen, the syntax of the sentence is harsh, even if we have other similar instances, e.g. in Jer. 1.1. It is therefore probable that the sentence as it now stands is the result of successive additions arising out of re-reading and that the original will simply have been 'Words of Amos of Tekoa, who was . . .' It is possible that this superscription was an ancient one. A second addition is perhaps the second relative clause 'which he received in a vision . . .'; that is doubtful because of the way in which it refers to the kings: in its present form the mention of them would allow Amos a ministry of about forty years; moreover the calculation based on the king of Judah presupposes a later redaction which could not be dated from Israel. The possibility that this is a redactional Deuteronomistic addition must therefore be taken seriously into account. However, the mention of the 'earthquake' is generally considered ancient, so that Wolff* would like to limit the original form of the superscription to 'Words of Amos of Tekoa which he saw concerning Israel two years before the earthquake'. The expression 'words . . . which he saw . . .' seems strange to us but is frequent in Hebrew, cf. Isa. 2.1; Micah 1.1, with *maśśa'*, 'oracle', in Isa. 13.1 and Hab. 1.1; in Isa. 1.1 we have $h^a zon$, 'vision', which seems more logical to us. Underlying the expression would seem to be the concept that the prophetic word, since it is largely a divine word, is also an event, in that it produces visible effects. However, the more frequent form is *d²bar/dibrē YHWH* . . ., 'Word(s) of YHWH', of whom the prophet is the herald.

This redactional work is sufficient evidence of constant rereading and of the interest that following generations had in anchoring the message of Amos to the official chronology of the kings, as well as to spectacular facts like a particularly disastrous earthquake. This is a concern for chronological verification which is frequent in the Old Testament, but not always successful.

A Detached Oracle

(1.2)

M. Weiss, 'Methodologisches über die Behandlung der Metapher, dargelegt an Am. 1, 2', *TZ* 23, 1967, 1–25; T. N. D. Mettinger, *The Dethronement of Sabaoth*, CB-OTS 18, Lund 1982, 31f.; Weiss**, 194ff.

---

1 [2]He used to say:
'YHWH is the one who roars from Zion,
from Jerusalem he makes his voice heard.'
Then the pastures of the shepherds shrivel,
the summit of Carmel withers.

'Used to say': a pausal form, cf. *GesK* § 68e. For the translation cf. R. Meyer II, § 100, 2b and S. Amsler*. Amos's words are emphatic; so it is also possible to render them 'When YHWH roars . . , when . . . makes his voice heard, then . . .', reading the consecutive perfect in v. 2b with Meyer II, § 101, 6a and S. Amsler*, H.-W. Wolff*. It does not seem that the future should be read, as has often been proposed (Weiser*), though that is grammatically possible. The saying emphasizes the pre-eminence of Zion over the other sanctuaries, an assertion which is evidently also polemic against the cult of Bethel and Dan. As Mettinger indicates, the image refers to the heavenly king enthroned in his sanctuary, whether heavenly or earthly, and exercising his power from there (cf. Pss. 14.7; 53.3, 6 and Joel 4.16 [EVV 3.16]). There is good reason for doubting whether it is authentic, all the more so since the first section also appears, as we have seen, in Joel 4.16 and, with variants, in Jer. 25.30; it is in fact interesting that in Joel the roaring of YHWH is connected with an earthquake. 'Roar'; the root *šā'ag* is attested in Ugaritic, *WUS* 2822 and *UT* 2627, as 'moo' (*ṯ'igt* or *ṯ'iqt*) and in Arabic (*ta'aǧa*) 'cry out', 'bleat', but in Hebrew it is typically used of the roaring of the lion, which is not the subject except in the passages cited (Maag**, 195). Given the fact that the oracle has no context, it seems better, as we have seen, to translate it as a present and not as a past or future, both of which would be possible on a purely grammatical level. 'Makes heard . . .', literally 'utters his own voice', an expression which is also found in Ugaritic, where it refers to thunder; cf. Job 37.4, where we

28

have 'makes his roaring heard' (literally 'his own voice roars'). So it is probable that the two verbs denote thunder, the roaring of YHWH *par excellence*, but also of other deities in the history of religions. The combination of 'Zion-Jerusalem' in parallelism is frequent throughout the Old Testament but not otherwise attested in the text of Amos, another element which makes the authenticity of the oracle suspect. That this is an oracle of judgment may appear from what comes next: the text does not seek simply to stress the tremendous character of the God of Israel but to announce what is about to happen. 'Wither': root *'ābal*, cf. Akkadian *abālu* (*AHw* 1, 3, cf. the parallelism with *yābeš*[v1], 'dry up', 'scorch') and not *'ābal*, 'struggle with' (thus the Italian Revised Version, Osty*, and Bic*). 'The pastures': *n^e'ōt*, plural of *nāweh*, a term already well known from the Western Semitic of Mari, where it denotes either pasturage or the encampments of semi-nomadic shepherds; *nawūm* (*AHw* II, 771).[2] Here the context suggests that we should render it 'pasture'. 'Carmel' is still a mountain covered with conifers and evergreen Mediterranean vegetation. Tg for some unknown reason (perhaps as an anticipation of the invective against the rich?) paraphrases it: 'The habitations of the kings . . , the fortifications of their castles . . .'

The connection of thunder with drought is far from obvious, but is not explained by the commentaries; cf. below.

Two features distinguish v. 2 (Wolff*): the formula 'He said', or better, 'He used to say', does not appear again in the book and does not belong to any of the literary genres attested there (cf. the introduction); this is not in fact either a 'messenger formula' (*Botenformel*) or the one in which the person who sends him is speaking in the first person, nor is it a 'testimony' (*Zeugenrede*), given that it is not addressed to any particular audience; there is no proper announcement, but this is replaced with an action-reaction pattern (Weiss). As A. Bentzen[3] has pointed out and Wolff* has confirmed, what we have here is, rather, a theme which is very reminiscent of the theophanies of ancient hymns: Deut. 33.2; Judg. 5.4f.; Ps. 68.8 [EVV 7]; cf. Micah 1.3; Hab. 3.3, where YHWH comes from a sacred place or a particular locality (often the desert or the

---

[1]For the whole problem cf. F. M. Abel, *Géographie de la Palestine* I, Paris 1933, 54, and A. van den Born, 'Erdbeben', *BL* ²1968, 408. Cf. also my 'Das Erdbeben von Amos 1.1 und die Chronologie der Könige Ussia und Jotham von Juda', *ZAW* 82, 1970, 17–21, for further details.

[2]Cf. M. Noth, *Der Ursprung des alten Israel im Lichte neuer Quellen*, Köln-Opladen 1961, 16 and 31 = *ABLAK* II, (245–72) 252, 265, who thinks of 'pasturage', and A. Malamat, 'Mari and the Bible', *JAOS* 82, 1962, 143–50, who thinks rather in terms of 'encampments'. But the word can evidently indicate both things, depending on the context.

[3]Cf. his article cited in the general bibliography to 1.3–2.16.

sanctuary of Sinai), here now the Jerusalem temple. And since this is a locality close to the audience, there is no need to use verbs of motion: it is enough for YHWH to roar, send forth his own voice, i.e. thunder, so that all can hear him without difficulty.

However, as Wolff* has rightly indicated, unlike the other theophanies mentioned, the natural disturbance caused by the intervention of YHWH is no longer one of the decisive features which favour the people of God, for example in a battle; it produces divine judgment on the people and the country, as happens, moreover, throughout most of the message of Amos. In other words, what we have here is something like a holy war in reverse: not against the enemies of the people of God but against God's own people, precisely as in Jer. 6.1ff.[4]

It is not easy to say anything about the origin of the oracle: the mention of Carmel clearly points towards the North, but the Jerusalem temple is also mentioned: the use of *ša'ag* with YHWH as subject instead of the lion is unique in the Old Testament outside the two other passages mentioned above, Joel 4.16 [EVV 3.16]; Jer. 25.30, and as we have seen, the literary genre is not attested elsewhere in the book. Wolff* thinks in terms of a redactional addition made in Judah, but it is also possible to suppose that this is a quotation taken from the description of an ancient theophany, reproduced here in a fragmentary fashion (thus A. Bentzen, cf. T. H. Robinson*, J. Fosbroke*). After E. Sellin*, only N. H. Snaith*, II 9ff., and V. Maag**, 4, have defended its authenticity.

We have seen that the voice of YHWH is probably identified with thunder and this creates a problem: the relationship between thunder and drought. Others have therefore thought in terms of the *ḥamsīn*, the famous east wind, a kind of dry sirocco (cf. Isa. 40.7), as the consequences might suggest (the main texts are in Weiss); we certainly cannot suppose that the imminent storm makes the flocks and shepherds leave the pastures to find shelter (Rinaldi*). Weiss is probably right in saying that the force of the metaphor lies in its paradoxical or downright contradictory character. And this character appears here not only in the lack of congruence between cause and effect but also in the divine intervention against the people of God rather than in its favour. In the sphere of nature and its fertility, then, the rains are always a divine gift (Hos. 2), but here the rain announced by the thunder becomes an element of justice; the pastures wither, evergreen Carmel becomes arid, and this further reinforces the sinister character of the scene: everything comes only by hearing; nothing is seen!

[4]For this theme see my 'Der prophetische Gedanke über den Heiligen Krieg als Gericht gegen Israel', *VT* 10, 1960, 79–83, ET in *Old Testament and Oriental Studies*, BiblOr 29, Rome 1975, 67–71.

The Oracles against the Nations
(1.3–2.16)

A. Bentzen, 'The Ritual Background of Amos I 2–II 16', *OTS* 8, 1950, 85–99; M. Weiss, 'The Pattern of Numerical Sequence in Amos 1–2', *JBL* 66, 1967, 416–23; M. Haran, 'The Rise and Decline of the Empire of Jeroboam ben Joash', *VT* 17, 1967, 266–97; id., 'Observations on the Historical Background of Amos 1.2–2.6', *IEJ* 18, 1968, 201–12; J. M. Ward**, 92ff.; S. Wagner**, 663ff.; M. Weiss, 'The Pattern of the "Execration Texts" in the Prophetic Literature', *IEJ* 19, 1969, 150–7; S. M. Paul, 'Amos 1:3–2:3: a Concatenous Literary Pattern', *JBL* 90, 1971, 397–403; D. L. Christensen, 'The Prosodic Structure of Amos 1–2', *HTR* 67, 1974, 427–36; J. Barton, *Amos' Oracles against the Nations*, SOS.MS 6, 1980; S. Segert, 'A Controlling Device for Copying Stereotyped Passages (Amos I 3–II 8, VI 1–6)', *VT* 34, 1984, 481f.; M. E. Barre, 'The Meaning of *lô' 'ašabynw* in Amos 1:3–2:6', *JBL* (forthcoming; I have not been able to use this article).

For the numerical formulae generally cf. S. Terrien, 'Amos and Wisdom', in *Israel's Prophetic Heritage, Essays J. Muilenburg*, New York and London 1962, (108–15) 109f.; W. M. W. Roth, 'The Numerical Sequence X/X+1 in the Old Testament', *VT* 12, 1962, 300–11; id., 'Numerical Sayings in the Old Testament', *SVT* 13, 1965, 63 n. 3; H. P. Rüger, 'Die gestaffelten Zahlensprüche des Alten Testaments und aram. Achikar 92', *VT* 31, 1981, 229–34.

The numerical formula, also called climactic parallelism, is characteristic of the whole of the section of oracles against the nations. This formula is well attested in Ugaritic as well as in Hebrew, cf. *CTA* 17 *II*, *'qht* II, 25–46, where we have an abnormal example of it.[1] In the Old Testament the formula appears mainly in the Wisdom literature, cf. Job 5.19; Prov. 6.16, etc., and seems so typical that Terrien sees its use as an indication that Amos knew Israelite wisdom and made use of its literary genres. However, there are only these two examples to allow a distinction between two types of such a formula; in two of the wisdom cases cited we do not have a rhetorical formula, and in fact there are six

[1] Translation in C. H. Gordon, *Ugaritic Literature*, Rome 1949, 87f. Segert, however, suggests that this is a form intended to avoid copying errors in stereotyped texts.

31

elements in the list, whereas in this case, the oracles against the nations, we have a purely rhetorical figure in which in fact only one element is listed. So to translate literally produces what we feel to be sheer nonsense, as was rightly pointed out in the 1920s by Giovanni Luzzi.[2] That explains why Roth and Rüger do not list the oracles of Amos against the nations among the numerical sayings.

1. Against Damascus (1.3–5)

A. Malamat, 'Amos 1:5 in the Light of the Til Barsip Inscription', *BASOR* 129, 1953, 25f.; K. N. Schoville, 'The Sins of Aram in Amos 1', *Proceedings of the Sixth World Congress of Jewish Studies . . . Jerusalem 1973*, Jerusalem I, 1977, 363–75; I. Willi-Plein**, 15–21; L. Markert**, 48–53; P. Höffken, 'Eine Bemerkung zum "Haus Hazaels" in Amos 1, 4', *ZAW* 94, 1982, 413–15.

---

1 [3]Thus YHWH has spoken: 'Because of the innumerable crimes of Damascus I will not go back on my decision: because they have thr.eshed [the pregnant women of (?)] Gilead with iron threshers, [4]I will set fire to the house of Hazael, so that it destroys the palaces of Ben-Hadad. [5]I will break the defences of Damascus, exterminate from Biqa't 'Awen him who is enthroned there, from Bēt´Eden him who holds the sceptre there, and the people of Aram shall go in exile to Kir', YHWH has spoken.

[3] 'Thus YHWH has spoken': LXX read καὶ εἶπε κύριος. This does not seem to be a variant proper but a theological interpretation: the prophetic word is the Word of God. The explanation of the hiphil of *šwb*, with YHWH as subject, depends on what the third person pronominal suffix denotes. There is a collection of the various possibilities in H.-W. Wolff*, 128, and K. Koch*, 106 n. 9. Some references which are grammatically possible should be excluded: for example to the Assyrians in the sense of a return behind their own frontiers or to the Aramaean population deported by them: comparison with other texts rules out this possibility. It is better to connect the suffix in question with the word, the decree pronounced by YHWH, a feature which seems irrevocable: literally 'I shall not make it turn back', or 'I shall not go back on my decision'. 'Threshed': the root *dwš* is a technical term for threshing, not by hand, but by means of special carts with wheels or sledges with points turned downwards,[3] implements which

---

[2]G. Luzzi, *I Profeti*, Florence 1929, 282ff. 'Just as Damascus has accumulated sin upon sin . . .' For the problem of these formulae cf., in addition to the bibliography above, G. Sauer, *Die Sprüche Agurs*, BWANT 84, Stuttgart 1963, ch. IV.

[3]There is an illustration in *BHH* 1, 1962, 356.

are partly still in use in the less developed areas of the Syro-Palestinian world. Applied to the population, the imagery indicates its decimation or even its total annihilation, whether this is meant figuratively or related to atrocities actually committed. The LXX no longer understood the verb but caught the atrocity signified by the expression: ἀνθ'ὧν ἔπριζον πρίοσιν . . , 'sawed with saws of iron'. 'Gilead': LXX prefixes 'the pregnant women of Gilead', τὰς ἐν γαστρὶ ἐχούσας, a variant which has a parallel in 5Q4.1[4]: hrw[t] hgl'[d], which the editors of the last text would prefer to consider authentic and as having fallen out by homoioteleuton (cf. the very short character of the line, already pointed out by N. II. Snaith*, though he accepted the variant of the LXX, the only one then known); however, it also seems possible that this is a phrase taken from 1.13; at all events the reference is more to total war than to cruelty in individual cases. Note how the term *pesă'* is used for the attitude of Damascus and the other nations.

[4] Does this begin a new sentence or is it a continuation of the previous one? In the former case the full stop is to be put at the end of v. 3 and we translate 'They have threshed'; in the latter case it becomes, 'Since they threshed . . . I shall set fire . . .' The second rendering seems better syntactically: as in the other oracles we then have the sequence of an announcement of an irrevocable decision, the reasons for such a decision, its substance and the way in which it was carried out. 'To the house' here seems to refer to the palace, not to the dynasty, see the parallelism with *'rmnwt*, a kind of palace-fortress. However, P. Höffken has suggested on the basis of Assyrian parallels that the reference is to the territory of Hazael, so that the oracle would precede Tiglath-Pileser III's invasion in 732. The second term is rendered more or less literally by Vg with *domos*, but by LXX with θεμέλια, foundations, by ' A and Σ with βάρεις, 'palaces', 'towers', by Θ with τὰς αὐλας, 'the courtyards', the 'rooms'. So the meaning of the term was already doubtful in ancient times.

[5]'Who . . . enthroned': it would also be possible to translate 'who lives there, who has his home there' (thus LXX and the ancient versions), but that would go against the subsequent parallelism.[5] Damascus is denoted in the Massoretic text with some terms the meaning of which is not always clear. *Biq'at 'āwen* and *bēt 'eden*, respectively 'plain' or 'valley of evil' and 'house of pleasure', have both been rendered by the ancient translations in forms which are not always comprehensible: for the first LXX has ἐκ πεδίου Ὠν; Vg *de campo idoli*; 'A ἀνωφέλους, 'useless', Σ ἀδικίας. The rendering of LXX confirms the consonants of MT, but On is the name of Heliopolis in Egypt (cf. Gen. 41.45, 50; 46.20). And since this name (Heliopolis) also appears for a Syro-Lebanese town, present-day Baalbek, situated between Beirut and Damascus, some writers have suggested this place. It is an

[4]*Discoveries in the Judaean Desert* III, Oxford 1962, 173.
[5]For this meaning of *yāšab* cf. W. G. E. Watson. 'David Ousts the City Rulers of Jebus', *VT* 20, 1970, 501f.

explanation which gives a reason for the LXX choice, but it cannot be used for MT: Baalbek is too far from Damascus. The second term appears in LXX as ἐξ ἀνδρῶν Χορράν, while Vg has *de domo voluptatis*, cf. Θ: ἐν οἴκῳ τρυφῆς, where *'eden* is translated as in Gen. 2.8 (but note the different vocalization); however, it confirms MT. The mention of Harran in LXX is interesting; for Wolff* this is not a textual variant but the trace of an autonomous tradition, inspired by Gen. 28.5ff., where we have Paddan-Aram and Harran. Cf. also II Kings 19.12, where Harran is mentioned among the places subjected by the Assyrians. T. H. Robinson* and, more recently, A. Malamat, have, however, wanted to identify *bēt 'eden* with the Aramaean state of Bir Adini, a name which the place was given after the Assyrian conquest, to which II Kings 19.12//Isa. 37.12 evidently refers, cf. also Ezek. 27.23, situated on the middle Euphrates. Its governor Šamši-ilu virtually succeeded in making it autonomous during the period of Assyrian decadence (cf. the introduction above, § 1) between about 780 and 746, so his sovereignty seems more or less contemporaneous with the reign of Jeroboam II. And that could be a good reason why LXX speaks of Harran.

Like the other 'oracles against the nations' in prophetic literature, this one too appears as a word of God, for whom the prophet assumes the figure of an intermediary. So here we have the 'messenger formula'. With the oracles against the nations the prophetic message assumes universalistic categories, even if for the moment they are purely negative.

The crime of Damascus does not lie in its having conquered Transjordan (there is an allusion here to the events which began with II Kings 8.11ff.; 10.32ff. and continued during the so-called Aramaean revival under Ben-Hadad III or IV, depending on the numbering, provided that we do not want to accept the improbable theory that the prophet is referring to events which took place about a century earlier), but to the way in which it did so: a total war of extermination. The curse is addressed first of all to those most directly responsible: they are told that their death is imminent in the burning of their own city. Then the curse takes in the whole people, less responsible and therefore condemned only to deportation. Barton has put forward the interesting theory that here and in some of the following texts we have a form of international law which put a limit on the acts of the victors towards the civil population.

The theme that a people must return whence it came does not appear elsewhere in Amos, so that Maag** thinks that this is a gloss on a general mention of the exile, but the idea is applied to Israel in Hosea, in the theme of the return to the desert (2.14ff.; 12.10ff.); in the first passage Israel retraces the route of the conquest, which passed through

Achor; in the second that of the exodus. For the Aramaeans that was in fact to happen some decades later (II Kings 16.9), in about 733–32. According to Isa. 22.6 Kir was in the direction of Elam, but we do not know precisely where.

2. Against the Philistines (1.6–8)

Willi-Plein**, 15; Markert**, 53–5.

---

1 [6]Thus YHWH has spoken: 'Because of the innumerable crimes of Gaza, I shall not go back on my decision: because they deported an entire people, to hand them over to Edom, [7]I shall set fire to the wall of Gaza, so that it devours its palaces. [8]I shall exterminate from Ashdod him that is enthroned there, from Ashkelon him that holds the sceptre. I will turn my hand against Ekron, so that the remnant of the Philistines perishes.' YHWH has spoken.

[6] For the translation cf. on vv. 3, 4, as also for the division of the sentence. Note how the construction is identical in form to that of the previous oracle. 'An entire': Hebrew $š^e l\bar{e}m\bar{a}h$, literally 'for their deporting of a complete deportation'. LXX rendered it τοῦ Σαλώμων, referring the whole passage to King Solomon, with an erroneous reading to be explained by the presence of a term which is written identically. But the other translations confirm the Massoretic vocalization. For the syntax cf. Brockelmann § 92a. 'To hand over': note the value of the root *sgr*, normally 'close', in the hiphil. **[7]** Here the terminology recalls that of v. 4. **[8]** The concluding formula of the oracle has an extra $^a d\bar{o}n\bar{a}y$ before YHWH over and above the previous oracle; the presence of the term, which is semantically otiose, is not attested in LXX but it does appear in Vg. It is interesting that it is already attested in a document from *wādī muraba'at*.[6] In Wolff* we find a series of cases listed in which the term has been prefixed to YHWH in Amos; but the phenomenon is frequent in all the prophetic books and is probably a prelude to the perpetual Qere for the tetragrammaton (i.e. its pointing with the vowels of $^a d\bar{o}n\bar{a}y$ to indicate that this is to be substituted).

The reasons why Philistia follows Syria in the oracles against the nations in Amos are far from clear, so it is not surprising that the subject has been a topic of discussion. It has been thought that the sequence could have been inspired by the Assyrian plans for conquest, but this

---

[6]*Discoveries in the Judaean Desert* II, Oxford 1961, 186.

explanation seems improbable, given that these plans are not mentioned anywhere. Others have suggested that the criterion is the degree of enmity towards Israel: the Aramaeans were the immediate danger while the Philistines were the traditional enemy. However, it should be noted that the times in which the Philistines were the enemy *par excellence* lay far in the past, that they had very soon parted from Judah (NB, not Israel) after the division of the united kingdom of David and Solomon, and again that they are censured here for a series of specific actions. Others have thought in terms of a geographical sequence from north to south, but in that case the Philistines are not evidently the first people that we meet after the Aramaeans, even if one does not want to exclude intermediary people like those of Transjordan.

The reference to the Egyptian execration texts made by A. Bentzen might resolve the literary problem here, if not all the others; Egypt follows a criterion which is apparently that of the cardinal points, but in reality is that of the caravan routes: it is these that Egypt seeks to protect by means of the curse.[7] However, the prophet's criterion does not seem to be national, political or economic, nor purely geographical and topographical, so that it seems better to suppose that he is using an ancient literary genre or something very similar, but in a completely new way: for example grading the people by the ferocity of their acts or by the degree of hostility they show to Israel.

It would also be interesting to know the facts which underlie this harsh invective. We know that the Philistines along with the Phoenicians had the reputation of trafficking in slaves, a reputation also attested in the OT in Joel 4.4–6 [EVV 3.4–6]. But we know nothing of the specific circumstances to which this passage could refer. In II Kings 12.18 Hazael of Damascus conquers Gath, but this is in the area of the Philistine Pentapolis which is not mentioned here, and the details there relate to more than half a century before the ministry of Amos. A suggestion by Osty* in his commentary does not take us quite so far backwards in time: he cites II Chron. 21.16ff., a passage which speaks of a Philistine attack on Judah in the time of king Joram (*c.* 849–42 or 847–45) accompanied with plundering, but this explanation brings up the chronological problem again to an even greater degree. Fosbroke* would prefer to post-date everything to the end of the eighth century, when in 711 Sargon II of Assyria conquered Gath (cf. *ANET*, 286, and *TGI*, 63ff.); and the lack of any mention of places here would be proof of its fall; the oracle, which in any case is not authentic, could refer to the remnant of the Philistines (v. 8b). So obviously it would have to be given

[7]W. Helck, *Die Beziehungen Ägyptens zu Vorderasien im 3. und 2. Jahrtausend*, Wiesbaden 1962, 62ff.

a later date. But there is a better explanation for the absence of any mention of Gath, which was put forward by T. H. Robinson*: Gath was closely allied to Judah from the time of David, who in fact recruited his own better and more faithful mercenaries from there (cf. II Sam. 15.18ff., the episode of Ittai of Gath); so it is probable that the place was no longer truly distinct from Judah, even when the Philistines regained their freedom. Be this as it may, as Rinaldi* notes, nothing in the text says that the prisoners sold were Judahites (far less Israelites); so here too, even if we do not know the circumstances to which the oracle refers, we have a condemnation of total war, whether this was directed against Israel or only involved other nations, total war which spared no one, though this time purely for gain: not extermination but the deportation of entire populations with the aim of selling them into slavery; in fact, war carried on with this particular aim, even if it was never declared.

3. Against Tyre (1.9–10)

W. Schottroff, '*Gedenken' im alten Orient und im Alten Testament*, WMANT 15, Neukirchen 1964, 157–9; E. Gerstenberger, 'Covenant and Commandment', *JBL* 84, 1965, (38–51) 40ff.; J. R. Priest, 'The Covenant of Brothers', ibid., 400–6; F. Vattioni, 'La terminologia dell'alleanza', *Riblos Press* 6, Rome 1965, (112–16) 115f.; W. H. Schmidt**; F. C. Fensham, 'The Treaty Between Israel and Tyre', *SVT* 17, 1969, 71–87; H. Cazelles, 'L'arrière plan historique d'Amos 1.9–10', in *Proceedings of the Sixth World Congress of Jewish Studies . . . Jerusalem 1973* I, Jerusalem 1977, 71–6; Willi-Plein**, 16; Markert**, 55–8.

1 [9]Thus YHWH has spoken: 'Because of the innumerable crimes of Tyre, I shall not go back on my decision: because they handed over to Edom whole groups of deportees, and did not remember the brotherly covenant, [10]I shall set fire to the walls of Tyre so that it devours its palaces.'

For the construction of the oracle cf. on vv. 3–4. [9] 'whole groups': see on v. 6. Some scholars (E. Sellin*, V. Maag**, T. H. Robinson* and S. Amsler*) would prefer to read *la*^{x}*rām* for *le*^{x}*dōm*, i.e. textual corruption arising out of the exchange of *res* and *dalet*, in order to match the geographical distance; in fact Sellin* would prefer to correct the text to read *g*^{e}*būl š*^{e}*lōmōh la*^{x}*rām*, 'they handed over the territory of Solomon to Aram', a reference to the cession of the territory in Galilee by Solomon to Hiram of Tyre (cf. I Kings 9.11–13), who in turn will have handed it over to the Aramaeans, though we know nothing of this last development. The two proposals, the first of which would resolve the geographical problem, have not found any critical approval. For 'brotherly covenant' see the commentary.

Apart from the mention of Edom (or Aram) the terminology which precedes and follows it in v. 10, clearly recalls vv. 6–8 and in fact seems to be an imitation of them. Only the destination of the oracle changes. For many scholars this is a clear sign that this is not an original oracle, with a formulation common to others typical of the same literary genre, but a genuine duplicate or a case of literary dependence (so most recently Willi-Plein** and Markert**). On the other hand, while it is true that there are remarkable analogies between the two sections, it is also true that we can find differences; in v. 9b we have a description of Tyre and its crimes in a clause with a verb, not a verbless one, and moreover it is shorter than others in this part of the book. Again, the conclusion 'YHWH has spoken' is missing; this could, though, have fallen out for textual reasons, as happens frequently throughout the Old Testament. Against the authenticity of the passage would be that oracles against Tyre are usually exilic, cf. Isa. 23.5ff., an addition to the ancient one against Sidon, whose authenticity a number of scholars doubt,[8] Jer. 47.4; and then in Ezekiel, cf. chs. 26; 27; 28. On the other hand W. Rudolph rightly points out that these arguments are not decisive. Like the Philistines, the Phoenicians were known as slave traders, so that what is said of one could be said of the other; and the mention of Tyre in the eighth century is not obviously illogical. At worst, I might add, if we think that the use of $b^e r\bar{\imath}t$ is typical of Deuteronomy and the Deuteronomist, we could conjecture an editorial gloss which arose in close proximity to these schools, a gloss which sought to describe (correctly) the nature of the relationships which existed between Israel and Tyre from the time of the united monarchy to the eighth century: similarly, H. Cazelles also offers a passionate (and convincing) defence of the authenticity of the passage.

To a condemnation of total war ending in the capture and sale into slavery of the defeated population, this passage adds as a Deuteronomistic-type gloss a reference to the violation of the 'brotherly covenant'. Whereas Kapelrud*, 24, Fosbroke* and Weiser* consider the expression inexplicable, more recent studies on covenants in the ancient Near East allow us to give an almost complete explanation of the expression and its implications.

Pedersen[9] already pointed out how the covenant serves to create brotherly relationships between outsiders who are not therefore bound by any relationship of kindred, a point which Dhorme* and Osty* recall

[8]Cf. my *Introduction to the Old Testament*, 263.
[9]J. Pedersen, *Israel. Its Life and Culture* I–II, Copenhagen 1926, 279ff.

in their commentaries. And this thesis has found ample confirmation in the terminology of international treaties in the ancient Near East:[10] the sovereigns bound by relationships of covenant and friendship were accustomed to call each other by the title 'brother', and this usage is attested among the Hittites, in Syria in the texts from Alalakh and also in the Akkadian world.[11] So the meaning of the expression was clear: there were brotherly relations between Israel and Tyre, which moreover are well attested over the centuries from the period of the united monarchy (David and Solomon, cf. II Sam. 5.11; I Kings 5.15ff., 26 [EVV 5.1f., 12]; 9.13) down to that of Ahab in the ninth century (I Kings 16.31), where the relations were sealed with the marriage of the king of Israel to princess Jezebel, daughter of the 'king of the Sidonians'.[12] Granted, a covenant is not specifically mentioned, and in addition it would be difficult to accept that Amos would have approved a relationship of this kind; he might well have revoked it (Snaith*, 23). However, as Schottroff rightly points out, such a relationship would seem inconceivable without the existence of a treaty of covenant. Be this as it may, such friendly relations were brusquely interrupted during the ninth century, but only by Israel, not by Tyre, during Jehu's *coup d'état*, which led to the abolition of the cult of Baal and the extermination of the royal family, including Jezebel (II Kings 9–10; cf. 9.30ff., and 10.1, provided, of course, that these notes, now presented in terms of the struggle against paganism and syncretism, count as historical evidence).[13] Another factor is that in 842 Tyre, Sidon and 'Jehu of the dynasty of Omri' (*sic*! a strange but significant expression for Israel) were subjected and made vassals of the Assyrians during the fourth campaign of Shalmaneser III (858–24), cf. the Assyrian annals in *ANET*, 280b, and *THI*, 50f. So even where the old covenant relationship had been interrupted, there was still one of co-vassalage which precluded any aggression. At any rate it does not seem probable that Tyre sought to involve Israel in its own foreign policy.[14]

Given this situation, it falls within the bounds of possibility that at the time of the Aramaean revival during the first years of Jeroboam II Tyre may not have felt itself bound by any pledge to Israel and may have

[10]D. J. McCarthy, *Treaty and Covenant*, AnBibl 21A, Rome 1978, 288; P. Kalluveettil, *Declaration and Covenant*, AnBibl 58, Rome 1982, 7f.

[11]For the Hittites cf. A. Goetze, *Kleinasien*, KgAO III.1, Munich 1957, 97f.; O. R. Gurney, *The Hittites*, Harmondsworth [3]1961, 77; for Alalakh D. J. Wiseman, *The Alalakh Tablets*, London 1953, no. 1, line 1; for the Akkadian *AHw* 1, 21. For all these problems see P,. Kalluveettil, *Declaration and Covenant*.

[12]Cf. the more recent histories of Israel.

[13]In addition to the histories of Israel cf. R. Bach, 'Jehu', *RGG* III, [3]1959, 574f.; 'Tyrus', *RGG* VI, [3]1962, 1098. I have examined these problems in detail in 'Jezebel oder die fremde Frau', in *Hommages à M. Henri Cazelles*, Paris 1982, 453–9.

[14]Thus for example A. van den Born, *BL* [2]1968, 1788f., s.v. 'Tyrus'.

sought to lay hands on places bordering on its own territory, deporting the population and selling them into slavery. In other words, the arguments used against the authenticity of this oracle are not conclusive, so the question must remain open. Rinaldi*, Dhorme*, Robinson*, Schottroff and Priest favour authenticity; W. H. Schmidt**, Weiser* and Wolff* do not.

4. Against Edom (1.11–12)

M. Fishbane, 'The Treaty Background of Amos 1.11 and Related Matters', *JBL* 89, 1970, 313–18; R. B. Coote, 'Amos 1.11, RHMYW', *JBL* 90, 1971, 206–8; Willi-Plein**, 16f.; Markert**, 58–61: M. E. Barre, 'Amos 1:11 Reconsidered', *CBQ* 47, 1985, 420–7 (which I have not been able to use).

---

1 ¹¹Thus YHWH has spoken: 'Because of the innumerable crimes of Edom, I will not go back on my decision: because he pursued his brother with the sword and killed all his compassion [LXX, ʾA, Σ and Jerome have: 'so that . . . he spilled his entrails on the ground!'] so that his wrath tore incessantly, and his anger kept watch for ever, ¹²I will set fire to Teman, so that it devours the palaces of Bozrah.'

For the construction cf. on vv. 3–4. **[11]** 'Compassion': instead of the Hebrew *raḥᵃmayw*, LXXᴬ read καὶ ἐλευμένατο μῆτραν ἐπὶ τῆς γῆς, while St Jerome in his commentary (*PL* 25,100) has *Sed violavit misericordiam sive vulvam eius;* ʾA read σπλάγχνα ἴδια, Σ (according to Jerome) *viscera propria* = ἔντερα αὐτοῦ. These last two translations evidently hinge on the twofold meaning of the term *raḥamim* in Western Semitic: 'internal organs' or 'entrails' or 'mercy', a dual meaning which also passes over into the Greek of the New Testament, cf. Luke 1.78. LXXᴬ then explains by means of an addition that this happened 'on the earth' or 'to the earth', ἐπὶ γῆς, perhaps an erroneous reading of ἐπίσην (Rudolph*), i.e. 'and thus violating the shared mother's breast'. The variant is interesting, first of all because it is evidence of the confusion between *raḥᵃmīm*, 'mercy', and *reḥem*, 'womb' (with a new corruption in LXXᴮ, which reads μήτεραν), easy with the suffix to the plural noun, but also because it perhaps preserves a recollection of violence which the Massoretic tradition thought it appropriate to suppress and which the relationship of kinship between the two people made even worse;¹⁵ the verb *šaḥat* in fact has a broad semantic horizon: 'exterminate', 'devastate', 'slay ritually', 'act in an infamous way'. So if we accepted the

---

¹⁵Cf. A. Jepsen, 'Gnade und Barmherzigkeit im Alten Testament', *KuD* 7, 1961, 261–71 = *Der Herr ist Gott, Aufsätze zur Wissenschaft des Alten Testaments*, Berlin 1978, 211–20, a suggestion taken over by W. Rudolph.

LXX reading we would no longer have a generic and incomplete formulation, as Weiser* and Wolff* complain in connection with the Massoretic text; we would have, rather, a description like 'he scattered his entrails on the ground' or 'he killed his mercy, thus violating the shared mother's womb', while T. H. Robinson* translates: 'Cast all his sympathy to the ground'; Rinaldi*, 'Mercy left him', without accepting the reading of LXX and taking the suffix as an object. 'Tore': LXX rendered the Hebrew *wayyitrop* with ἥρπασεν, 'seized, snatched', while 'A translates it ἤγρευσεν, 'chased', or ἐθέρευσεν, 'tore to pieces'; Vg has *tenuerit*. All the ancient translations other than Vg thus more or less confirm MT. Despite that, it has become the custom (cf. Snaith*, Osty*, Robinson*, Maag**, Amsler* and Weiser*) to follow Vg and emend to *wayyittor*, '(Edom) has kept, maintained its own anger constantly' (root *natar₁*). 'Incessantly': for *la'ad* LXX has εἰς μαρτύριον, i.e. *lā'ēd*, which would also give good sense: his anger tore 'to give an example' (literally 'and his horror snatches as a testimony'). However, the remaining translations confirm MT. 'Kept watch for ever': for *šᵉmārāh neṣaḥ*, subject 'anger'; on the basis of LXX, Vg and perhaps Θ which read the third person masculine suffix, the reading *šāmar lᵉneṣaḥ*, with Edom as subject, has been proposed, cf. LXX εἰς νίκος (confusion of the two meanings of *neṣaḥ* 'glory, victory', and adverbially, 'for ever'; but the term also appears without the preposition, cf. Pss. 13.2; 16.11) and Vg which has *in finem*. In that case we should have a third person masculine with a third person feminine pronominal suffix (without *mappiq*, GesK § 29e and Joüon § 31c). That would give 'his anger is kept perpetually', whereas in MT it is indicated that the anger remains over the lacerated prey. For an analysis of the problem cf. H.-W. Wolff*, who leans towards keeping MT, which he rightly regards as the *lectio difficilior*. Moreover, the oracle is constructed like the others, and the people to whom it is addressed has to remain subject right through the reasons given for the judgment on it.

With Edom we come to the first people traditionally 'related' to Israel. The problem of authenticity is similar to that of the preceding oracle, even if this time the exact wording of the preceding oracles is not repeated: here, too, we have the special feature of the enlargement of the description of the crime by means of a clause with the finite verb (cf. v. 11c with v. 9c), and here too the phrase 'YHWH has spoken' is missing at the end. Moreover here too we have a feature which militates against authenticity: the fact that all the oracles against Edom (Isa. 11.14; 34.1ff.; Jer. 25.21; 40.11; 49.7ff.; Ezek. 25.12ff.; Obadiah)[16] always appear in exilic or post-exilic contexts. But if a similar observation can

[16]For the Isaiah text cf. my *Introduction*, 363.

quite easily be countered for Tyre by means of a series of historical data, the question in the case of Edom is much more complex. In the middle of the ninth century Edom succeeded in liberating itself from Israel (cf. II Kings 8.20–22//II Chron. 21.8ff.). However, about fifty years afterwards it was attacked and defeated by Amaziah king of Judah (c. 800–783 or 801–787, cf. II Kings 14.7, 22; II Chron. 25.11ff.). In fact the Judahites occupied Petra and massacred a contingent of prisoners of war. And even if it is not said in so many words that Edom was reduced to the status of a vassal, the reconstruction by Judah of the port of Eilath on the Red Sea (II Kings 14.2) seems to indicate that something of the sort happened. So it would not seem strange that at the time of the Aramaean revival Edom, too, tried to regain its independence and perhaps went over to the offensive against Judah. Be this as it may, here too the author is opposed to the concept and the practice of total war. However, the real problem of this passage is not historical, but rather that of its essentially Judahite orientation. Moreover, whereas in the case of Tyre the prophet could justify the extermination by Jehu of Jezebel and the rest of the royal family related to the Phoenician city state, so that Tyre would not have had any good reason for denouncing and violating the covenant, there would have been even less reason for such a violent reaction by Edom to the atrocities committed by Judah, and a reminder by the prophet of piety and mercy (according to MT) or of the bond of kinship which united the two people would seem at least irrelevant. In reality an oracle like this would seem to have clear motivation if it were related, at least as far as v. 11b β is concerned, to an attack by Edom on Judah in 587–86, cf. Obadiah 10ff.; Ps. 137.7; Joel 4.19 [EVV 3.19], but not II Kings 24.1. So in this case the presumption is that the text is not authentic. Teman and Bozrah are respectively a region and a city to the east and south-east of the Dead Sea (coord. 197–971 and 297–016); the latter is present-day Buṣeirah.

5. Against Ammon (1.13–15)

J. de Waard, 'A Greek Translation-Technical Treatment of Amos 1:15', in *On Language, Culture and Religion: In Honor of Eugene A. Nida*, The Hague 1974, 111–18; Willi-Plein**, 17; Markert**, 61–4.

1 [13]Thus YHWH has spoken: 'Because of the innumerable crimes of the Ammonites I shall not go back on my decision: since they have ripped up the pregnant women of Gilead to enlarge their territory, [14]I shall set fire to the wall of Rabbah so that it devours its palaces; like the war-cry in the day

of battle, like the whirlwind in the day of tempest. [15]Then their king [Milkom] shall go into exile, along with his leaders [priests]!' YHWH has spoken.

[13] 'Have ripped up': *bāqaʿ* is a verb denoting cleaving, cutting, dividing. In this sense it appears essentially in the piel. 'The pregnant women': mediaeval Jewish exegesis (Kimchi) wanted to understand *hārōt*, 'pregnant women', as if it were *hārīm*, 'mountains', cf. nowadays Sellin*, though he would prefer to read the singular *har*; however, the expression recurs in II Kings 8.12; 15.16 and Hos. 14.1, so this correction, evidently intended to reduce the atrocities, is not to be commended (Rudolph). 'To': *lᵉmaʿan*, the term is often considered to overburden the metre (most recently Willi-Plein** and Markert**), as well as being a preposition which appears often in Deut., Dtr and Ezek.[17] Be this as it may, it expresses the aim of the action well. **[14]** 'I will set': the root *yaṣat* (perhaps *ṣwt*) is rare in Hebrew and unknown in Western Semitic; it is therefore the *lectio difficilior* and should not be replaced by *šālaḥ*, the term which appears in the other oracles, as Wolff* would prefer: the same literary genre can have the same words but does not need to (Rudolph*). 'As': the two prepositions *bᵉ* in 14b are *bet essentiae*, cf. *GesK* § 119i, Joüon § 133c, and should therefore be translated in this way. 'The war-cry': the Hebrew *terūʿāh* can mean a variety of things: a cry of joy, applause, acclamation, the sound of the trumpet; it often appears in relation to a liturgical action.[18] 'Tempest'; LXX read συντελείας αὐτῆς, i.e. *sopah*, 'of its end'. **[15]** MT reads 'their king'; LXX has the singular noun and the plural suffix, but LXX, ʾA and Σ read μελχομ, thus Vg *Melchom*, cf. a similar problem in Jer. 49.1, 3 and Zeph. 1.5; the former is also an oracle against Ammon. Milkom is attested as the Ammonite deity in I Kings 11.5, 33; II Kings 23.13,[19] cf. also the explanation given by Jerome in his commentary, *PL* 25, 1002: . . . *et idolum Ammonitarum quod vocatur Melchom id est rex eorum, feritur in Assyrios*. This is an exact allusion to the Assyrian and Babylonian custom of also deporting the statues of the deities of conquered peoples. On the other hand, as Rinaldi*, Robinson* and Rudolph* rightly point out, 'their king' forms a good parallel to 'their leaders', but cf. again LXX which has οἱ ἱερεῖς αὐτῶν (ʾA, Σ, Θ, αὐτῆς), i.e. *kōhᵉnayw* instead of 'their princes'. But MT is usually considered better (Wolff*).

[17]Cf. the information in H. W. Wolff*, 134, on 2.7.

[18]For the term, the exact meaning of which is not important for understanding this passage, cf. P. Humbert, *La terouʿa. Analyse d'un rite biblique*, Neuchâtel 1946, and, recently, E. T. Moneta Caglio, 'Lo jubilus e le origini della salmodia responsoriale', *Jucunda laudatio* 15, Venice 1976–77. I am grateful to F. Luciani of Milan for pointing out this second study to me; unfortunately I have not been able to consult it.

[19]The name has meanwhile appeared also in Ammonite inscriptions, cf. among others that of the fortress of Amman, line 1, for which see provisionally E. Puech and A. Rofe, 'L'inscription de la citadelle d'Amman', *RB* 80, 1973, 531–41.

In its proto-history Israel had had contacts with Ammon in the time of the Judges (ch. 11) and in the time of Saul (I Sam. 11), when the Ammonites were settled in their territory in Transjordan trying to enlarge their possessions at the expense of the Israelites living in the region of Gilead. Under David and Solomon they had been reduced to vassal status, but then, like the other peoples of Transjordan, they succeeded in liberating themselves with the break-up of the personal union between Israel and Judah, though in what circumstances we do not know. In II Chron. 20.1ff. they fight against Jehoshaphat of Judah (c. 873–849 or 868–847), but are defeated. The situation of the Ammonites is therefore similar to that of the Edomites, though in their case, too, we cannot accept a campaign in relation to the Aramaean revival, but only directly against Israel. Here too we are confronted with total war, this time fought to gain space; but in this case, too, the war is accompanied with cruelty, this time aimed at providing the new occupants with a territory stripped of its original inhabitants. Rabbah, also called Rabbat ($b^e n\bar{e}$) Ammon, is the site of present-day Amman, capital of the Hashemite kingdom of Jordan (coord. 238–151), and has partially kept the old name.

6. Against Moab (2.1–3)

Willi-Plein**, 17; Markert**, 64–7; G. Pfeifer, 'Amos und Deuterojesaja denkformanalytisch (sic!) verglichen', *ZAW* 93, 1984, 439–43.

---

2 [1]Thus YHWH has spoken: 'Because of the innumerable crimes of Moab, I shall not go back on my decision: because they burned the bones of the king of Edom to lime, [2]I shall send fire against Moab, so that it destroys the palaces of Kerioth, and Moab shall perish amidst uproar, amidst the war-cry and the sound of the trumpet. [3]I shall destroy the ruler from its midst and will slay his princes with him.' YHWH has spoken.

[1] 'To lime'; so this is not the practice of cremating corpses, but the plundering of tombs. The text is therefore clear and there is no point in emending. [2] Keriot is a place in Moab also mentioned in the Mesha inscription from the end of the ninth century, KAI 181, line 13,[20] the present-day el-Qereiyāt (coord. 215–105). LXX read τῶν πόλεων αὐτῆς, i.e. *qiryōtēhā*, similarly Tg, but that has the singular, a confusion which is possible in an unvocalized text. 'Perish': literally 'die'. For 'war-cry',

---

[20]For the text see my *Introduction*, 476.

Hebrew *terū'āh*, cf. on 1.14. **[3]** 'The ruler': the earliest meaning of the root *šāpat*, usually 'judge',[21] already attested in the Mari texts of the eighteenth to seventeenth century BC and perhaps at Ebla at the end of the third millennium. 'From its': the feminine suffix refers to Kerioth, so an emendation is not necessary.

We do not know to what episode of the history of relations between Edom and Moab this text refers. However, it must have been a matter which caused something of a sensation: to violate a tomb has always been considered an act of grave impiety throughout the civilized world. It is interesting to note that Moab is not regarded as guilty towards Israel, a fact which appears completely in line with the whole tendency of the oracles against the nations: these always deal with crimes against humanity, whether or not they have been committed against Israel, so that it seems that there is no nationalistic approach to the matter.

7. Against Judah (2.4–5)

S. Wagner**, *passim*; Willi-Plein**, 17f.; Markert**, 67–71; G. Pfeifer, cf. on the previous section.

2 [4]Thus YHWH has spoken: 'Because of the innumerable crimes of Judah, I shall not go back on my decision: because they have forsaken the teaching of YHWH and have not observed his commandments, because their lying [gods] (which already their fathers followed) have led them astray, [5]I shall send fire against Judah which shall destroy the palaces of Jerusalem!'

[4] 'Have led them astray', root *ta'āh*. 'Gods': to be understood, though the text avoids mentioning them directly. LXX adds ἃ ἐποίησαν, referring to the statues, the images, but this element does not seem implicit in the text.

From Wellhausen onwards this oracle has been considered inauthentic. That seems evident from v. 4bβ and perhaps also from v. 4bα, given the presence of marked Deuteronomistic terminology. However, it need not necessarily be the case, as Rudolph* notes, although it is possible to trace elements of a similar re-elaboration here. Rudolph wants to explain it by saying that language of this kind must already have existed

[21]W. Richter, 'Zu den "Richtern Israels"', *ZAW* 77, 1965, 40–72, and recently my 'Osservazioni sulla radice *špt* e sul termine *šōpᵉṭīm* in ebraico biblico', *OA* 19, 1980, 57–9; also my *Judges*, OTL 1981, 2ff.

and does not arise from one year to the next, but this is clearly an inadequate explanation of the phenomenon. It is clear that the invective is automatically suspect not least because it would be the only one which does not speak of some form of atrocity, but only of transgressions which we could call 'theological'. On the other hand it is evident that in the context, in which virtually all the peoples of the region including Israel are mentioned, an oracle against Judah would in fact seem necessary, as Rudolph* rightly points out. If this argument is correct, we must accept that an original text was lost and replaced by this one, and that there is no hope of reconstructing the old text.

8. Against Israel (2.6–16)

E. A. Speiser, 'Of Shoes and Shekels', *BASOR* 77, 1940, 15–20 = *Oriental and Biblical Studies*, Philadelphia 1967, 151–9; M. A. Beek, 'The Religious Background of Amos II 6–8', *OTS* 5, 1948, 132–41; H.-J. Kraus, 'Die prophetische Botschaft gegen das soziale Unrecht Israels', *EvTh* 15, 1955, (295–307) = *Biblisch-theologische Aufsätze*, Neukirchen 1972, (120–133) 295ff./120ff.; R. Bach, 'Gottesrecht und weltliches Recht in der Verkündigung des Propheten Amos', in *FS Günther Dehn*, Neukirchen 1957, 23–34; H. Gese, 'Amos II 13 und die hebräische Wurzel "WQ"', *VT* 12, 1962, 417–24; S. Wagner**; J. Vollmer**, 20–26; Willi-Plein**, 18–21; R. Rendtorff, 'Zu Amos 2, 14–16', *ZAW* 85, 1973, 226f.; Markert**, 71–83; J. L. Sicre**, 112–16; B. Lang, 'Sklaven und Unfreie im Buch Amos (II 6, VIII 6)', *VT* 31, 1981, 482–8; S. M. Paul, 'Two Cognate Semitic Terms for Mating and Copulating. 2. Amos ii 7', *VT* 32, 1982, 492–4 and H. S. Barstad** 1984, 14–36.

---

2 [6]Thus YHWH has spoken: 'Because of the innumerable crimes of Israel I shall not go back on my decision; because they sell the innocent for silver, the needy for the equivalent of a pair of sandals. [7]They trample in the dust of the earth [they look for a speck of dust on] the head of the humble, they hinder the wretched from gaining access to legal proceedings.

Father and son go to the girl and thus profane my holy name. [8]On garments taken in pawn they lie down before every altar; they drink the wine of those who have been fined, in the temple of their God. [9]And for love of them I uprooted the Amorites, whose height was like that of the cedars and whose strength was like that of the oaks. Nevertheless, I destroyed their fruit above and their roots beneath. [10]And I was the one who had brought them up from the land of Egypt, who had led them through the desert for forty years, to occupy the land of the Amorites. [11]And it was I who made some of your sons prophets and some of your young men Nazirites. Is it not indeed so, O Israelites? Says YHWH. [12]But you gave the Nazirites wine to drink and you forbade the prophets to prophesy. [13]Therefore, behold I will make the soil tremble [split] under you as a cart trembles [makes it split] when it is full of sheaves; [14]then every way of escape shall vanish for the swift, the strong man will no longer be able to use his strength, the brave man will no longer be able to save his life; [15]the one who draws the bow will no longer be able to stand, the swift man will no longer be able to run away on foot nor the horseman succeed in saving his life. [16]Even he who is most stout of heart among the brave will flee away naked in that day.' Oracle of YHWH.

[6] 'Sell': *mik'rām* for *mok'rām*, cf. *GesK* § 61b, Joüon § 65, 5 and Meyer II, § 85g. The verb is characteristically used for the selling of slaves. 'The innocent': *saddīq* in the context of a trial indicates the innocent party, the one who is in the right, whose cause ought to win (cf. Deut. 25.1). 'For the equivalent . . .': the expression, which recurs with variations in 8.6, is usually understood as 'sell for a small debt' (most recently Sicre**) which has subsequently grown as a result of usurious interest, whereas the law in Ex. 22.1–3 provides such a penalty only for one who has committed a theft and cannot recompense the damage and pay the penalty provided for it. Moreover in Babylonia,[22] too, a region which economically was more advanced, interest of 20% to 25% was exacted on loans in cash and 30% on advances in kind to countryfolk. However, others think that the reference is to the corruptibility of judges (a plague which is still acute today in the Near East), whom small sums (*bet pretii*) are enough to influence (V. Maag**). Another explanation has been proposed by Speiser and accepted by Snaith*: the starting point is the usage attested in Ruth 4.7 and Ps. 60.10, cf. Deut. 25.9f., of taking off a sandal and giving it to someone else or throwing it over an object: this is the sign or the pledge for a legally valid transaction, given the low value of the object, which cannot therefore denote a form of barter or payment. Moreover in the Nuzi texts (middle of the fifteenth century) there was a way of circumventing the law which prohibited the alienation of land. This was by means of a fictitious adoption: the adopted person thus inherited the property; transactions of this kind were sealed with a pair of shoes or a garment. Speiser rediscovers such concepts in a reading attested by LXX for I Sam. 12.3 (it is confirmed by Sir. 49.19). Here we read: 'From whose hand did I take bribes or shoes? Tell me, I am ready to restore them', a reading which is generally considered better than MT. According to Speiser's explanation Samuel denies ever having accepted money to corrupt him or having been a party to fictitious transactions (even if they were legally valid), concluded with the above-mentioned pledge, the sandal. The phrase will thus have been proverbial:

[22]Cf. R. de Vaux, *Ancient Israel*, London 1961, 170f.

by means of transactions valid on the formal legal level but in essence fictitious, the poor and the lowly are put in the position of always being in the wrong. The phrase would thus reveal one of the most specific aspects of oppression, all the more serious in that it is conducted with legally unexceptionable means. This is a very interesting explanation, but the parallelism would seem rather to favour a reference to the venality of the judge or to the exorbitant amount of interest on the loan. **[7]** 'Trample': the Hebrew *haššoʾpīm* comes from the root *šāʾap*, 'breathe painfully', 'puff', 'pant', sometimes 'fly off' (to bring something or someone, always with an object). But LXX read τὰ πατοῦντα ('trample') ἐπὶ τὸν χοῦν τῆς γῆς, καὶ ἐκονδύλιζον, i.e. the Hebrew *šwp₁*, which is also attested in Gen. 3.15 in another context which is less clear. The Greek text also sees them 'slapping the faces of the humble', probably a secondary amplification, as is the MT addition 'in the dust of the ground': these are both attempts to show in a vivid way how the lowly are ill-treated. V. Maag suggests**: 'Look for specks of dust on the head of the humble', i.e. find a pretext for being able to condemn them. Given the legal context of a trial, Wolff* understands *derek* as in the phrase 8.12: any recourse to the law, any legal *iter* will be useless in a situation of injustice, formally legalized by those in power. This is a better rendering than that arising from the reading *midderek*, 'and put off the wretched from the road', much more generic and with moral connotations. 'Father and son', literally 'a man and his father', is meant to indicate the spread of these practices among old and young, in other words among all members of society, and not the sharing of the sin in the nuclear family. The text does not, however, say that they go to the *same* woman (although it seems to imply it); in all probability the article with 'woman' also indicates that this is a current term for sacred prostitute, and is therefore a synonym of *qᵉdēšāh* (Snaith). At all events it is clear that illicit sexual acts are involved here, as Paul[23] has demonstrated. For Beek and Maag** (cf. Markert**, 79f.), however, this would be the general abuse of lowly people of female sex in domestic service, by violating them (Ex. 21.7–11; Lev. 12.17). 'And profane': a clause preceded by *lᵉmaʿan*, a term which normally introduces a final clause, but here, as *KB²⁻³*, Snaith* and Amsler* rightly observe, it serves to present the consequences of an act rather than the intentions of the one who commits it. On the other hand, as Rinaldi* points out, this does not exclude the intention of engaging in a fertility cult of other deities, and therefore bestiality. At all events this is a terminology typical of Deuteronomy, Dtr and Ezekiel, also in the mention of the divine name. **[8]** 'On garments . . .': the preposition is lacking in LXX, which has 'They stretch out the garments . . .', thus implying yet another crime: but it is attested in all the ancient translations. In MT the expression indicates the continu-

---

²³Cf. already A. B. Ehrlich, *Randglossen zur hebräischen Bibel*, Leipzig V, 1912, 232 (pointed out to me by S. M. Paul). For the social position of the 'girl' see now the exhaustive study by Barstad**.

ation of the orgy. 'Garments': a generic term for a probable reference to Ex. 22.25–26//Deut. 24.12–13, texts which require the restoration of the cloak before the evening to anyone who has given it in pledge for a loan. The application of this law also seems to be confirmed by the now famous ostracon of Yabneh Yam[24] from the end of the eighth and beginning of the seventh century BC, a text which, despite all the aspects which are still obscure, deals with the problem of a cloak given in pledge for a debt which has not been restored by the evening. 'Of their God'; it is grammatically possible also to translate this 'of their gods'; but we should remember that Amos is not dealing with problems of paganism or syncretism,[25] so that the reference to YHWH gives the speech a note of sarcasm (Snaith*, Amsler*) when the text would otherwise be pale and colourless. There is no mention here of the Jerusalem temple, as Dhorme* would like to see.

[9] 'For love of them . . .', literally 'before them', 'in their presence'. For the height of the Amorites cf. Num. 13.32, a text from which this one differs somewhat.

[11] Note the partitive value of *min*: 'Some of . . .' For the Nazirites cf. Num. 6.2ff.

[13] 'Split', Hebrew *meʿiq*, is a well-known *crux*. V. Maag** renders it 'shake', M. A. Beek, 'jolt', similarly Markert**, 81ff.; in which case it will be a reference to the earthquake. Another valid translation, though rejected by Amsler*, comes from Gese**'s study: the root *ʿwq* is a *hapax legomenon*, since it only appears here, albeit twice. LXX[B] has the verb κυλίω, 'roll', cf. 'Α with τριζήσω, Vg *stridebo* and Arabic *ʿyq*; these are images connected with the movement of a laden cart on a bad road. Hence the suggestions that it should be translated 'jolt' or 'creak'. LXX[A] has κωλύω, 'hinder', i.e. the Aramaic *ʿwq*, Hebrew *swq*, from *dwq**, 'be afraid', 'preoccupied', in the causative 'compress' or 'oppress', 'put stress on', cf. Arabic *ʿwq*, but this seems a spiritualizing solution and therefore makeshift. Gese, however, beginning from the idea of the overburdened cart (*lāh* would then be a *dativus commodi*, cf. *GesK* §§ 119s, 135i; Joüon § 133d) recalls the rabbinic terms *ʿūqāh* and *ʿawāq*, 'splits', 'fissures', 'ditch', connecting the expression with a split in the earth caused by the track of the wheels. Here, too, we have an image of what the earthquake would be (cf. 1.1). This explanation is clearly better than all the others (Wolff*), even if evidence for the use of carts for transporting crops or straw has yet to be found (Osty*). Rinaldi* therefore prefers the more generic and less specific 'press' on the ground by the overloaded cart.

[14–16] These repeat conventional themes (cf. Jer. 46.5, 12; Ezek. 32.21); moreover the end contradicts the beginning. They are clearly additions.

---

[24]*KAI* 200, cf. my *Introduction*, 479, for a translation and examination of the problems in the text.

[25]Cf. my *Introduction*, 244.

This pericope is clearly meant to form the climax of the oracles against the nations; it also gives the impression that what has been said about the other peoples has been said essentially as preparation for the oracle against Israel. This is a well-attested method among the prophets, cf. here 3.2; also Isa. 5.1ff.; II Sam. 12.1ff.; namely, to obtain the assent of one's audience to a series of assertions and then force them to accept one directed against them; if YHWH punishes the guilty among the other peoples, he will also punish those of his own people (Vollmer**). A number of features of form and content mark this oracle out from the others. Formally it is much longer: in content the conventional description of punishment by means of fire is missing at the end, while the crimes of Israel are in fact four in number, so that the numerical oracle is no longer a rhetorical figure. However, the oracle has in common with the others the introductory formula and the theme of imminent punishment introduced by the preposition *'al* with the infinitive: according to Bach's study these crimes are to be connected with elements in the apodeictic formulation of law.[26]

The charge is introduced (v. 7a) by a participle, followed (v. 7bα–8aα) by three imperfects, in turn amplified by formulae of a typical ethical and cultic type (vv. 7bβ, 8aβ, bβ) aimed at making the crimes appear even more abominable, in that they have been committed within the sacral sphere. The introduction of an argument with a participle is also attested elsewhere in the book, cf. 5.18; 6.1, 3–6, 8, 14, and can easily be connected with the numerical formula, which we examined in 1.3ff. And all this could be a feature in favour of the authenticity even of the evident amplifications in vv. 7b–8. However, the obvious change of theme is a strong point against such authenticity, despite the stylistic affinities. In vv. 9ff. we then have a series of formulae which stress the contrast between the divine work and Israel's response: these are typical 'contrast motives' which have been examined by Westermann;[27] Wolff* wants to attribute the material to the prophet, and in fact in v. 9 we find traditions which have every appearance of being original; they differ from others in the Pentateuch and the former prophets by attributing to the Amorites the possession of all Palestine and saying that they were extraordinarily tall, features which we do not find elsewhere. By contrast, as W. H. Schmidt**, 179ff., points out, vv. 10 and 11 are conventional, as perhaps is also v. 12, and certainly to be connected with a redaction which is Deuteronomistic or from a similar origin. Verse 13 finally announces the punishment; not, however, in

[26]For this kind of law in ancient Israel cf. my *Introduction*, 152ff.

[27]C. Westermann, 'Die Mari-Briefe und die Prophetie in Israel', in *Forschungen am Alten Testament*, Munich 1964, (171–88) 182.

terms of fire against a place in Israel, but as an anticipation of the imminent earthquake, a theme introduced by the term *hinneh*, 'Behold . .', which is a term attested several times in Amos, always in connection with judgment. Verses 14–16 also appear to be conventional, while the conclusion has the formula *n^e'um YHWH* instead of *'āmar YHWH* (cf. the introduction, § 3a). The formula appears particularly in Jeremiah and Ezekiel, but Wolff* does not see why it should not go back to Amos himself, since it serves well to conclude the series of oracles against the people. At all events it is a formula which is difficult to trace back to Amos and the more ancient traditions.

So originally the oracle against Israel seems to have been composed of vv. 6 and 13, then amplified successively, though still in ancient times, from v. 7a on. Verses 7b–9 form a later addition which may be old, but it is hard to attribute it to the prophet or to circles round him, while vv. 10–12 are probably Deuteronomistic or from a related school, and vv. 14–16 belong to a later amplification, perhaps two, from the exilic period: which of these is the case is not easy to determine.

The text is also noteworthy for some points of content. First of all, the invective criticizes the internal situation in Israel and not acts committed to the detriment of other peoples; and secondly, on the level of biblical theology and the religion of Israel, it seems of supreme importance that here we have the earliest attestation of what we can call a harsh criticism, and therefore an invitation to the people of God to practise self-criticism. For the first time the election of Israel appears as something for which the people of God has to give account, a theme which is clearly developed in the additions and perfected by them. The life of Israel should not be, and therefore cannot be, like that of other peoples. If they commit atrocities in war, Israel commits atrocities within what should be a community; the total war of the others therefore does not appear much worse than Israel's own radical injustice.

The technique followed by the prophet in his preaching is typical in this respect and reappears, albeit on a much smaller scale, in 3.2 (a passage which precisely for this reason Maag** prefers to consider an integral part of the present one); the oracles against the nations and the condemnation of the nations can also appear to the audience as the theological seal on the revivalist policy of Jeroboam II. Having thus aroused the theological and nationalistic enthusiasm of his audience, the prophet explains that a true preaching cannot be exhausted in condemning the atrocities of others but must also take account of those of its own. As we have seen, Isa. 5.1ff. took the same line some decades later.

In v. 13 we would have an earthquake, instead of fire as in the other

51

oracles, which appears as the instrument of punishment. And the earthquake is a feature which often accompanies a theophany, especially if it refers to the divine interventions by YHWH in prehistorical times on behalf of his own people (Judg. 5.4b–5; Ps. 68.8a; 97.5; cf. Isa. 6.1ff. and, much later, Ezek. 19.16–19). The fear which accompanied a phenomenon of this kind, which in any case was terrible, was therefore dialectically overcome by the certainty that God was acting for the salvation of his own people. However, in this case the theme appears with the opposite function, that of a judge against his own people, and that also explains the fear of Isaiah in the vision in ch. 6. Thus the ancient salvific phenomena are reversed; they are directed against the people of God rather than against its enemies, and whereas in the holy war those affected are the enemies who cannot resist, here it is the people of God, as the addition of vv. 14–16 rightly indicates.[28] And whereas in 1.2 everything still remains hidden, here it appears in manifest form; the reason for the punishment is here given as a law which has become an instrument of corruption and oppression rather than of equity and justice. We can see the additions as a series of later interpretations of these themes: syncretism, which combines manifest immorality with offences against YHWH and one's neighbour (cf. Hos. 4.14); the ancient forms of the cult (of course as they were seen by the redactors) now void of its meaning and its content; the rejection of the Torah, in other words of the word of God. The redaction is thus able to pursue the theme of a history from salvation to ruin; if it came to such a conclusion, all the preceding history of the people, the divine interventions on its behalf, its promises, have been useless and are therefore annulled. Rather, Israel will feel from the saving hand of its own God the harshness of the Holy War directed against it. And in this way the ancient past, re-read many times by the generations to follow, also takes on an ideologically uniform character.

[28]For the Holy War see the now classic study by G. von Rad, *Die Heilige Krieg im alten Israel*, ATANT 20, 1951 and reprints. The only objection that has been made to it is that it dates to an early period material which is for the most part Deuteronomistic. For the holy war as a judgment on Israel see my study cited in n. 4 (p. 30) above. For the whole problem, see my forthcoming article in *Theologische Realenzyklopädie*, 'Krieg – Altes Testament'.

The 'Words of Amos of Tekoa' I

(Chapters 3–6)

1. The election of Israel (3.1–2)

Y. Gitay, 'A Study of Amos's Art of Speech: A Rhetorical Analysis of Amos 3, 1–15', *CBQ* 42, 1980, 293–309.

The 'words of Amos' begin with a brief digression on the problem of the election of Israel; however, this is not a testimony but still a messenger formula. For this reason, as I noted in the last lines of the previous section, V. Maag** would prefer to classify these two verses with the previous section, given that the theme is similar. But in that case what is to be done about the superscription? The alternation of persons, here the first person and there the third, is not a problem, since it is also well attested in Ugaritic. On the other hand, in a basic examination of the two texts it immediately emerges that the theme is only similar and not identical; 2.6–16 are concerned essentially with the oppression of the wretched and not with election, a feature which is only added at a later stage and therefore seems secondary; nor does it have the verb *yāda'*, used here, as we shall see, in quite a special sense. It might also be added that v. 1b is an addition of a Deuteronomistic kind, even if that is not completely certain because of the use of the verb *'ālāh* in the hiphil instead of the verb *yāṣā'* in the hiphil which is typical of Deuteronomy and Dtr. Gitay argues that the whole section vv. 1–15 presupposes a speech given to an audience.

E. Baumann, 'YD' and seine Derivate', *ZAW* 28, 1908, 22–41 and 110–43 (still valid despite its age); J. Pedersen, *Israel. Its Life and Culture* I–II, Copenhagen 1926, 278; G. J. Botterweck, 'Gott erkennen', in *Sprachgebrauch des Alten Testaments*, BBB 2, Bonn 1951, 21f., 37f.; T. C. Vriezen, *Die Erwählung Israels nach dem Alten Testament*, ATANT 24, Zurich 1953, 36ff.; W. Eichrodt, *Theology of the Old Testament* II, London and Philadelphia 1967, 291–3; J. Lindblom, *Prophecy in Ancient Israel*, Oxford 1962, 326; S. Herrmann, *Die prophetischen Heilserwartungen im Alten Testament*, BWANT 85, Stuttgart 1965, 119; T. R. Hobbs, 'Amos 3, 1b and 2, 10', *ZAW* 81, 1969, 384–7; H. B. Huffmon, 'The Treaty Background of Hebrew *yāda'*', *BASOR* 181, 1966, 31–7; id. and S. B. Parker, 'A Further Note on the Treaty

Background of Hebrew *yāda'*, *BASOR* 184, 1966, 36–8; F. Gaboriau, 'La connaissance de Dieu dans l'Ancien Testament', *Angelicum* 45, 1968, (145–83) 176f.; M. O'Rourke Boyle, 'The Covenant Lawsuit of the Prophet, Amos III 1–IV 13', *VT* 21, 1971, 338–62; W. Schottroff, *yāda'*, *THAT* 1, 1971, (682–701) 692ff.; J. Vollmer*, 29–33; Willi-Plein**, 20f.; Markert**, 83–6; Y. Gitay, art. cit., above.

---

3 [1]Hear this word that YHWH has spoken against you, O people of Israel, against the whole family which I brought up out of the land of Egypt: [2]'With you alone of all the families of the earth have I had a special relationship; therefore I shall call you to account because of your transgressions.'

[1] ' . . . the family' is an unusual expression in a context like this; but this is explained by the mention of 'all the families' in the following verse, to which it is an introduction. That demonstrates the late character of the verse, unless the beginning of YHWH's speech is transposed to the middle of the verse, producing ' . . . O Israelites, of all the family that I brought up out of Egypt, only you . . .' [2] 'have had . . . a special relationship': *yāda'ti* is clearly the key term of the phrase. Given the vast semantic range of *yāda'* (from 'know' on the intellectual level to 'have sexual intercourse with'), it is not surprising that translations differ. We can immediately reject the literal rendering 'You only have I known' (Dhorme* and others) because it is clearly wrong: on the one hand God knows all people, cf. the preceding section; on the other it burdens the unknowing reader with a problem which has to be confronted and resolved in the translation phase. Wellhausen*, Nowack*, Marti* and Snaith* want to render 'have intimate relations with', cf. Snaith's 'With you alone I have been intimate', thus indicating at the same time the relationship the concept has with election; similarly J. A. Bewer*, T. H. Robinson*, W. Rudolph* and V. Maag**. Others have looked for possible sexual implications of the phrase, seeing in it an echo of the marriage ideology which appears in Hos. 1.3. However E. Baumann (*'huldreiche Erwählung, bzw. Berufung'*, 34, i.e. 'gracious election or calling'), G. Rinaldi*, A. Weiser* and E. Osty* all opt for the concept of election, choice, also attested indirectly in 9.7 and in Hos. 13.5 with the same verb; we also have the verb *wadū//edū₁* in Akkadian, *AHw* I, 187f., to denote either the knowledge or the divine election of king and people (Rinaldi*). Lindblom thinks in terms of being 'occupied with', 'interested in . . .', 'preoccupied with . . .' Now there can be no doubt of the fact that *yāda'* serves also to express the concept of election in the theological sense of the term, cf. Gen. 18.19; Jer. 1.5; in the latter text the prophet is 'known' and 'sanctified' by God before his birth. The root also appears in the language of the international treaties of the Ancient Near East, first those of

Mari in the eighteenth-seventeenth century BC, then in the Hittite treaties and others from the second half of the second millennium, in which the vassal asks the great king to recognize him and the great king pledges to do this (Huffmon, 24, in fact stresses that here we have an allusion to the covenant as in Hos. 13.4f.; Deut. 9.24 in the emended text, so that there would be a very close link between covenant and election). 'Of the earth': Vollmer** and Markert** would prefer to translate 'fertile land', thus distinguishing *'ªdāmāh* from *'ereṣ*; however, this is useless pedantry. The text does not seek to distinguish between the inhabitants of the cultivated land and those, for example, of the desert and to translate in this way introduces a new concept which is irrelevant to the text. 'Call to account': *pāqad* is the verb of visitation, but very often with the negative sense of inspection with the subsequent punishment of one who is found wanting: and it has this sense here through the use of the preposition *'al*, in this context 'against'.

This short oracle speaks of the theme of the election of Israel directly rather than indirectly through the mention of or allusion to episodes in the history of salvation. What we find in v. 1b is, as we have seen, of doubtful authenticity, and in any case appears in the superscription, not in the oracle proper. The latter is composed of a very brief text of two lines linked together, but in the perfect tense, denoting completeness. The audience appears in the first part of the superscription, v. 1a: the 'Israelites'. This is clearly a reference to the North and not to the twelve tribes, as Herrmann, 119, rightly observes; in particular it is to the Joseph group, Ephraim and Manasseh, the central nucleus of the kingdom from time immemorial who bore the name Israel in the strict sense. It was only after the fall of the Northern Kingdom (722–20 BC) and especially after the exile that Judah claimed the name 'Israel' for itself, notwithstanding the opposition of those who were soon to become the Samaritans. Nor is it strange that both the theme and the audience appear in Amos and Hosea, the only prophets who address the north. This is an argument in favour of the antiquity of the first part of the superscription, which probably goes back to the first redaction of the book.

The concept of election or at least a special, privileged relationship is here expressed with the root *yāda'*, as we have seen. It is not exactly the same as that expressed in 9.7, contrary to what is sometimes claimed; 9.7 tends rather to discredit the concept or rather to reduce its dimensions, stressing that Israel is not superior to the other peoples, who are also the object of divine vocation. Rather, this passage fully accepts the validity of the concept, which moreover is presupposed by the discourse which follows, but challenges the conclusions that the people draw from it. The people obviously seem to have considered the election in static terms, as an indefeasible privilege conferred in a distant past, the validity of which lasted over the centuries and in which they thought they could trust without any fear: the one who had elected Israel would also be disposed to pardon its transgressions and come to its aid (cf. Ex. 20.5–6//Deut. 5.9–10); 34.6f. and again Hos. 6.1ff., a text which for many scholars is a liturgical expression of the current view. And it is reasonable to suppose that this concept of election found its main support precisely in the cult, in which the glorious acts of God in the past were celebrated. Moreover, Deuteronomy also rails against similar notions, cf. 10.15; 27.16–19; 28.1f. For the prophet, election implies the responsibility of the people towards their Lord, who has the right to make demands on them in return for gifts received: the New Testament also knows a similar concept when in Luke 12.48 Jesus states: 'The more someone has received the more will be asked of him.'

Some scholars (most recently Huffmon) have argued that election here is synonymous with a relationship regulated by the covenant. But these are two different things which are not necessarily connected: election can (but need not) be expressed in a covenant, especially in the context of the reinterpretation of Israel's traditions made by Deuteronomy and Dtr (cf. the cases of Abraham, Moses and much later Jeremiah). But in such cases the covenant, when it is present, clearly forms an interpretation of the event, not an original component. Moreover election is always a unilateral act of the deity towards the faithful, whereas the covenant is by nature a bilateral act, with a second party or, in the case of vassal treaties, a fictitious party, which simply suffers it.

The thought of the oracle is very significant, though if the surface meaning is clear, some of the ultimate implications escape us. It has been argued that in reality the passage is the conclusion of a dispute (Rinaldi* and Weiser*), but it is impossible to say anything of that kind for certain.

2. Causes and effects (3.3–8)

H. S. Gehman, 'Notes on *mwqš*', *JBL* 38, 1939, 277–81; H. Junker, '*Leo rugiit, quis non timebit? Deus locutus est, quis non prophetabit?*', *TTZ* 59, 1950, 4–13; G. R. Driver, 'Hebr.*môqeš*', *JBL* 73, 1954, 131–5; D. W. Thomas, 'Note on *nōʿādū* in Amos 3. 3', *JTS* NS 7, 1956, 69f.; H. Reventlow, *Das Amt . . ,* 25ff.; H. Gese**, 424f.; H.-W. Wolff**, 6f.; W. H. Schmidt**; S. Mittmann, 'Gestalt und Gehalt einer prophetischen Selbstrechtfertigung (Am. 3, 3–

56

8)', *TQ* 151, 1971, 134–45; Willi-Plein**, 21f.; Markert**, 86–94; H. H. Schmid, *Der sogenannte Jahwist*, Zurich 1976, 33f.; W. Eichrodt, 'Die Vollmacht des Amos', in *Beiträge zur alttestamentlichen Theologie, FS W. Zimmerli*, Göttingen 1977, 124–31; J. M. Ward**, 1969, 37ff.; Y. Gitay, cf. the preceding section; B. Renaud, 'Génèse et théologie d'Amos 3, 3–8', in *Mélanges bibliques et orientaux . . . M. Henri Cazelles*, AOAT 212, Kevelaer-Neukirchen 1981, 353–72; M. J. Mulder, 'Ein Vorschlag zur Übersetzung von Amos III 6b', *VT* 34, 1984, 106–8; A. Schenker, 'Interpretation von Amos 3, 3–18', *BZ* 30, 1986, 250–6. For *ya'ar* = 'scrub', cf. C. Houtman, 'De jubelzang van de struiken der wildernis in Psalm 96:12b', in *Loven en geloven, FS N. H. Ridderbos*, Amsterdam 1975, (151–74) 164–72.

---

3 [3]Do two people walk together unless they have first met [made an appointment]? [4]Does a lion roar in the scrub without having any prey? Does a young lion grunt from his den without having taken something? [5]Does a bird fall into a trap on the earth, when there is no bait in it? Does a snare spring up from the ground when it has taken nothing? [6]Or, if the trumpet sounds in the city, will the people not be afraid? Or does evil happen in the city without YHWH being the author of it? [7]Surely the Lord YHWH does nothing without having first revealed his intention to his ministers, the prophets. [8]The lion roars, who will not be afraid? Lord YHWH speaks, who will not prophesy?

Leaving aside v. 7, this passage is made up of six questions. Five of them are introduced by the interrogative particle *h^a* and are in five linked lines; two are introduced by *'im*, vv. 3–5 and 6. We also find the second construction in 6.6, 12; for it cf. *GesK* §§ 150c–i, Joüon § 161d and Meyer II, § 86, 3a-b; Meyer stresses its disjunctive value. For that reason in the translation I have introduced the conjunction 'or' in v. 6. [3] For Gese**, 424, preceded by K. Marti*, the whole verse has differences in style from what follows (there is no parallelism, the sinister tone of the others is missing and the content is somewhat conventional); therefore it is not authentic but only serves as a link between 3.2 and 3.4, so that it could logically belong to the preceding unit. These arguments are not conclusive; the lack of parallelism could also arise from the loss of half a line. 'Met' or 'made an appointment': *nō'ādū*, from *yā'ad*, which denotes both terms; it is confirmed by '*A*, *Θ*, Vg and Tg. But LXX translated γνωρίσωσιν (cf. *BHK*[3]), and therefore read *nōdā'ū*, root *yāda'*, i.e. 'without knowing one another'. For some scholars this reading is preferable to MT, cf. the study by Thomas, who wants to connect the possible *yd'* with the Arabic *wd'*, which in some patterns means 'be reconciled'; but here we would have a concept of litigation and reconciliation which is alien to the context. [4] 'Scrub': *ya'ar* in ancient times, in addition to the meaning which it has in modern Hebrew, often denoted ground covered with shrubs and bushes, rather than a 'wood'. 'From his den': the expression is deleted by some scholars because it overloads the metre of the line; however, the preceding line also has an indication of place. Another reason for deletion is that it is zoologically inaccurate (Snaith): the lion roars only when it is pouncing and not when it is eating. But the text says only that the young lion 'utters his sound' or 'his voice', which can also be rendered 'his grunt'. **[5]** 'Into a trap' is lacking in LXX, which only has τῆς γῆς. What is literally 'on the snare of the earth' refers, as Gehman pointed out, to a particular implement, distinct from the noose or the net held in the air. 'Prey': the Hebrew *mōqēš* is translated thus by some scholars: BDB, Gehman, Rinaldi*, Robinson*, Amsler*, Rudolph*: G. R. Driver differs and it is better than 'trap' in the economy of the phrase, even if it can have that meaning in other contexts. LXX and Tg have 'bird-catcher', i.e. the participle of *yāqaš*. **[6]** M. J. Mulder, 1984, suggests a new translation: 'Can something evil happen in the city without YHWH reacting to it?' This is an interesting suggestion. **[7]** This prose verse interrupts the context with an explanatory comment on the relationship between decision and divine action and the part which the prophet has in them; cf. already W. R. Harper*, 1895. This is a comment which nowadays is generally understood to be Deuteronomistic (Schmidt** and Schmid) and is an arbitrary amplification of the text. It is probably the echo of discussions like that in Deut. 18.19ff., whereas the expression 'his ministers (or his servants) the prophets' usually appears in a Deuteronomic or Deuteronomistic context. Sellin* would prefer to postpone the verse to v. 8, while Dhorme* suggests joining the two syntactically, and making one sentence. However, the first approach would markedly interfere with the text without any justification, and the second mixes two different literary genres without resolving the basic question, that of content. Reventlow**, 28, is the only one to consider the verse authentic. 'Intention', literally 'plan', 'secret discourse': Hebrew *sōd*; LXX translated παιδείαν, probably 'project, educative plan'.[1] 'A has ἀπόρρητον, mystery; Σ ὁμιλίαν, discourse; Θ βούλην, will, and Vg *secretum*. **[8]** *ᵃdōnāy*, 'Lord', is an interruption as in 1.8; here, too, it is probably a precursor of the perpetual Qere of the divine name.

This passage has often been seen (Rinaldi*) as the final discourse in a dispute on the legitimation of Amos in his prophetic ministry. It is often entitled 'causes and effects', and that is what I have called it here. In reality these are rhetorical questions (in the sense that they do not expect an answer), a genre which we often meet in 'wisdom disputations'.[2] As Schmidt** observes, this genre, like that of the didactic question, as Wolff prefers to call it,[3] is therefore not one of establishing causal nexuses,

[1]Cf. G. Bertram, παιδεύω, *TDNT* 5, (596–624) 603ff., 610ff.
[2]Cf. S. Terrien, 'Amos and Wisdom', in *Israel's Prophetic Heritage. Essays . . . J. Muilenburg*, New York and London 1962, 108–15.
[3]H. W. Wolff**, 6ff.

connections between cause and effect, which are typically Western categories, but simply of showing the link between two or more events and thus leading the interlocutor to accept step by step the final statement that is made to him, in itself less obvious than the others. This may also explain the difference in the introductory formulae in vv. 3–5, 6b: from effect to cause and from cause to effect (Reventlow**, Weiser*). That seems better than to begin from the suggestion made by Renaud, who points out the contrast in the passage between 'doing' (vv. 4–5, 6b) and 'saying' (vv. 6a, 7, 8). This contrast is evidently present in the text but it does not seem advisable to use it as a basis for establishing strata and phases in the additions.

So the prophet wants to proclaim the inevitability of the prophetic message when there is a divine word to transmit. And in vv. 3–5 he begins by proclaiming truths so obvious as to be almost banal, however, in vv. 6a, 8a his position changes: the reaction to the action is instinctive and thus not intrinsically necessary or always verifiable. Hence finally the jump to the last statement, the author's real thesis. This progression renders the prophet's view well: that his ministry appears in intuitive, instinctive, uncontrollable categories like fear and anxiety at a particular type of sound. Other problems do not exist for the prophet: for example that there may be people who will not obey, who are not disposed to lend themselves to being divine heralds, or that there are others who in good or bad faith either travesty a real divine message or proclaim an apocryphal one. But v. 7 which, as we have seen, is usually assigned to a Deuteronomistic redaction,[4] is in fact occupied with this problem, which we see appearing in the immediately pre-exilic period (cf. the confrontation between Jeremiah and Hananiah in Jer. 28). For the first instance see Jer. 1.7; 20.7–11, where in the second passage the prophet has actually to be 'seduced' so that he becomes a docile instrument of the divine will. These are problems which seem to have become acute shortly before the exile, when, confronted with what was clearly a desperate situation, many people put forward solutions and presented themselves as prophets sent by God without being able to identify themselves clearly to the people.

So in this case the prophet has followed a tactic which we have already been able to note on other occasions. First of all he leads the people to agree to certain obvious truths by means of instinctive categories, for the most part inaccessible to logic; then finally he presents the final thesis of his speech.

[4]S. Lehming, 'Erwägungen zu Amos', *ZTK* 55, 1958, (145–69) 152f.; W. H. Schmidt**.

3. Against the kingdom of Israel (3.9–12)

J. Reider, 'DMSQ in Amos 3.12', *JBL* 67, 1948, 245–50; G. R. Driver, 'Difficult Words in the Hebrew Prophets', in *Studies in Old Testament Prophecy . . . T. H. Robinson*, Edinburgh 1950, 69; G. S. Glanzman, 'Two Notes: Am. 3, 15 and Os. 11, 9', *CBQ* 23, 1961, 227–9; J. Rabinowitz, 'The Crux at Amos III 12', *VT* 11, 1961, 228–31; H. Gese**, 1962, 427–32; R. Fey, *Amos und Jesaja*, WMANT 12, Neukirchen 1963, 38–40; H. W. Wolff**, 56ff.; N. H. Pelser, 'Amos 3.11 – A. Communication', in *Studies in the Books of Hosea and Amos*, Pretoria 1965, 153–5; L. A. Sinclair, 'The Courtroom Motiv in the Book of Amos', *JBL* 85, 1966, 351–3; J. F. A. Sawyer, 'Those Priests in Damascus', *ASTI* 8, 1970–71, 123–30; W. Rudolph**, 1973; Willi-Plein**, 23f.; Markert**, 94–9, O. Loretz, 'Vergleich und Kommentar in Amos 3, 12', *BZ* NF 20, 1976, 122–5; S. Mittmann, 'Amos 3, 12–15 und das Bett der Samarier', *ZDPV* 92, 1976, 149–67; J. L. Sicre**, 110–12; G. Pfeifer, 'Die Denkform des Propheten Amos (III 8–11)', *SVT* 34, 1984, 476–81.

---

3 [9]Proclaim to the palaces of Ashdod – to the palaces of the country of Egypt, in these terms: 'Assemble yourselves upon the mountain[s] of Samaria, observe the great disorder that prevails within her, the oppression in her midst. [10]They are not capable of acting rightly (oracle of YHWH), those who store up products of violence and robbery in their palaces.' [11]Therefore thus says the Lord YHWH: 'Adversity [An enemy] is now surrounding the country and will trample down your power, and your palaces will be plundered.' [12]Thus says YHWH, 'As a shepherd manages to rescue from the mouth of the lion two legs or a piece of ear, so shall be the people of Israel who dwell in Samaria in the corner of a bed, on inlaid couches from Damascus.'

[9] Whereas MT read 'Ashdod', the Philistine city, LXX has 'Assyria', as a geographical area opposed to Egypt. MT is supported by Vg and Tg and is without doubt a *lectio difficilior*; on the other hand the reading makes little sense and could be an error arising out of a confusion between *res* and *dalet*. But in favour of the Massoretic reading there is more than the principle of the *lectio difficilior*: Assyria is never mentioned explicitly in Amos, whereas Ashdod appears at least one other time in 1.8. 'To the palaces': *'al* ('on' or 'within') is clearly used here for *'el*, 'to': the palaces are addressed; they are not the theme of the proclamation. In the latter case LXX has only 'to the regions of Egypt'; moreover the line is overloaded and we should delete either 'palaces' or 'the country of', probably the latter. Pfeifer observes that the distance of the two regions already implies something like a world horizon for the prophecy in the book. 'On the mountain': MT, Vg and Tg

have the plural 'on the mountains', not a nonsensical reading as some scholars would argue: in fact it denotes the mountainous region around the capital, on the hills of which the enemy are gathering for a better view (Snaith*), but it is also possible that here we have what has been called a generalizing plural (*GesK* § 124a and Joüon § 136j), in which case the reference is to the mountain on which the capital was built and the translation should be in the singular, as in LXX.

[10] 'Oracle of YHWH' seems to be an erroneous addition: the prophet is still speaking: some scholars would prefer to put the expression at the end of v. 11. [11] Difficult. 'The adversity' seems to be a better rendering than 'the enemy' (Snaith*, with Tg); it stresses the sinister character of the announcement. But LXX and 'A read 'Tyre' (*ṣōr*), which is certainly a possible reading in an unvocalized text. 'Surround'; the Hebrew *ūsᵉbīb* has been regarded for about a century now as the corruption of an original *yᵉsōbēb* (confusion between *waw* and *yod*), an original which still appears in LXX and Vg. MT 'Adversity (or 'the enemy') and the siege of the country will trample down . . .' is heavy, even if the meaning is clear. Moreover *Σ* has πολιορκία, i.e. siege, whereas *Θ*, quoted by St Jerome, has *fortitudo*; the two readings would confirm MT which is supported by *Θ*: περικύχλωσις τῆς γῆς, which would make good sense if we deleted the *waw* (perhaps a dittography with *res*?): we would then have a reference, again sinister in its indeterminacy, to Assyria, which in fact 'surrounded' Israel.

[12] Some scholars consider this to be part of the following section; others would prefer to limit this connection to v. 12c, or even postpone the whole of the verse until v. 13; for yet others it is an independent unit. In any case it is possible that v. 12 is an autonomous oracle, inserted here because of its similar theme. The conclusion is difficult because of the use of an obscure technical term, in addition to which the text is perhaps corrupt; it is therefore a classical *crux interpretum*. The difficulties already appear in LXX which simply transcribed, rather than translated, with ἱερεῖς; the Hebrew *'āreś*, a term which 'A and *Θ* have by contrast translated well but without understanding the meaning. In any case the translation confirms MT, cf. *BHK³*. The literal translation of the expression is 'in Damascus on a bed', not intrinsically impossible, but not completely convincing given that the expression does not appear either in Hebrew or elsewhere in the Semitic languages of the period. Some scholars (Maag**, 17, and *KB²*, have suggested inverting the terms, thus giving 'bed, sofa of Damascus', i.e. damask, but here too it should be noted that there is no evidence for Damascene silk for furniture and other uses before the Hellenistic period, whence it passed to the Arab world, thus making the region famous. Gese**, 430f., has proposed another possibility, followed by Markert**, 100, namely that of reading out of the expression discussed *bᵉ'ameśet*, a Hebrew term which would derive from the neo-Babylonian *amašut* (*AHw* 12, 40b) and which denotes 'arm' or 'side of a seat'. Thus the Israelites

accused would be sitting here. However, this proposal is clearly problematical, as Willi-Plein** rightly observed. W. Rudolph* and already **1973 suggested correcting to $w^e r\bar{o}b^e d\bar{\imath}m$ *šen '$\bar{a}r\bar{e}š$*, 'and which are covered with fur, inlaid with ivory'. So there are various possibilities and I have chosen only the least improbable. For a complete list cf. W. Rudolph* and K. Koch*.

The rendering of LXX is a straight transcription of '$\bar{a}r\bar{e}š$, but, as Sawyer demonstrates, it has been done perhaps with the intention of attacking the priests of Qumran. That is a problem with which I cannot deal here. The 'corner of the bed' or 'divan' seems to be a special back of an ottoman kind for reclining on, as Mittmann has shown with a wealth of examples.

Loretz has a completely different way of coping with the problem. He regards as authentic only the lines:

kh 'amr YHWH	Thus says YHWH
kysyl hr'h mpy h'ry	As a shepherd rescues from the claws of
kn ynslw bny yśr'l	lion, so the Israelites will be saved!

whereas all the rest would be a late addition by way of commentary. But the problem of the last words of the verse remains, even if it is transposed to another level.

In this passage we find the typical structure of the 'messenger formula': the analysis of the situation made by the prophet is followed by two oracles of judgment. The difference between these two elements in the prophetic preaching appears clearly from the fact that the first oracle makes only a partial reference to the prophetic analysis while the second makes no reference at all. Thus the introductory discourse serves to create the justification, if one can put it that way, for the oracle of judgment.

The discourse begins with the invocation addressed to the hypothetical heralds, sent in turn to Egypt and to Ashdod (or to Assyria), i.e. to the two nations to the north and the south, to concentrate themselves on the hills of Samaria (or, according to the other possibility that we have examined, on the hill itself), to watch what is happening in the capital of the kingdom of Israel. And these witnesses are invited to analyse the situation which is described in vv. 9b–10 with a few decisive words. The style is closely reminiscent of other prophets who call on distant lands or on heaven and earth to be involved in the trial of his own people which YHWH has instigated: Micah 6.1ff.; cf. Hos. 4.1ff.; Isa. 1.2ff.; 3.13ff. This time the invitation is addressed to mountains, hills, islands and so on. This involvement is envisaged either as bearing witness against the people of God, making accusation against it or being present at the trial. The situation is similar in this text, in that it often speaks (Sinclair) of a trial to which the witnesses are summoned. However, the image of the trial is not exploited to the full: those called are invited only to see the situation which is being created and the way in which YHWH reacts to it. And we also have the idea here that what YHWH does to his own people has a paradigmatic value for all the others. This situation also seems to be repeated in v. 10. One particularly interesting point is that noted by Terrien, 112f., and Wolff**, 57 n. 125: that the terminology in the text is, at least, in part and with different shadings, that which appears in wisdom literature. Cf. Prov. 15.16, where we have the pair *'ōṣār* and *mᵉhōmāh* (treasure and disorder, vv. 9f.), and Prov. 8.8f., where we have *da'at* and *nᵉhōnīm* (knowledge and rectitude, v. 10). For the judicial context cf. II Sam. 15.3, where Absalom calls the words of the one who seeks justice and does not find it 'good and right', cf. also Isa. 30.10, where the terms are combined in the prophet's preaching. So these would be features of popular or court wisdom, well known to the public whom the prophet addressed. Again, in a study of the social message of the prophets, H. Donner[5] thinks of members of the clerical classes, of Canaanite origin, who in the time of David and Solomon moved over from the city states to Israel and continued the administrative practices current there. 'Violence . . . and robbery' (v. 10) would then be expressions not to be taken literally but intended as synonyms of oppression in the economic sphere. This would also explain how the people in question had palaces and precious furniture. Again, however, it must be stressed that we hardly have ethnic contrast here: it is not Canaanite practices versus Israelite ones, but something which must be explained as a development within Israel, even if the texts often tend to put the blame on the Canaanites.

Now that the reasons for his preaching and the judgment that arises out of it have been made plausible, Amos can go on to pronounce the two oracles contained in vv. 11 and 12. The first, with its mention of palaces, partly links up with the analysis that has been made and announces their destruction as retaliation; the second, however, speaks of the possibility that a remnant will remain, albeit in a very bad shape. But even this possibility seems extremely remote to the prophet: the recovery of a few pieces of an animal devoured by a wild beast is clearly not a valid basis of hope for the shepherd[6] and the same goes for Samaria. The expression of doubt in 5.15 does not seem very different, though its formulation is less radical; here, moreover, the text foresees that God will have pity on the people if they are converted and substantially change the way they behave.

[5]H. Donner, 'Die soziale Botschaft der Propheten', *OA* 2, 1963, (229–44) 234–7.
[6]S. Herrmann, *Die prophetischen Heilserwartungen im Alten Testament*, BWANT 85, Stuttgart 1965, 125 n. 25.

4. Against the sanctuary of Bethel and the palaces (3.13–15)

Willi-Plein**, 24f.; Markert**, 103–6. For the nature of the goods mentioned see Mittmann's article cited in the previous section.

---

3 [13]Hear, be witnesses in [against] the house of Jacob (oracle of the Lord YHWH of hosts):
[14]'In the day that I call Israel to account for its crimes and punish the altars of Bethel, the horns of the altar will be cut off and fall to the ground. [15]I shall smite the winter palace and the summer palace; the palaces adorned with ivory shall perish and the numerous houses shall come to an end.' Oracle of YHWH.

[13] 'Be witnesses': root $'wd_{II}$ is usually 'proclaim', but here is rightly rendered by Maag** and KB^3 'be witnesses', cf. $'ed$, 'testimony'. b^e here can denote either the place in which the testimony is given or the one against whom the testimony is directed. There is no textual reason for deleting v. 13b or part of it on grounds of metre or content; the same goes for v. 14, where bα may be a gloss on 14bβ. One feature in favour of deleting the latter clause could be the alternation of the plural and the singular in relation to the altars, but in the former clause, the plural can refer to an actual plurality of altars in the cult centre mentioned (we know nothing about its topography and shape); the latter can refer to the genus 'altar' in a more vague and generic sense. The only feature in favour of deleting the two lines is the length that they give to the verse, double that about the altars; but at least in the second case we would have to take seriously into account the possibility that a line has fallen out (Rinaldi*, Robinson*) and that the part which seems to inflate the text is simply a remnant of that line. Moreover references to Bethel in Amos are quite frequent (4.4; 5.5; cf. 7.10–14 and perhaps also 9.1, where the reference is to an altar generally but Bethel is probably implied). In v. 13 the expression $YHWH\ \check{s}^e b\bar{a}'\bar{o}t$ can create difficulties, but here too it should be remembered that it is used another six times in Amos, even if it is usually associated with a typically Judahite object, the ark. [15] 'Numerous': the term *rabbīm*, which does not appear in parallelism with any other element and is banal, even if not impossible, has often been corrected, from the Marti commentary onwards, to *hobnīm*, 'of ebony' (cf. Ezek. 27.15, which speaks of 'tusks of ivory and ebony'); instead Sellin* proposed $Y^e erob'am$, 'of Jeroboam (II)', while H. Donner[7] would prefer to read $b^e r\bar{o}m\bar{\i}m$, 'embroidered fabrics', cf. Ezek. 27.24. But notwithstanding the weakness of the final expression, there is no textual reason here for emendation, so that Rinaldi*, Fosbroke* and Rudolph* reject any change in the text.

After the preceding oracle of judgment the prophet goes on to look at

[7]Donner, 'Soziale Botschaft', 237 n. 19.

other elements in the transgressions of Israel. These are features which he considers intimately connected: the illicit cult, a feature to which he has already alluded in the previous passage, so that some would prefer to take either all or part of v. 12 as the beginning of this passage. The second feature is luxury. According to the argument of the text these two elements, like the injustice in 2.6–16, are the effective cause of the spiritual and moral wretchedness of Israel.

According to I Kings 12.16 the cult of Bethel, which the tradition derives from the patriarchal period (Gen. 28), had been elevated by Jeroboam I to the dignity of a state cult when the empire of David and Solomon was divided at the end of the tenth century BC. Given the extent of the sources we are not in a position to pronounce on the character of the cult during the empire and in the immediately preceding period; however, it is reasonable to suppose that it functioned as a sanctuary, even if not a national sanctuary. The Judahite origin of Amos can be glimpsed through this global condemnation of the cult of Bethel, a condemnation repeated often through the book and which according to 7.10–17 led to the expulsion of the prophet from the sanctuary in question. Here, too, v. 14c seems to refer to the earthquake as an instrument of judgment, as in 2.13, cf. again 9.1ff. and the purely chronological reference in 1.1. The fall of the horns from the altar[8] seems to be a sign of the intensity of the earthquake, but at the same time it denotes that nothing in Israel, not even the altar, can offer a safe refuge. Moreover the theme of the breaking of the altar appears in the Deuteronomistic history work (II Kings 23.15ff.), though there it does not happen through an earthquake, but by means of king Josiah and his reform. Hence this is probably a *vaticinium ex eventu*.

The mention of the palaces is generally understood as an indication of the transformation of Israelite society by patterns of the Canaanite city-state which recall those of feudal times. This transformation will have led to a revolution in tribal solidarity making inoperative the institution of usufruct in the tribal territory, at least in the north, where it has been thought until recently, on the basis of studies by A. Alt, that the Canaanite population will have been preponderant and the city state will have succeeded in regaining the upper hand in politics as well. However, these suggestions can now be considered outdated:[9] there are

[8]For the shape of this kind of altar cf. *BHH* 1, 1963, 63; *ANEP*, 575; and *BRI* ²1977, 5–10. A four-horned altar of remarkable dimensions has been discovered during the 1973 excavations at Beer Sheba, cf. Y. Aharoni, 'The Horned Altar of Beer Sheba', *BA* 37, 1974, 2–6: a similar construction has been found at Tell Dan, but in fragments, cf. ibid., 106ff. For the problem generally cf. recently F. J. Stendelach, 'Altarformen im kanaanäisch-israelitische Raum', *BZ* NF 20, 1976, 180–96.

[9]I myself proposed it in the Italian edition of 1982, 92f. See meanwhile S. Timm, *Die Dynastie Omri*, FRLANT 124, Göttingen 1982, 270–3.

no explanations of an ethnic type for the phenomenon. The luxury described here is well attested in the region and surrounding areas: inlays of ivory have been discovered in excavations in Samaria (cf. *BHH* 1, 1962, 393f.) and in other places: Amos also mentions inlaid furniture in 6.4, cf. I Kings 22.39; Ps. 45.9 [EVV 8]. Bar-Rakib, king of Sam'al in northern Syria near present-day Zinjirli, writes around 733/32–728 on his stele of having beautified his ancestral home like the palaces of monarchs much more powerful and richer than himself, a simple vassal of Assyria. The same text also speaks of a summer and winter residence (*KAI*, 216). Jeremiah 36.22 also speaks of a winter residence for Jehoiachim, but he is the king, not just any citizen. Moreover Rinaldi* recalls the present-day practice of Arab emirs of having a summer parlour and a winter parlour in the same building. This situation has a remarkable parallel in the discoveries made in the excavations.[10] It follows from them that apart from a few palaces the country was remarkably poor, especially in Judah, even if the situation of Israel, a country with a firmer economic base and close to the trade routes, was notably better. At all events the destruction of the tribal structure, now inadequate for the new monarchical form of government, simply aggravated the many problems of the region.

The context thus appears relatively clear and corresponds well to that described in the oracles of Amos: a few rich and powerful landowners bound to the court, who lived in luxury and lorded it over a few merchants and a mass of manual labourers.

In this oracle the Israelite cult and the deterioration of the economic and social situation are closely connected, and that should not be surprising: both were the fruit of the government politics which, according to biblical tradition, from the time of David onwards had been in the process of encouraging assimilation between Israelites and Canaanites so as to make the north a coherent national state. Another factor was respect for the position of the city state, incorporated into the empire of David and Solomon in circumstances of which we have no knowledge. This respect necessarily led those with property in the cities, which were economically stronger and more progressive, to expand and therefore to become pre-eminent. If we discount all the legendary elements which have been attached to the narrative, the episode of Naboth's vineyard in I Kings 21 gives an interesting example of a conflict between the king, now the main landowner, and a usufructuary of tribal land. It is true that the new system could provide a degree of economic and political stability, but it was obtained at a high price: the

[10]For a confirmation, albeit limited to Judah, cf. G. Pettinato, 'Isaia 2, 7 ed il culto del sole in Giuda nel sec. VIII a.c', *OA* 4, 1965 (1–30), 1ff.

suppression of liberty and independence so characteristic of ancient Israelite society as it is described in the sources, probably idealistically.[11]

In vv. 13–14 Jacob and Israel are mentioned in parallelism. However, the reference is again not to the twelve tribes, as Osty* would have it, since Judah never had dealings with Bethel, but rather to the need for the old system of tribal possession of land to be restored, thus producing common property again. To what point such demands are to be classed as utopian is a matter for debate.

5. Against the rich women of Samaria (4.1–3)

S. J. Schwantes, 'Note on Amos 4, 2b', *ZAW* 79, 1967, 82f.; D. N. Freedman and F. I. Andersen, 'Harmon in Amos 4.3', *BASOR* 198, 1970, 41; M. O'Rourke Boyle, 'The Covenant Lawsuit of the Prophet Amos: III 1–IV 3', *VT* 21, 1971, 338–62; S. M. Paul, 'Fishing Imagery in Amos 4.2', *JBL* 98, 1928, 183–90; A. J. Williams, 'A Further Suggestion for Amos IV 1–3', *VT* 29, 1979, 206–11; H. M. Barstad**, 37–47.

---

4 [1]Hear this word, you cows of Bashan, who have lived on the mountain of Samaria, who oppress the lowly, ill- treat the poor, who say to your lords, 'Bring us something to drink.' [2]The Lord YHWH has sworn by his holiness, 'Behold, the days are coming upon you when they shall take you away with nose-rings, and your remnant with fish-hooks. [3]You shall go out through the breaches in the walls one after another in file, and you shall be driven towards . . .' Oracle of YHWH.

[1] 'Hear': for the verb in the masculine addressed to those of female sex cf. *GesK* § 145p. Both in the verb (especially in the imperfect and cognate forms) and with the pronominal suffix (especially in the plural) note the tendency to replace feminine suffixes with masculine ones. 'Who have lived . . .': *ªšer* presupposes a verb or should be deleted. 'Your' for Hebrew 'their'. 'Bring': for the form cf. *GesK* § 72y. [2] This is a difficult verse and it is impossible to translate the conclusion in the present state of research. For the divine oath cf. the comments on 6.8. 'They will take you away': Hebrew *wᵉnissaʾ* can be either niphal or piel; for a discussion cf. *GesK* § 75,oo. LXX probably read the niphal: λήμψονται ὑμᾶς, 'will seize hold of you', while Vg seems to suggest the piel: *et levabunt*. At all events, in the Hebrew we have an impersonal form which LXX and Vg render with the third person plural. It is probably better to understand the impersonal niphal with *'et*, following *GesK* §§ 121a–b: 'it will be carried away' or something of that kind.

---

[11]A comparison with the so-called segmentary society of non-Arabian Africa has recently been made by F. Crüsemann, *Der Widerstand gegen das Königtum*, WMANT 49, 1978, ch. IV.

'Your remnant': for this rendering of *wā'aḥerīt^eken* cf. Gese's study. 'Nose-ring': Hebrew *ṣinnōt* is a *hapax legomenon* which seems to mean shield, but the idea of women carried away on the shields of the victors, whether alive or dead, seems improbable. Vg has *in contis*, 'on the pikes', Θ ἐν δόρασι, 'on the javelins', both obvious references to the Assyrian practice of impaling a certain number of prisoners,[12] while LXX, 'A and Tg ἐν ὅπλοις confirm the Hebrew text. So the term would seem already to have been difficult in ancient times: an interesting attempt at a solution has been made by Schwantes, though it was rejected by Rudolph: *sinnāh* is said to derive from the Akkadian *sinnatu* (which is not in *AHw*), 'nose-ring and rope'. Moreover the LXX term ὅπλα can also mean 'ropes', cf. the inscription on the Portico of Athene at Delphi, while Herodotus IX, 121 speaks of Persian implements hung up in the temple. So in this case we would have a foreign practice denoted with a non-Hebrew term, hence the difficulty of understanding the technical term. This explanation would also match the parallelism 'with fish-hooks' (or 'gaffs'); when real rings run out, they resort to substitutes. However, as I have said, this solution is rejected by Rudolph*, who translates 'goad' (in the sense of an artificial thorn), while S. M. Paul rejects it outright: he would prefer to translate: 'And you will be transported in chests – the last of you in fishermen's pots.' 'Gaffs' or 'hooks': *sīrōt* is the plural of *sīrāh*, 'gaff', in a botanical context 'thorn', but normally this plural is used for *sīr*, 'pot', 'pan', while *sīrāh* normally makes its plural as *sīrīm*. However, on this last interpretation the phrase again makes no sense, as the LXX translation shows: 'And fiery destructors will throw those with you (i.e. *aḥ^aēreken*, 'following you') into boiling cauldrons', a version which refers to a practice of which we are totally ignorant. So the meaning of the text would appear to be this: the women, accustomed always to being served and doing little or nothing, are now led off as though they were cattle, with rings in their noses, while those who survive (better than 'posterity') are forced to travel bound together with hooks or gaffs. This is a practice attested for Assyria, cf. *ANEP*, 447. Some scholars (most recently Paul) have wanted to translate the passage as though the women were transported in chests or pots for fish, like the mothers on shields; others have read 'they will carry you away on nose-lances (reading *'app^eken* for *'et^eken*) and with hooks (fish: gloss?) to sit on', but this imagery makes trivial and scurrilous a fate which is tragic, even if it is deserved (Amsler*). Other possibilities are that they are brought together and driven with goads and objects of that kind. So the reference is to deportation and, moreover, in particularly appalling conditions. That is all that we can say clearly.

[3] LXX read: 'You will be carried outside naked', hence the passive of the verb and the term *^arummōt* for 'breaches'. 'Will be driven': read the hophal with LXX and Vg against MT, which has 'drive' (hiphil). The last

---

[12]Cf. *ANEP*, 362, 368, 372–3.

word cannot be translated in the present state of research. At all events it should indicate a place or a zone which are the goal of the deportation, but places and regions of this kind are unknown. Dhorme*, Osty*, Weiser*, Amsler*, Rudolph* and perhaps Rinaldi* would prefer to vocalize *hāhermōnāh*, 'in the direction of Hermon', on the road to Syria, but this is the easier reading; others (Robinson*) think of *hammadmēnāh*, 'towards the rubbish heap' (a confusion between *res* and *dalet*) from *dōmen, madmān* (cf. *KB*³). The ancient translations almost all have transcriptions of the term which do not help.

Another invective against the inhabitants of Samaria as in 3.9ff., but this time the objects of it are the women who are considered to share responsibility with their husbands in that (v. 1b) they actively participated in the oppression of the humble and profited from the benefits that this brought them. In fact commentators are agreed in seeing their continual demands as one of the elements which goad the men on towards corruption, oppression and violence. That also emerges from the construction of the text: the women make their demands; never satisfied, they goad on their husbands to expect more and more. 'To drink' is equivalent to 'feast', cf. the term *mišteh* which often denotes 'orgy', so that we have an uninterrupted sequence of banquets and feasts. The situation is therefore not substantially different from the one we looked at in 3.9–12 with its palaces and valuable furniture. And the expression 'cows of Bashan' is well fitted to it. This is present-day Hauran, on the south-east of Lake Tiberias, on both sides of the Yarmuk. It was a region proverbial for its fertility: it had the best pastures and therefore the best cattle (Deut. 32.14; Ezek. 39.18; Ps. 22.13 [EVV 12]), cf. the relevant articles in the lexica. Robinson* therefore aptly renders the term 'prime beasts'. But since even today in the Near East the quality of meat is associated with the fatness of the animal, the expression clearly indicates the fatness and therefore the physical weakness of the women in question, a feature which must obviously aggravate the inconveniences of deportation, which are inevitable anyway.

H. M. Barstad** in his recent monograph is now opposed to this almost universal exegetical consensus. An exhaustive examination of the texts leads him to the conclusion (40): 'there can be no doubt that the expression *prwt hbšn* in 4, 1 is a paraphrase for the whole of the Israelite people/inhabitants of Samaria', cf. moreover the preceding *bhr šmrwn*. Rather, the mention of 'lords', instead of referring to husbands (never called by this title), would refer to the pagan deities worshipped in place of the one husband/lord YHWH. The term 'cow' also appears frequently for Israel, accompanied by pejorative adjectives. Barstad devotes a long and detailed excursus to the theme of the cow in the ancient Near East, from which it appears that the animal is a symbol of fertility. The two theories are certainly interesting, but it does not seem to me that the author has yet established the relationship between these elements, or at least made them the basis of a probable view.

The conditions of the text do not allow us to go into detail here, but it seems clear that something terrible is happening. Or perhaps we should understand Bashan not as the mountain chain, but as a cognate of the Arabic *baṭne* or *baṭane*, 'prosperous'. That would not alter the meaning of the discourse substantially, even if the image would appear less picturesque.[13] In fact, if we could keep the rendering of the last word with 'rubbish heap' (though as we have seen, this is one of the less probable renderings) we would have an allusion to the killing of those who proved completely unable to make the long journey.

So here too, as in 3.9ff. we have an announcement of inexorable judgment, without a remnant being able to survive and escape.

6. The cult as sacrilege (4.4–5)

R. Hentschke, passim; W. Brueggemann, 'Amos IV 4–13 and Israel's Covenant', *VT* 15, 1965, 1–15; J. L. Crenshaw, 'A Liturgy of Wasted Opportunity', *Semitics* 1, 1970, 27–37; J. Vollmer**, 9–20; W. Rudolph**, 1973, 158; Willi-Plein**, 27–30; Markert**, 111–119; H. W. Barstad**, 49–54.

---

4 [4]Come to Bethel and commit sin,
to Gilgal and sin even more;
bring your sacrifices every morning,
your tithes on the third day;
[5]burn a sacrifice of thanksgiving with leavened bread,
and proclaim free-will offerings in a voice that can be heard.
Thus it pleases you, Israelites!
Oracle of the Lord, YHWH.

[4] 'To Bethel'; the verb *bw'* can be transitive of the place. Bethel is identified with present-day Beitin (coord. 172–184). 'And commit sin . . . and sin . . .' Coordination sometimes indicates in Hebrew the purpose or consequence of an act, so we should perhaps render 'to commit sin . . . and sin . . .' or 'with the result of committing sin and sinning'. The same goes for the following line. 'To Gilgal and . . .;' the conjunction, absent in Hebrew, is necessary in a Western language. Gilgal is perhaps present-day *ḫirbet el*

[13]For topographical information cf. Y. Aharoni, *The Land of the Bible*, London 1967, the table on 371ff. For a complete examination of the information available from the two sanctuaries see now the study by Barstad**, 29–54.

mefg̱ir near Jericho (coord. 193–143). 'Sin even more': literally 'multiply through sinning . . .', a form explained in *GesK* § 114n. The daily sacrifice and the offering of the tithe every third day are actions which reveal an almost exaggerated zeal: I Sam. 1.3, 7, 21 speaks of a sacrifice once a year, while according to Deut. 26.12 the tithes were presented only in 'the third year, the year of the tithes'. That is, of course, assuming that *yāmīm* here does not have the meaning 'years' as it does often (Robinson*); that is improbable, cf. the parallelism. **[5]** 'Burn': infinitive absolute with finite value, Hammers-haimb* and Rudolph*, cf. *GesK* § 113bb; so it is unnecessary to emend as some scholars would prefer, cf. *BHS* and Vollmer**. The root *qāṭar* (piel or hiphil) is a technical term for a sacrificial offering by fire, usually used for incense or other forms of perfume, with the accent on the smoke. 'Leavened bread': note the use for offerings of ordinary food, not unleavened bread, specially for the cult LXX has a different text: 'They read the law openly, publicly (ἔξω)', probably arising from a wrong reading of the Hebrew, not a different original, cf. Rudolph*. The expression fits well and should not be corrected to 'unleavened bread' (privative *min. GesK* § 119y) as Snaith* and Robinson* would prefer. 'Offer free will offerings': LXX read ὁμολογίας, perhaps the Hebrew *n^edārīm*, 'vows', with a confusion of *res* and *bet*. 'Thus': or should we understand *kēn* as a noun: 'The right thing is what pleases you', bitter sarcasm (cf. G. R. Driver in Robinson*, Maag**, 20, 157, and Rudolph*, who takes serious account of the hypothesis)?

In the present redaction, vv. 6–13 are connected directly with vv. 4–5; but they are separated from them by the fact that refrain does not appear in these verses.

1. In the redaction this text, which Barstad** considers to be a continuation of the preceding pericope, is meant to be an introduction to vv. 6–13, but we have seen that the two sections must at least have been separate to begin with. We have what we might call a caricature of the *tōrāh*, of the prophetic or priestly teaching.[14] The exhortation to zeal and piety is here changed into its sarcastic opposite: zeal and piety are not understood here in a positive way but only negatively: 'This is what pleases you', as the conclusion of v. 5 has it, either 'It is this that pleases you' or, if we accept the proposal made by G. R. Driver, 'The right thing is what pleases you', a rendering which stresses the sarcastic character of the affirmation. The cult offered at Bethel and Gilgal is therefore not the product of divine decisions but of human decisions, and therefore illegitimate.

It is probable that the discourse was uttered in one of the two temples, probably that of Bethel, in the presence of pilgrims in the course of a

[14]A literary genre studied for the first time by J. Begrich, 'Die priesterliche Torah', in *Werden und Wesen des Alten Testaments*, BZAW 66, Berlin 1936, 63–88 = *GS*, Munich 1964, 232–60.

feast which we can no longer identify; so as Amsler* rightly observes, we have a situation similar to that of Jer. 7. The speech is characterized by the paradoxical introduction: those who come to the sanctuary end up by sinning, by committing actions the consequence of which is a rebellion against the very God whom they seek to celebrate and adore. These are weighty statements to those who have faced risks, weariness and expense to complete the journey.

2. Bethel is a sanctuary which the patriarchal tradition derived from the vision of Jacob (Gen. 28.10–22); it then became the national sanctuary of the North after the break-up of the empire of David and Solomon under Jeroboam 1 (I Kings 12.25–32) and as such it appears explicitly in the narrative of Amos 7.10–17. But Gilgal, too, boasted ancient traditions: here the Israelites set up the twelve stones after the crossing of the Jordan and established the first sanctuary in the holy land, Josh. 3; 4 and 5; here they celebrated the first Passover,[15] and here the first king of Israel, Saul, was crowned (I Sam. 11). We know nothing of any special relations between Bethel and Gilgal.

3. This text has obvious affinities of content with Amos 5.4–5, 21–27, cf. also 8.14; and with Hos. 6.6; 8.13; Isa. 1.10–17; Gen. 6.19–21; Mal. 1.10; 2.13, in its criticism of the cult. In the Isaiah passage this criticism is explicitly connected with social injustice; there cannot be a legitimate cult in a society in which injustice reigns; in the present text, however, we do not have any motivation for the harsh judgment on the praxis and the zeal which animated those who assisted at the cult. Certainly the conclusion of v. 5 could seek to indicate that this was an arbitrary cult, wanted not so much by God as by the faithful for the satisfaction of some of their needs, whether or not these were religious (Weiser* and to some degree also T. H. Robinson*). But we may well ask whether these explanations are not too theological or modern, not to say Pauline. The key to the explanation is probably to be found in 5.4–5 (and 9), a text which should also be consulted. Barstad**, 58, has recently made an interesting proposal: at a time when only a small part of the population adhered to Yahwism as it had been presented by the prophets, Amos appears in the role of a missionary of this faith. Barstad finds this theory illustrated by the later passage.

Be this as it may, it is impossible to establish whether Amos was attacking the cult *per se* (which is highly improbable) or whether as a good Judahite he had wanted to maintain the legitimacy of the Jerusalem sanctuary; but this position would be at least premature and therefore totally anachronistic.

[15]Cf. my *Joshua*, OTL 1972, ad loc.

7. The useless quest (4.6–13)

Cf. the works cited in connection with the previous section. Also F. Horst, 'Die Doxologien im Amosbuch', *ZAW* 47, 1929, 45–54 = *Gottes Recht*, Munich 1961, 155–66; J. M. Ward**, 112f., 121ff.; G. W. Ramsay, 'Amos 4:12 – A New Perspective', *JBL* 89, 1970, 187–91; W. Rudolph, 'Amos 4, 6–12', in *Wort-Gebot-Glaube, FS W. Eichrodt*, ATANT 59, 1970, 27–38; R. Youngblood, 'LQRT in Amos 4:12', *JBL* 90, 1971, 98; J. L. Crenshaw, *Prophetic Conflict*, BZAW 124, Berlin 1971, 81f.; W. Berg**; Vollmer**, 9–20; Willi-Plein**, 27–30; Markert**, 119–24; F. Foresti, 'Funzione semantica dei brani participiali di Amos: 4.13; 5.8f.; 9.5ff.', *Bibl* 62, 1981, 168–84; H. Barstad**, 58–75.

4 [6]I for my part have left you
with an empty mouth in all your cities,
a lack of food in all your places,
yet you did not return to me, oracle of YHWH.
[7]I for my part withheld the rain
when there were yet three months to harvest,
or made it rain on one city
but not rain on another;
one field received the rain,
and the other which did not receive it was withered!
[8]Then two, three cities agreed |wandered|
with [towards] one city, to find drink,
but did not quench their thirst;
yet you did not return to me, oracle of YHWH.
[9]I smote your grain with blight and mildew,
I made worse your gardens and vineyards:
the locusts devoured your figs and your olives,
yet you did not return to me, oracle of YHWH.
[10]I sent against you the plague
in the manner of Egypt,
I killed your best young men with the sword;
together with your captured horses;
I made the stench of your encampments go up your nostrils,
yet you did not return to me, oracle of YHWH.
[11]I worked among you destruction,
like the more terrible destruction,
that of Sodom and Gomorrhah,
so that you became like a brand plucked from a fire,
yet you did not return to me, oracle of YHWH.
[12]Therefore thus I will act towards you, Israel,
with a judgment that I have made ready:

prepare to meet your God, Israel!
[13]For lo:
he who has formed the mountains and created the wind,
and declares to man what is his intention,
who makes morning from the darkness
who treads on the heights of the earth,
his name is the Lord, the God of hosts!

[6] 'For my part', *gam* adversative;[16] the formula also appears in v. 7. 'I have left', literally 'I have given cleanness of teeth', in the sense that there was nothing to eat because of the famine. LXX, cf. Vg, Tg and Syr read *qihyōn*, root *qāhāh* (post-biblical), 'broken teeth': γομφιασμόν – *stuporem*. 'Return': *šwb* is also the verb of conversion, so it could also be rendered 'You were not converted to me'; there is probably a deliberate play on words. 'To': note the use of the preposition *'ad*, 'up to', which is stronger than *'el*. Here we have a refrain which is repeated in vv. 8, 9, 10, 11.

[7] Vollmer** would like to delete the first two words, but without specific reasons. It is possible that there are later additions in 7aβ–8a, cf. *BHS*; for Rudolph* this would only be 7b, which separates 7aβ from 8a: for other possibilities cf. Vollmer** and Markert**. 'Three months': the harvest falls between the end of April and the beginning of May, so the rains have stopped right in the middle of the winter, in January-February. [8] 'And their thirst is not quenched': Hebrew has the same root *šāba'* for hunger being satisfied and thirst quenched. 'Are agreed' or 'go wandering': the second translation is the usual one, meaning those who wander for weakness, but the imagery seemed strange to LXX, which read συνασθροισ-θήσονται, 'are met together', i.e. Hebrew *no'adu*, from *ya'ad*, a root which was examined as an alternative in 3.3. But a study by O. Eissfeldt[17] has made probable the rendering 'make an agreement', i.e. a meaning similar to that in LXX. [9] 'Blight' and 'mildew', Hebrew *yērāqon* and *šiddāpōn*, contrary to LXX, which has πυρώσει and ἰκτέρῳ, 'inflammation' and 'jaundice', are two diseases of cereal crops, the first as a result of a microfungus, the *Puccinia graminis Persoon*, which grows in excessive humidity, the second a product of drought, cf. Vg which is already better: *in vento aurente et in aurugine*. In both cases the ear remains empty. So these are not human maladies, as LXX suggests.[18] 'I made worse' is not an easy expression to translate and many scholars consider it corrupt. LXX has ἐπλεθύνατε, i.e. Hebrew *hirbētem*, 'have multiplied'; Vg has *multitudinem*, i.e.

[16]C. J. Labuschagne, 'The Emphasizing Particle *gam* and Its Connotations', in *Studia Biblica et Semitica T. C. Vriezen . . . dedicata*, Wageningen 1966, 193–203.
[17]O. Eissfeldt, 'NUAH, sich vertragen', *STU* 20, 1950, 71–4 = *KS* III, Tübingen 1966, 124–8.
[18]Descriptions in G. A. Dalman, *Arbeit und Sitte in Palästina*, Gütersloh I.2, 1928, 326; II, 1932 (reprinted 1964), 33.

rᵉbābāh or *rᵉbābōt*. This is an infinitive construct hiphil from *rābāh*, to be understood either as if it were an infinitive absolute with finite meaning or as a secondary rare form of the infinitive absolute (Rudolph*), to be translated adverbially, as dependent on 'have smitten'. Others correct to *hehᵉrabtī*, 'have withered' (from Wellhausen on) or *herabtī*, 'have dried up'. An assured translation will never be possible, but the context suggests that the discourse continues with agricultural catastrophes, depending on the previous clause. 'The locusts' is understood by some scholars as an addition from Joel 1.4 because it introduces a new theme and does not continue that of the scant or excessive rain. **[10]** 'In the manner of Egypt': also attested in Isa. 10.24–17, though there it has a different and more distinct meaning, is deleted by many scholars, most recently Vollmer**; however, with Rudolph⁺, I do not see the need for this. If anything, here we have an independent tradition about a plague of Egypt to which Ex. 5.3 seems to allude, where the plague is threatened. 'With the sword . . .' does not seem to fit in with the text and is perhaps a dittography (Amsler* and Rudolph*). 'Captured horses': very uncertain; the Hebrew is literally 'together to the prison (or *sᵉbī*, 'flower') of your horses', a phrase which does not make much sense; Rudolph, who thinks of an Arabic root *šbw*, the 'whitening' of the horses, hence 'although your horses are whitened'. 'The stench', Hebrew *bēʾōš*, understood by LXX (ἐν πυρί) as *bᵉʾēš*, but to be preferred because it is a rare term: the idea is that the decomposing bodies make the encampment uninhabitable. 'Your nostrils': delete the *w* with Rudolph*.

[11] Something seems to be missing at the beginning of the verse, which I insert with Rudolph and others. 'Most terrible': *ᵉlōhīm* sometimes has a superlative significance, in which case it clearly should not be translated literally,[19] cf. Ps. 36.7; 80.11 [EVV 10]; Isa. 14.13 and perhaps also, according to some scholars, Gen. 1.2 ('raging wind', instead of 'Spirit of God'). The great majority of scholars see here one of the many references to the earthquake in 1.1, a theory rejected by Wolff*, who, as we shall see in the commentary, would prefer to date all this section about a century later. **[12]** 'To meet': for the root with a *h* as third consonant conjugated as if it were a ' see *GesK* § 74h. Ramsay would prefer to understand the text as if it said 'Prepare to meet your gods', which is grammatically possible, while Youngblood corrects to *liqrōt ʾet* *ᵉlōhāyk*, where the particle would have fallen out by haplography, i.e. ' . . . to meet your gods'; but the text does not speak of other deities. 'Which I have prepared for you': MT has a 'colourless repetition' (Rudolph) of the previous phrase; usually either v. 12 is deleted (*BHS*) or the verb is read in the second person masculine. The presence at the end of the verse of an exhortation where we would expect a description of what God plans to do is perhaps a sign that this part of the

---

[19]Cf. D. W. Thomas, 'A Consideration of Some Unusual Ways of Expressing the Superlative in Hebrew', *VT* 3, 1953, 209–24.

text is also secondary; probably this line originally took the place of another much harsher line which was therefore unacceptable to the redactors (Vollmer**). For another explanation see the commentary below on Wolff's theory. **[13]** 'Formed', root *yāṣar*, typical of the work of the potter; it also appears for the creation of the first man, Gen. 2.7. ' . . . created': the verb *bārā'* appears in exilic or immediately post-exilic contexts like Deutero-Isaiah and the Priestly Codex. 'Intention' is a form which is phonetically different and a *hapax legomenon*: here we have *śēᵃḥ* for the more frequent *śīᵃḥ*.

1. The beginning of this passage with the words 'I for my part' logically suggests a connection with something which has gone before, but whatever it was is missing here since it does not seem to be contained in vv. 4–5, which are a criticism of the cult. The presence of a refrain, however, suggests some form of public recitation of this text, perhaps in a liturgical context, as Crenshaw has shown to be probable in his important studies; so it would have been this *ad hoc* composition which gave a unitary character to a variety of minor themes (Robinson*). We find another similar case in Isa. 5.25–30; 9.7–20. So despite some fragmentary elements this text proves to be substantially a self-contained unity. The theme is simple: it deals with the divine attempts to lead the people to conversion, to repentance, by admonishing them and punishing them with what we can call 'plagues', i.e. partial catastrophes, circumscribed in area and limited in time, which announce the final definitive catastrophe if the people does not return to its Lord. That will be a catastrophe for which there will be no remedy. Here, in fact, we have a kind of history of salvation turned upside down: a history of the disasters undergone by the people so that they become attentive to the demands of God: but always in vain, as A. Weiser*, followed by many scholars, has indicated. The structure of these past plagues is based on the number six: as Rinaldi* rightly observes, 'we have six plagues of Israel in growing degrees of severity', collected in five groups or strophes, each one ending with the refrain. And the list of the plagues endured by the people has an aim to it: 'to discover the lesson of the facts, the purpose that they have', as Rinaldi* again puts it.

Drought in one area matched by excessive rain in another has ruined the crops of grain and fruit and caused a famine. The plague, perhaps caused by enemy invasions (if this is how we are to understand v. 10, though not everyone takes it this way, cf. Amsler*, and doubt remains because of the condition of the text) has done the rest; to this is probably added a powerful earthquake (v. 11), again the earthquake of 1.1; now the country resembles the proverbial cities of Sodom and Gomorrah after their destruction (cf. Gen. 19). But all these divine warnings have been useless; the people has not returned to its God. In reality, however, if this is how we can understand the difficult v. 12, it has been the people that has ruined itself with its own hands, has brought on itself the terrible trial that it is undergoing, so now there is nothing for it but the last definitive judgment which the prophet sees as being imminent. That is perhaps how we should understand the enigmatic v. 12c: the encounter with God as the final settling of accounts. And the people does not believe that God does have the power to do this: it is not for nothing that he is the creator! The presence of this doxology at the end of the passage is therefore fully justified, even if the literary genre is different.

On the other hand, and this is one of the great difficulties posed by the text, we are not in a position to establish to which particular events the prophet is referring, and that explains why some scholars have wanted to see the whole passage as an eschatological text. But it would seem evident that the reference is to events in the past. The whole passage could certainly also be quite simply a rhetorical figure centred on the three classic catastrophes of famine, sword and pestilence, but as Rudolph* rightly objects, that would have made the prophetic preaching extremely ineffective it would hardly be credible, other than pointing out the specific verifiable character of the phenomena described (Reventlow**, 77f.) In any case, this is a problem which is difficult to solve. Rudolph makes an interesting proposal. He begins from the fact that around the middle of the eighth century BC the country enjoyed a long period of peace and prosperity or of wars carried on outside its territory, wars which allowed it to reconquer a large part of the territory of Gilead. These are times which normally we would connect with notable economic prosperity. But the prophet pointed out at the same time that all that glittered was not gold: famine had struck the country despite the favourable political situation; the war (if that is how we are to understand part of v. 10) had not spared all the country and had been followed by an epidemic – despite the general well-being. On the other hand the information that we have on Jeroboam II, who is said to have been a notable ruler, is somewhat scarce (cf. II Kings 14.23–29), even if it does indicate that he did a good deal in the military sphere.[20] So it is only possible to use the words of the text as a basis: despite the good political and economic situation shadowy zones seem to have remained which were vaster than the official theory was disposed to admit; moreover, this situation must also have been

---

[20]I have examined the problem of the relationship between Amos and the foreign policy of Jeroboam II in my study 'Amos VI, 13–14 und I, 3 auf dem Hintergrund der Beziehungen zwischen Israel und Damaskus im 9. und 8. Jhdt', in *Near Eastern Studies in Honor of W. F. Albright*, Baltimore 1971, 433–41 and my *History*.

notorious among the population. This is the situation to which the prophet now refers. Moreover famine was frequent and has remained so almost down to the present day as a result of drought, locusts and other natural causes; for some biblical instances cf. I Kings 17.1, 12 (under Ahab), II Kings 4.38; 8.1 (under Joram). And such phenomena were often attributed to divine judgment, cf. Jer. 14 (drought) and Joel 1–2 (locusts).

2. This time it is no longer the ruling class of Israel that is the object of the invective but all the people (vv. 6, 12); nor, as would seem logical in a situation in which those addressed do not hold power, is the crime described in terms of oppression and corruption at the expense of those who are weaker. This time the transgressions of the people are connected with the cult, and to this element is added another: that the people have refused to repent, although they have been severely admonished many times. But whereas in 2.6–16 the transgressions are indicated clearly, so much so that successive redactions were able to broaden their scope considerably, here there is no certain indication of what the transgression of the people really was, and why it called for such severe admonitions first, and the threat of such a heavy punishment. That whatever it was involved practices approved by the faithful, i.e. considered just and pious by those who engaged in them, appears clear from the invective, cf. the sarcasm of v. 5b. Another characteristic which distinguishes this text from 2.6–16 is the absence of relevant political features when plagues are mentioned. The catastrophes are limited to the natural sphere: drought, excess of rain, locusts, pestilence, with perhaps the exception of v. 10b, which is in any case corrupt. But we are told nothing about the nature of the transgression committed by the people.

3. However, this explanation does not find unanimous support. In his commentary H. W. Wolff* does not believe that the text can have come from Amos. Its construction is obscure and differs markedly from 2.6–16, as also from the visions in 7.1–6, 7–9; 8.1–3; 9.1–4. In original texts of Amos it is in fact relatively easy to distinguish the original part from the additions (e.g. 2.6–7a from 2.7bff.), whereas in this text such distinctions, as we have seen in connection with 4.7aβ–8a, are doubtful and therefore controversial. In reality, if this text can be related to any Old Testament text it is to Lev. 26.14–33, while language which is very similar, if not exactly the same, appears in the treaty of Sephireh, between Arpad and KTK (the vocalization is unknown) in the middle of the eighth century BC, written in Aramaic (*KAI* 222, 1–A–21ff.). The text of Lev. 26 is particularly important because we find a repetition of the phrase 'if you are willing to hear' followed by other parallels (26.14, 18, 21, 23, 27), which seem to fit well with the refrain in this text: 'But

you did not return to me . .', vv. 6, 8, 9, 10, as has been rightly pointed out by Reventlow**, 83ff., and Brueggemann, 7f.; and in Lev. 26, as here, $^x n\bar{\imath}$ is also used for $^x n\bar{o}k\bar{\imath}$, which is the usual form in Amos. Again, the classical triad hunger, sword, pestilence appears in Lev. 26.16b, 26 (hunger) and 20b, 25 (sword and pestilence) together with other scourges (cf. Jer. 14.12; 21.7; Ezek. 6.11f.; 12.16 and other passages); while on the positive level we have the promise: 'I will give you your rains in their season, and the land shall yield its increase, and the trees of the field shall yield their fruit. And your threshing shall last to the time of vintage . . .' (vv. 4, 5). Finally, I would add, the use of the term $b\bar{a}r\bar{a}$', for creation, as it appears in v. 13, a term not attested in Israel before the middle of the sixth century, would also seem to be a sign of later composition, even if of course we should consider the possibility that it is a technical term originally belonging to the doxological genre, from which it will have passed to Deutero-Isaiah, to Job and to 'P'. The hypothesis put forward by Horst, 1929, that the literary genre is to be connected with the proclamation of sacral law, has now generally been abandoned, because of the impossibility of finding adequate evidence and because of its intrinsic improbability. However, Foresti 1981 has put forward important arguments for dating this and other doxologies (5.8f.; 9.5ff.) at a time between Deutero-Isaiah and the book of Job.

Moreover the plagues which are listed here also reappear, in terms of content if not on a formal level, in Deut. 28 and in the prayer of Solomon (I Kings 8.33–37). The phrase in v. 11, 'Like that most terrible destruction, that of Sodom and Gomorrah', appears, applied to Israel, in Deut. 29.22–23, albeit with variants, while for other peoples the comparison appears in Isa. 13.19 and Jer. 49.18, 40. The difference, as Wolff* rightly notes, lies in the fact that whereas Lev. 26 and Deut. 28 threaten these plagues if pledges are not fulfilled in the future, this text presents them as already having taken place: moreover for this text they are not just a punishment, as they are in others, but rather a warning that issues an invitation to conversion. Again, in I Kings 8 they are connected with intercession in the temple (v. 33). Everything thus seems to indicate that here we are a short distance from the exile, in the context of the accusations made against the North, accusations made in the context of Josiah's reform and the desecration of the altar of Bethel (II Kings 23.15–20). So we would find ourselves in the early Deuteronomic period and the encounter with God would need to be connected with Josiah's reform.

4. However, these theories are rejected by Rudolph, who maintains the originality of the greater part of this passage. Here, too, it is possible to recognize the additions, and if it is true that this text has some features in common with Lev. 26 and Deut. 28, that does not mean

anything, given that lists of plagues and catastrophes always tend to be very similar, because of the similarity of the material and the literary, and hence sterotyped, character of the lists. Moreover the term 'sword', on which the reading of the triad pestilence, sword and hunger is based, is probably an interpolation (cf. the text of v. 10) or simply the product of a dittography. Nor does Rudolph accept the indirect reference to the destruction of the altar of Bethel by Josiah, which he considers a sheer guess by Wolff*. Here, moreover, as Wolff also recognizes, we do not have plagues as an announcement of future judgment but as an indication of the warnings received in the past.

Clearly a balanced solution is not easy. But one thing is certain: Crenshaw's theory that the refrain is an indication of later redaction indicates a public, perhaps liturgical recitation. Now the composition with the refrain would have been made *ad hoc* on the basis of early material – and why not material going back to Amos? So we should accept at least the principle of doubt and consider this text one of controversial authenticity.

8. Funeral lament over Israel (5.1–3)

Willi-Plein**, 30ff.; J. M. Berridge, 'Die Intention der Botschaft des Amos, exegetische Überlegungen zu Amos 5', *TZ* 32, 1976, 321–40; Markert**, 125ff.; J. de Waard, 'The Chiastic Structure of Amos V 1–17', *VT* 27, 1977, 170–7 (de Waard and Berridge are relevant for all or part of chapter 5); Barstad**, 76f. For a rhetorical analysis of 5.1–17 cf. N. J. Tromp, 'Amos V 1–17', *OTS* 23, 1984, 56–84.

One of the main problems of this chapter is whether it is basically made up of fragments (which is generally accepted) or is a substantial unity (despite the existence of various breaks), as Berridge would hold or as has been argued by Markert** and de Waard for the first seventeen verses. The latter has shown that there is the following chiastic structure in vv. 1–17:

```
A 1–2–3
      D 4–5–6
            C 7
                  D 8abc
                        E 8d
                  D'      9
            C' 10–12 (13)
      B' 14–15
A'      16–17
```

While the symmetry and coherence of structures of this kind are always impressive, there is no need for them to go back to the author himself or even to the earliest phase of the redaction; nor should one argue differently for the organic character which Berridge finds throughout the chapter, notwithstanding the breaks that he notes between vv. 6 and 7, 14 and 15, 17 and 18, 20 and 21, 24 and 25; these would in fact be breaks which do not prejudice the basic organic character. All the more so since vv. 25–27 are generally recognized, from W. H. Schmidt's study onwards, as belonging in whole or in part to a Deuteronomic redaction, and Berridge takes over the result of this study.

On the other hand Berridge notes an important feature when he stresses that logically speaking there cannot be a break between vv. 3 and 4; it would not in fact make sense to sing the parody of the funeral song if the people did not have any possibility of a conversion, and an alternative of this kind is in fact offered by vv. 4–5 (and perhaps 14–15). But again, it is not in fact certain that 5.4–5 (14–15) were originally the continuation of 5.1–3; why not for example, of 4.4–6, to which it would provide the alternative (erroneous, sinful cult – the right alternative) that is missing and thus also implicitly the reason why the cult of Bethel and Gilgal has not turned to YHWH?

So it would seem prudent, at least in a first phase, to proceed analytically and if necessary to restate the problem at the end of this phase.

5 ¹Hear this word which I take up over you: a funeral lament, O house of Israel:
²'Fallen, no more to rise,
is the virgin Israel;
she lies outstretched on her ground,
no one can make her rise up.'
³Thus the Lord YHWH has in fact spoken:
'The city that put into battle a thousand men
shall keep only a hundred,
and that which put only a hundred
shall keep only ten for the house of Israel.'

[1] 'This word': LXX adds κυρίου, wrongly, because it is the prophet who pronounces the discourse. [2] 'Fallen': the root *nāpal* appears in contexts like this, especially for those who have fallen on the battlefield (cf. II Sam. 1.19b; 3.34; Jer. 9.21; 14.17f.; Ezek. 29.5; Lam. 2.21), and is often accompanied by the expression *baḥereb*, 'by the sword'. Note the so-called

prophetic perfects, which in reality refer to the future, *GesK* § 106n. [3] 'Into battle': this is one of the technical meanings of the root *yāṣā'*, 'go out'. 'For the house of Israel': an added phrase.

1. The literary genre of the funeral lament is the easiest to identify, in terms of metre as well: every line is formed of 3 + 2 stresses. Hence it immediately becomes evident that v. 2 is the original lament, while v.3 is a comment or sequel. As in 4.4–5 with the 'priestly instruction', here too we have the anomalous use of a literary genre; the difference is that here the sarcasm is completely missing; note, rather, between the lines the accuracy of the scene which stands out before the eyes of the prophet. This is the picture of a dead young woman, laid out on the ground where we would put the catafalque, whom the tears and laments of the grieved parents and her betrothed can no longer revive. And the image refers to the future of Israel, a future which envisages the certain death of the people. This text, too, seems understandable only if pronounced before a great audience, a large assembly, whom the prophet thus invites to join in the lament, drawing the logical consequences. The assembly had probably come together in the sanctuary of Bethel on the occasion of one of the great religious and national feasts; in fact it would not be surprising if it had been precisely a saying like this which provoked the reaction of Amaziah mentioned in 7.10ff. In other words, in the midst of all the enthusiasm of the feast the prophet produces a kind of anticlimax; instead of the salvation which is celebrated along with the glorious acts of God in the past, there is an announcement of death. As he might have said, 'You are already dead and do not know it.' The song therefore has clear prophetic and political connotations, well brought out by O. Eissfeldt,[21] and taken up by T. H.Robinson*. The expression 'virgin Israel' is again used in Jer. 18.13; 31.4, 21; cf. Isa. 37.22; Lam. 2.13, where it is transferred to the South, so that we read, 'The virgin, daughter of Zion' or ' . . . of Jerusalem'. The mention of 'on her ground' refers to the fact that a particular place is prepared for the watch over the corpse; but the term can also denote 'her country', so that the domestic image becomes national. In a society in which every woman is married, the 'virgin' is at the same time very young.

And as a virgin, she has not yet, at least in the opinion of the time, realized her own femininity (cf. Judg. 11.37–40, where Jephthah's daughter bewails her virginity), just as Israel as a nation has not succeeded in realizing the maturity for which the election and the

---

[21]O. Eissfeldt, *The Old Testament: An Introduction*, Oxford 1965, 96.

experiences of the past have led her to hope (Rudolph*). The verbs, too, have been carefully chosen, since, as we have seen, they usually denote the body of one who has fallen in battle.

2. In the present context, where someone may have wanted to contradict the prophet, pointing out the generally favourable situation, the prophet explains the sources of his information. This is not particular political acumen or a particular gift of looking into the future, but a message received from YHWH. The text does not necessarily belong in this context, at least originally; it may, however, already have been composed during the discussion which followed the preaching of Amos. The terminology is again military, so the reference is not to the citizenry generally but to the troops which the various places would put in the field. The point of view is that of someone who stands at the gate of the city and counts the troops going out and coming back. On their return only ten per cent of them appear,[22] of course a conventional formula which is not therefore to be taken literally, but one which effectively describes the magnitude of the catastrophe. And it is the death of the majority of the able-bodied men which leads the prophet to intone the funeral chant. In 8.14 the same theme is applied to the illicit cults, for which it appears as a punishment (cf. ad loc.)

It remains doubtful whether the text regards ten per cent survivors as an elect remnant or not. H. W. Wolff* thinks not, otherwise the funeral lament would not be justified; H. D. Preuss[23] thinks rather that it does: the lament over the fallen would not exclude survivors, the ten per cent, and this last theory would seem reasonable. But the problem cannot be resolved in either-or terms: the text announces an absolute, definitive judgment on the state; and if it is true that some will escape, it is also true that there is not the slightest stress on this fact. These are individual exceptions, there is no longer a structure among the survivors, nor a new theological category which takes the place of the previous one.

9. The quest for God (5.4–6, 14–15)

F. Hesse, 'Amos 5, 4–5.14f.', ZAW68, 1956, 1–17; R. Hentschke**, passim; K. W. Neubauer, 'Erwägungen zu Amos 5, 4–16', ZAW78, 1966, 292–316; Willi-Plein**, 31ff.; J. M. Ward**, 86ff.; A. de Pury, Promesse divine et légende cultuelle dans le cycle de Jacob, Paris 1975, I, 220 n. 38, 232 n. 99; Markert**, 125ff.; G. Crocetti, '"Cercate me e vivrete". La ricerca di Dio in Amos', in

---

[22]For the terminology and the military question see R. de Vaux, Ancient Israel, 231ff.
[23]H. D. Preuss, Jahweglaube und Zukunftserwartung, BWANT 87, Stuttgart 1968, 159–81.

Quaerere Deum – Atti della XXV Settimana biblica, Brescia 1980, 89–105; J. Lust, 'Remarks on the Redaction of Amos V 4–6, 14–15', *OTS* 21, 1981, 129–54; Barstad**, 77–88.

These are two brief sections, evidently connected by a central common concept, the quest for God, root *dāraš*. They are probably to be connected with 4.4f., in which the two sanctuaries are mentioned and to which they seem to offer the alternative missing there. So with a large number of scholars I am treating them together.

5 [4]For thus YHWH has in fact spoken to the house of Israel:
'Seek me, if you want to live,
[5]but do not seek Bethel,
nor enter into Gilgal
nor pass through Beersheba,
for Gilgal will have to go into exile
and Bethel be reduced to nothing.
[6]Seek YHWH if you want to live,
lest he break out on the house of Joseph like a fire
which will devour Bethel, and no one will be able to quench it.

[14]Seek good and not evil
if you want to live:
only thus will YHWH, the God of hosts, be with you
as you claim!
[15]Hate evil, love good,
make justice prevail in the court,
so that YHWH, the God of hosts, may have pity on the "remnant" of Joseph!'

[4] 'In fact' is one of the meanings that *kī* can have. 'Seek me': the pronoun constructed as a verbal suffix, and not emphatic (e.g. *'otī dirᵉšū* and similar forms), suggests that emphasis should be avoided in the translation. 'If you want', cf. *GesK* § 110f for this form, which expresses a condition, 'seek', for what follows. **[5]** 'Do not . . . nor . . . nor': note how *'al* and *lō*, the first used for the occasional contingent prohibition, the second for an absolute prohibition, are here used indiscriminately. 'To nothing': *'āwen*, often 'evil', 'iniquity', can also indicate nothingness, cf. Vg *inutilis*. Bethel is often called *bēt-'āwen*, even if sometimes the texts would seem to distinguish the two terms as relating to different places (Josh. 7.2; 18.12; I Sam. 13.5; 14.23; Hos. 4.15; 10.5). If we maintained this attribution to two different places the second would be closely connected with the first, although in that case its location would seem uncertain. For a similar phrase against the sanctuaries of the north cf. Hos. 4.15. Plays on words are noted for both Gilgal and Bethel and are impossible to render in a translation. Beersheba,

a sanctuary in the northern Negeb (coord. 134–072), and therefore belonging to the South: LXX renders φρέαρ τοῦ ὅρκου, 'well of the oath': the translation of the expression is given in Gen. 21.31 whereas in 8.14 LXX uses the actual name. Perhaps LXX felt the incongruity of the mention of a southern sanctuary in the context of a northern sanctuary and in a discourse addressed to people in the north. Note also that the destiny of Beersheba is not announced here. Is it an addition, a Judahite gloss, as some authors have suggested (Wolff*, Willi-Plein**)? Grammatically note how the names of places, normally construed with verbs in the feminine, here appear with verbs in the masculine. H.-W. Wolff attributes this to the fact that the text is meant to refer to the populations, but it seems more logical to think of the general tendency to replace the forms of the feminine imperfect with those of the more active masculine.
[6] 'Will burn': ṣālaḥ is normally the verb which indicates success; it is evidently wrong here, so that a number of emendations have been proposed (cf. Wolff*; BHS): LXX has μὴ ἀναλάμψῃ, 'which does not go up in flames', similarly Vg conburatur, and Tg and Syr are similar. This sense fits well with the mention of fire. However, a long time ago (cf. Rudolph*) the root was connected with the Akkadian ṣālu/ṣelu, 'light (a fire)', cf AHw III, 1090: in that case we would have to accept the existence of a hapax legomenon ṣālaḥᵤ. 'Bethel' is corrected by some scholars on the basis of LXX to bēt-yiśrā'ēl (Weiser), while others delete it (Amsler*). The whole verse looks like a later addition.

[14] 'Only thus': ken here cannot be, as Maag and KB^{2-3}, cf. Rinaldi*, would have it, 'that which is right and good', thus producing, 'And that happens which is good, that YHWH   ' Many scholars want to delete 'God of hosts' here and in the following verse, because the text is overloaded. **[15]** LXX has the verbs in 15a in the first person plural, making the Israelites confess: 'We have hated the evil, loved the good', but then puts the other verb in the second person. This sort of rendering is a mistake, not a variant which presupposes a different archetype. 'In court': literally 'at the gate' of the city, an edifice with a complex structure with an open place in the middle of which the court met, cf. Ruth 4.1ff. The place had the same function as the Greek agora.[24]

1. A number of formal characteristics mark out this passage from the rest: first of all we have a series of prohibitions, but then a command: seek YHWH instead of the sanctuaries (vv. 4b, 6a). A promise seems to be connected with this command, though conditional upon its observance: live. This is a unique instance in Amos and therefore

---

[24]For the topography of the typical Israelite city gate during the first half of the first millennium BC cf. recently S. M. Paul and W. G. Dever, *Biblical Archaeology*, Jerusalem 1973, 18–20, 89–94 and 97–101, and *BRL* ²1977, 346–8.

important, all the more so since it does not appear in a passage which cannot be attributed to him.

As it now stands, as Rudolph* rightly points out, the text presents a scene in which the prophet is replying to the people. To the people who have already objected to the incongruity of a funeral lament over their imminent death when by contrast they have received promises of election and life, the prophet retorts that these promises are subject to a condition: that the people really seeks YHWH and is not content with palliatives like feasts in the sanctuary. But this is imagery which the text offers in its present form, as the product of a long redaction, probably lasting over centuries. Note that the structure of this text seems much more complicated – cf. the examination of it by H. -W. Wolff*. And in fact it is reasonable to argue that only v. 4b can be considered authentic, whereas the rest would be the product of later additions: v. 5, which declares that things should not be like this; v. 6, which takes up in the second person what appears in 4b as the word of God in the first person; while vv. 14, 15 seek to explain positively and negatively the meaning of 'seeking YHWH' (in vv. 6b, 15b we still have the unusual 'house of Joseph', which appears only in 6.6, clearly an addition, cf. ad loc.).

In other words, in the face of a divine oracle by Amos which was considered enigmatic or at least open to other developments and interpretations, successive commentators will have tried to explain the meaning that the divine word proclaimed by Amos in his time had for them and for their contemparies.

2. In the Old Testament the root *dāraš* connected with YHWH has three basic meanings:[25]

(a) Seek a cult place or go to it;
(b) consult YHWH by means of an oracle, a prophet or other charismatic:
(c) keep faith with YHWH and his commandments.

With God or a cult place as its object, but without oracles, it appears from the time of Deuteronomy and Dtr onwards: Deut. 4.29; 12.5; Jer. 29.13; 30.14 and also other passages, all exilic and post-exilic. The situation seems different when it comes to consultation through an oracle given by a prophet, a sanctuary or in some other way; Gen. 25.22–23;[26] I Kings 14.1–6, 12–13, 17–18; II Kings 8.7–15 and other

---

[25]R. S. Cripps*, 1929, 180ff.; C. Westermann, 'Die Begriffe für Fragen und Suchen im Alten Testament', *KuD* 6, 1960, 2–30 = *Forschungen am Alten Testament* II, Munich 1974, 162–90; G. Gerleman, 'DRS', *THAT* 1, 1971, (460–7) 463; cf. also S. Wagner, 'DRS', *TDOT* III, 1978, (293–307) 304f.

[26]For dating to the period of the monarchy cf. C. Westermann, *Genesis II*, 12–36, Minneapolis and London 1985, 413.

passages; all these passages go back to pre-exilic times. The third instance also reflects situations which are immediately pre-exilic and later, but not earlier. So in this case we would still have the rejection of the sanctuaries, but an invitation either to return to God through the prophet (Wolff*) or to practise the commandments as a visible sign of faith in YHWH (Rudolph*). Then follows the declaration that such an attitude is a *conditio sine qua non* for salvation and life, here probably meant primarily as the survival of the people in the face of the political catastrophe which seemed imminent, well symbolized by fire (v. 6), already threatened many times to the nations in chs. 1–2, fire that will take hold of the sanctuaries which seem to be regarded as an alternative to YHWH. So this set of problems has been constructed by the redactors through a context in which the speech seems to be a reply by the prophet to an objection made to the funeral lament.

3. 'Seek the good', as Rudolph* explains, cannot denote a philosophical concept of the kind we find in Western thought, nor is it an immediate identification of God and the good, thus bringing together faith and ethics in a single cell (as Rinaldi* would seem to think). The good which at the same time saves and gives life is the observance of the divine commandments, i.e. the human response to the saving act of God, as this is developed in the prologue to the Decalogue, Ex. 20.1–2// Deut. 5.6–7. In other words it is that basic attitude through which the people accept that they are the people of God in accordance with the vocation that they have received, in that first God has become their God. And that does not happen by means of the celebration of festivals or participation in pilgrimages, occasions which, even presupposing the purest Yahwistic faith on the part of the participants, were always mixed with paganism, although celebrated with the intention of showing gratitude: rather gratitude is demonstrated in daily life, as is pointed out by Micah 6.8, another passage later than the prophet in question. And as v. 15 shows, this is not only a matter of not doing evil but of hating it, rejecting it, and instead loving the good. And to avoid a theoretical discourse it is suddenly asserted that the abuses of justice will be rooted out, a development already mentioned in 2.6–7a (cf. 5.11).

The mention of the 'remnant' at the end of the section (v. 15b) shows that the prophet considers that the mass of the people are now incapable of fulfilling the demands that might lead the Lord to have mercy: so a minimum of them will be able to survive the imminent disaster. And here too the formula expresses doubt: 'Perhaps'. The mention of 'Joseph' is unusual in Amos, as we have seen, cf. v. 6 above and 6.6 where it seems to be an addition (see ad loc.). Perhaps it presupposes that Israel is now reduced to living in the central hill country, having lost the territory of Galilee and the plains (Joseph is in fact the collective name for Ephraim and Manasseh, who settled in the hill country). In that case the earliest date would be after 733, when the Assyrians occupied these regions under Tiglath-Pileser III.

10. The first invective (5.7 + 10–13, 16–17 and 8–9)

G. Hoffmann, 'Versuche zu Amos', *ZAW* 3, 1883, (87–126, 279–80) 110; F. Horst, 'Die Doxologien im Amosbuch', *ZAW* 37, 1929, 45–54 = *Gottes Recht*, Munich 1961, 155–66; J. D. W. Watts, 'Note on the Text of Amos V 7', *VT* 4, 1954, 215f.; H. Gese**, 432–6; J. J. Glück, 'Three Notes on the Book of Amos', *Studies in the Book of Amos*, OTWSA 7–8, 1964–5, (115–21) 115–19; J. M. Ward**, 74ff., 112ff.; W. Berg**, 18f. and passim; I. Willi-Plein**, 33ff.; Markert**, 140ff.; F. Foresti, 'Funzione semantice dei brani participiali in Amos: 4, 13; 5, 8f.; 9.5ff.', *Bib* 62, 1981, 169–84; L. Zalcman, 'Astronomical Allusions in Amos', *JBL* 100, 1981, 53–8; H. N. Barstad**, 77–88.

We are again confronted with a section which is far from simple, having been altered in a redaction the criteria of which now escape us. The situation is complicated by the presence in vv. 8–9 of one of the doxologies of Amos which some scholars (e.g. S. Amsler* and W. Berg**) regard as a separate section; others prefer to put it at the end of the passage, so that 'the Lord', with which v. 17 concludes, can appear as the subject of the participle with which v. 8 begins.

5 [7]Woe to those who turn justice to bitterness,
who cast down justice to the earth,
[10]who hate him who judges justly in the courts,
and abhor him who makes true depositions.
[11]Therefore because you collect rent from [trample down] the poor,
take from him exactions of grain,
you have built houses of hewn stone,
but you shall not live in them;
you have planted precious vines,
but you shall not drink the wine.
[12]Indeed I know how many are your transgressions,
how heavy your sins,
what they do with those who are in the right;
they accept bribes,
prevent the poor from gaining access to the courts!

[13]Therefore in a time like this the prudent will keep silent,
it is indeed an evil time!
[16]Therefore thus says YHWH, the God of hosts, the Lord:
'In all the squares there shall be a lamenting,
in all the streets they shall cry "Alas, alas",
they shall finally call to mourning those who labour,
to the funeral lament the experts in lamenting.
[17]Finally in the vineyards lamentation will prevail,
when I pass through the midst of you', says the Lord.
[8]He who has made the Pleiades and Orion,
and turns the deepest darkness into morning,
darkens the day into night,
calls the waters of the sea,
to pour them out on the surface of the earth,
YHWH is his name.
[9]Who makes destruction come upon the powerful
[Who makes the 'Bull' come upon the 'Goat'],
brings destruction upon the fortified cities
[raises the 'Bull' behind the 'Grape Gatherer'].

[7] Since this verse is clearly separate from vv. 4–6, the participle at the beginning is left without a subject. This is usually remedied either by inserting or understanding a *hōy*, 'woe . . . to', the technical term which introduces the genre of literary invective, as does G. A. Smith* 1896, [2]1928. 'Bitterness': Hebrew 'wormwood', *artemisia absinthus*. However, LXX read a different text: 'It is he who performs judgment on high – who has established justice on the earth', a phrase which makes YHWH the subject as the author of justice; perhaps it goes back to a different archetype which sought to connect v. 7 with the doxology in vv. 8–9. It is accepted by Watts. [10] 'Who judges', cf. Zorell and *KB*[3] *yākah*. 'Justly': cf. the parallelism. 'In the tribunal', cf. above on v. 15a. The forensic context suggests this translation: 'depositions': Hebrew has 'the fullness'. [11] A root *bāšas* is attested only here in the Old Testament; J. Wellhausen suggested emending it to *būs[e]kam*, an orthographic variant of *bws*, 'trample', thus producing 'Since you trample', while H. Torczyner, *JPOS* 16, 1936, 6f., followed by Maag**, suggests connecting the term with the Akkadian *šabāsū* (*AHw* III, 1119), 'require contributions in kind' in the sense of exorbitant rent or contributions (metathesis from *bšs* to *šbs*). The two explanations are not incompatible, but the first is general, thus contrasting with the precision of the other passages (cf. 2.6–7a; 8.4ff.), so that again in view of the parallelism the second possibility seems better. 'Exactions': Hebrew *maś'ēt*, root *nāsā*: LXX has δῶρα ἐκλεκτά, perhaps *maśśā'*, probably with the stress on the corruption. 'Precious', literally 'of beauty, grace'. [12] 'Your transgressions': note the feminine plural with the noun predicate in the masculine, so

that some scholars would prefer to correct to *ḥaṭṭa'ēkem*, but inconsistencies of this kind between the subject and noun predicate are frequent, especially if the latter precedes the former (*GesK* § 145o). Hence emendation does not seem necessary. Note the change from first to third person in 12b. 'Who are in the right': for this meaning of *ṣaddīq* see above on 2.6–7a. 'Bribes': *kōper₄*, 'baksheesh'. 'Prevent': cf. on 2.7. 'Courts': cf. on v. 15a. **[16]** 'Those who labour' (in Hebrew the singular collective): *'ikkār* is the farmer who does not own his land, cf. Gese and *KB³*, but not *KB²*, which has 'countryman'.[27] 'The experts in lamenting . . .'; note the two terms used in Hebrew for 'lament': the text is confused and needs to reverse some terms, cf. Gese** and Rudolph* for the various problems. 'The experts': Rinaldi* would prefer to read *lō'* for *'el*, thus producing 'those who are not experts' and a paradoxical text.

[8] This perhaps lacks a beginning. 'Deepest darkness', Hebrew *ṣalmāwet*, often wrongly translated 'shadow of death', but it is now known that *māwet* and *mōt*, 'death', can, like *'elōhīm*, serve to indicate the superlative (cf. 4.11).[28]

[9] 'Brings . . . upon': Hebrew has the root *bālag*, 'be, become cheerful', but this does not fit well. Σ suggests 'make ridiculous','A and Vg 'deride', thus seeking to keep the basic meaning but adding a humorous or sarcastic note. LXX, however, has διαιρῶν, 'dividing, spacing', in Hebrew the root *pālag*, 'separate, divide', but this is also a makeshift solution while Tg and Syr have a paraphrase pure and simple. Here we probably have a root *bālag₂*, only in the hiphil, 'make lightning come, flash', 'make shine', Glück, Rudolph*. 'Destruction' is repeated, not an impossible form but one that is stylistically heavy, so that some scholars would prefer to replace this with *šeber*, 'ruin, breach'. 'Carry': read *yābī'* (hiphil) with all the translations. An interesting suggestion which is by now quite old is that the astronomical discourse begun in v. 8 is continued in v. 9, thus avoiding its isolation from the context and its somewhat conventional formulae. This was made in 1883 by G. Hoffmann[29] and has been taken up again by Snaith*. Contemporary authors also regularly flirt with it, as for example recently *KB³*, Amsler*, Mays* and Koch along with *BHK³* and *BHS*. However, this is a rendering which finds no echo in the ancient translations, so it cannot be proved. In any case it would have to be checked by an astronomer, and this is where its weakness lies. Hoffmann suggests correcting *šōd* to *šōr*, 'the Bull',

[27]For their social position see the basic study by T. N. D. Mettinger, *Solomonic State Officials*, CB.OTS 5, Lund 1971, 87.
[28]Cf. D. W. Thomas, 'SLMWT in the Old Testament', *JSS* 7, 1962, 191–200.
[29]G. Hoffmann, 'Versuche zu Amos', see bibliography to this section. The theme was taken up, with some variants, by B. Duhm, 'Anmerkungen zu den zwölf Propheten', *ZAW* 31, 1911, 1–43, 91; W. Nowack* and H. Gressmann*, and recently by G. R. Driver, 'Two Astronomical Passages in the Old Testament', *JTS* NS 4, 1953, 208–12: J. D. W. Watts, *Vision and Prophecy in Amos*, Leiden 1958, 55f. For the problem cf. Berg**, 40–52; he too is against this proposal, cf. Salomon **1981.

i.e. the constellation Taurus (confusion between *rēs* and *dālet*), *'az* to *'ēz*, 'the Goat', Capricorn, which would rise (root *bw'*) behind the *m'baṣṣēr* (for *mabsīr*), 'the Grape Gatherer' (from the constellation of Virgo) or *mabsīr*, 'Arcturus'. If such explanations, arrived at with minimal textual modifications (L. Zalcman**), could be substantiated, they would in fact resolve all the problems of the text and its context.

1. It seems very difficult to consider this passage a unity. If a unity does exist it is thanks to the redactors. Here too the main theme is that of the inefficiency and corruption of the courts, a feature also discussed, as we have seen, in 2.6–7a and in 8.4ff. We can therefore consider it to be one of the dominant themes in the prophet's preaching. We do not have information to evaluate the details of the denunciations made by the prophet, but the general framework which emerges is disconcerting: in fact justice must have functioned in such a way that the poor did not have access to it except to be condemned, as in 2.7. Various reasons have been given as to why the first 'woe to' appears in the text at this point. H.-W. Wolff* thinks that it can be explained by the fact that *hōy*, like *'ōy*, sometimes also introduces the lament, when it then has the significance of 'alas', so that there would be an affinity, albeit formal, with 5.1–3. But W. Rudolph* sees v. 7b rather as the continuation of 15a: making justice prevail in the tribunal is a necessary condition for the Lord to have mercy on the remnant of Joseph. So seeing that in reality the opposite happens can only lead the prophet to exclaim 'Woe to . . .' However, it could simply indicate, as Rudolph* continues, that the redactors had found a suitable place for the invective. In reality it is not necessary to connect this text with any preceding passage: the faults in the procedure in the courts and in the application of the law must have been a problem of the utmost seriousness in ancient Israel, as is evident from Amos's criticism of the courts, one of the leading themes of the book.

2. So v. 7 is invective against the courts and most particularly against the judges who pronounced sentence. The law and the administration of justice, which have always and in all places had the aim of giving society a just and rational order by protecting those who were weak and incapable of protecting themselves, and limiting to the greatest possible degree the power of the powerful, especially if it were malevolent, excessive or devious, has here become the shield, the excuse for the prevarication of the strong and the wily at the expense of the weaker and poorer and in general of those who, while manifestly having right on their side, resorted to the offices of the tribunal to get it recognized. In v. 10, however, we have an invective against those who persecuted the just judges (so that there must still have been some of them) and the

witnesses in the tribunal who spoke the truth and nothing but the truth. Verses 11 and 12 go on to speak of oppression, probably by corrupt judges, who found the innocent guilty, influenced as they were by bribes (baksheesh) and also, if we can consider v. 11 to be part of the original context, by interests created and rights acquired through which they demanded from the poor rent and tribute in kind much in excess of what had been agreed, or which even was not owed. These people were precisely the ones who had no other defence than the courts, and those were not effective. So it seems possible to read between the lines that these judges had private interests which were manifestly incompatible with the exercise of a public function or with the cases that they were hearing. This practice led to exorbitant profits, as was shown by their possession of fine houses built of hewn stone instead of common rough bricks made of mud.[30] However, the possibility remains that v. 11 is a redactional addition to this section (Weiser*, Robinson* and Wolff*), although many scholars (Sellin*, Maag*, Amsler* and Rudolph*) see it as the logical continuation of v. 10. The problem lies in the fact that rather than continuing the invective against the corrupt magistrates, the verse speaks of the exploitation of the poor by the rich through swindling and improper exactions: so these would be authentic words but in the wrong part of the book. As Rudolph* rightly notes, underlying v. 11 is the violation of the prohibitions against charging interest on loans (Ex. 22.24; Lev. 25.26; Deut. 23.20; cf. Prov. 28.8), laws made to defend the lowly and the poor. The difference here is that the interest did not consist in sums of money but in contributions in kind, and in such quantities as to put in question the economic survival of those who had to pay them. These exploiters are threatened with a kind of retribution, a harsh remuneration: they will not be able to enjoy the fruits of their misdeeds even if they have invested their money in luxurious buildings and precious vines. Verse 16 turns the screw further: the invective intoned by the prophet will soon be caught up in the general lamentation, with cries of anguish (Hebrew *hō, hō*, 'Alas, Alas', only here) even in the vineyards (v. 17), a traditional place for demonstrations of joy (cf. Judg. 9.27; Isa. 16.10; Jer. 48.33; Cant. 8.13). The lament here seems meant to include everyone and not just the 'mourners' mentioned in Jer. 9.16, cf. II Chron. 35.25 (Barstad** brings out interesting parallels with the fertility cult which can still be found in the sphere of Syrian Christianity).

Verse 13 is the clearest of all the interpolations, limiting itself to

[30]Cf. H. K. Beebe, 'Ancient Palestinian Dwellings', *BA* 31, 1968, 38–58.

noting the silence of the prudent man in such adverse circumstances. Things could have been difficult for Amos, but he did not keep silent here.

3. As Rudolph* rightly noted, the doxology is an interruption in its present position and so various scholars put it in different places, as, moreover, do some of the redactors. Others would prefer to treat it independently as a fragment separated from the other doxologies, and that is perhaps better. God appears in the fragment as creator and guarantor of the laws of nature, a concept which some scholars would want to deny that Israel ever had, and rightly so, if by it we understand the harmony of the components of the cosmos in an Aristotelian sense. But Israel does know of an order willed by God for nature; everything is in fact attributed to him: not only the alternation of day and night and the cycle of the seasons, but also the rising of the constellations and their movement. The Pleiades are the 'seven' stars, an old translation which has now become traditional, though LXX read ' . . . every house', a literal translation of *kīmāh*, 'family, mass'; Orion, too, is an almost universal rendering, though there are those who prefer Sirius (which in any case is connected with Orion), while Vg reads 'Arcturus' (for the discussion see Rudolph* and Berg*). Note that the explanation is not mythical (and scientifically more exact), differing from that of P which sees the rain as the product of openings in the celestial vault (Gen. 7.11; 8.2; cf. Isa. 55.10; Job 36.27–30; 38.34–38). Moreover it is possible, as Rudolph* indicated, that here we already have an implicit protest against the divinization of the stars as in P and Deutero-Isaiah: here we have (A. Weiser*) a substantial unity between God as judge and as creator, a concept which was probably widespread at the time of Amos and which the prophet made his own.

We considered in the discussion on the text the possibility that the astronomical discourse begun in v. 8 continues in v. 9.

11. The second invective: the 'Day of YHWH' (5.18–20)

Seierstad**, 17f., L.Černy, *The Day of Yahweh and Some Relevant Problems*, Prague 1948, passim; G. von Rad, 'The Origin of the Concept of the Day of Yahweh', *JSS* 4, 1959, 97–108, cf. id., *Old Testament Theology* II, London 1975, 119–25; F. J. Helewa, 'L'origine du concept prophétique du Jour de Yahvé', *Ephemerides Carmeliticae* 15, 1964, 3–36; S. J. deVries, *Yesterday, Today, Tomorrow*, Grand Rapids, Mich. and London 1974; M. Weiss, 'The Origin of the Day of the Lord Reconsidered', *HUCA* 37, 1966, 41–5; J. M. Ward**, 83f.; C. Van Leeuwen, 'The prophecy of the *yōm yhwh* in Amos V

18–20', *OTS* 19, 1974, 113–34; Willi-Plein**, 31; Markert**, 153ff.; Y. Hoffmann, 'The Day of the Lord as a Concept and a Term in the Prophetic Literature', *ZAW* 93, 1981, (37–50) 40–3; Barstad**, 89–110; K. A. D. Smelik, 'The Meaning of Amos V 18–20', *VT* 36, 1986, 246–8.

---

5 [18]Woe to you who expect the day of YHWH:
what will the day of YHWH be for you?
It will be darkness and not light.
[19]It will be as if a man escaped from a lion
and a bear met him,
or went into a house and leant on the wall
and a serpent bit him.
[20]Indeed the day of YHWH will be darkness and not light,
gloom with no brightness in it.

A particularly clean text. **[18]** For some scholars this is an addition which anticipates v. 20; but if one notes the chiastic structure of the composition it is evident that this would be disturbed if even the smallest part of it were deleted. **[19]** The animals, rather than representing real dangers in everyday life (thus G. Rinaldi* and others), seem to be rhetorical figures, and the image corresponds to our 'out of the frying pan into the fire'.[31] **[20]** Here MT understands the terms in the second line as attributes of the day of YHWH, while LXX understands them as nouns. But this is probably a matter of style rather than a variant. 'Indeed': I read the particle $h^a l\bar{o}$ as an emphatic *lamed*; a question which does not expect an answer makes no sense here (e.g. 'Perhaps the day of YHWH will not be darkness and not light?), given that the invective presupposes that the people have a completely wrong idea as to what it will be.

As we have seen, a particularly clean text with an organic structure here presents the second of the 'woes' announced by Amos. First of all it says what the day of YHWH will be; it seems that there were substantial differences between the prophet and his audience. It has even been proposed recently (Smelik 1986) that the problem arises from the preaching of 'false' prophets, as we find them later in Jeremiah and Ezekiel, a suggestion which deserves to be elaborated upon. But it must be remembered that *yōm* does not necessarily mean a day of twenty-four hours: the term is also used for years and epochs generally; here it is the era in which God himself will take the reins of history into his hand to guide it to its proper end. This is something that Israel had experienced in its traditional protohistory and which was taken up in the actualiz-

[31]Cf. A. Caquot, '*DOB*', *TWAT* II, 1977, 74–6.

ation of the history of salvation in the liturgy of the cult; at the end of time the glorious acts of God in the past will again be manifested. So the people envisages a time of light (vv. 18, 20), a time in which YHWH will manifest himself for the salvation of his people. Thus the times which are now about to come and are ardently expected will be great ones. For the prophet, however, this will be a time of 'utter darkness', of constant peril which it is impossible to escape (v. 19); having avoided one danger people will immediately be confronted with another.

This is probably the earliest datable discussion of an eschatological theme, a theme which, moreover, seems to have been well known to the people and therefore cannot just have emerged then. So here too we have the old contrast, one of the characteristic features of this book: the prophet is pessimistic, as he already has been on other occasions, as to whether there is any saving element in the faith of Israel, while the people seem confident and even cocksure: the next manifestation of God (there was no doubt that there would be some form of divine manifestation) could not but turn out for its own good. The prophet sees only a life lived without coherence, sometimes an impious life, a life which could not in any case lead to blessings but which could only end up in disaster. And so it is that he can now intone his second invective.

In his now classical study of 1905 Gressmann,[32] nowadays still basically followed by W. Rudolph*, spoke for the first time of a 'popular eschatology' characterized by hope for a time when God himself would have established his Lordship over the earth and brought to his own elect people, for ever and publicly, before all the nations, the eternal salvation he had promised, a salvation which the events of history had always kept delaying. This discussion was taken up by von Rad: he claimed that the optimistic eschatology derived from the concept of the holy war in which God fought on the side of his own people, so that was how he was expected to fight at the end of time (cf. the texts of Isa. 13.6–8, 34; Joel 2.1–2; Ezek. 7.7ff.). However, in considering this argument we must note that the concept of the holy war is no longer considered to be an ancient institution: in fact virtually all the texts which speak of it are of Deuteronomistic origin. Gressmann, however, was not necessarily right in deriving this eschatology from outside: in reality the religion of Israel contains all the elements for the rise and development of such a faith. It is expressed in phrases like that of v. 14, 'YHWH is with us'. Now for Amos the disasters which the people have had to face in its history are not a return to the time of salvation but the

[32]H. Gressman, *Der Ursprung der israelitisch-jüdischen Eschatologie*, Göttingen 1905; id., *Der Messias*, FRLANT 40, Göttingen 1929; cf. recently H. D. Preuss, *Jahweglaube* (n. 23), 170–9.

warning signals of the final and irreversible disaster that is approaching. For popular beliefs cf. Hos. 2.20; 14.6–8; Isa. 11.6–8. We cannot enter into a detailed examination of the origins of this concept here (in any case Barstad** has considered them thoroughly); it is enough to note that we find one of the earliest attestations of it here. It is important to note that in the circumstances the prophet rejects any form of optimistic nationalist eschatology which may have been widespread among his audience, perhaps also encouraged by the recent victories of Jeroboam II in the military sphere. The prophet does, however, proclaim the tremendous and indeed inescapable character of the 'day of the Lord', whose coming no one will escape, a concept fully illustrated in the text by the image of the three savage creatures.

12. Cult and injustice (5.21–27)

E. Würthwein, 'Amos 5.21–27', *TLZ* 7, 1947, 143–53 = *Word und Existenz – Studien zum Alten Testament*, Göttingen 1970, 55–67; E. A. Speiser, 'Note on Amos 5.26', *BASOR* 108, 1947, 5f.; J. P. Hyatt, 'The Translation and Meaning of Amos 5.23–24', *ZAW* 68, 1956, 17–24; R. Hentschke**, 73–88; R. Dobbie, 'Amos 5.25', *TGUOS* 17, 1957–58, 62–4; E. Würthwein, 'Kultpolemik oder Kultbescheid?', in *Tradition und Situation . . . FS A. Weiser*, Göttingen 1963, 115–31 = *Wort und Existenz*, 144–60; W. H. Schmidt**, 188–91; S. Gevirtz, 'A New Look at an Old Crux', *JBL* 87, 1968, 267–76; J. M. Ward**, 138ff.; J. McKay, *Religion in Judah under the Assyrians*, SBT II, 26, London 1973, 68; J. Vollmer**, 37–43; I. Willi-Plein**, 37ff.; W. Rudolph**, 1973; M. Cogan, *Imperialism and Religion*, SBL.MS 1974, 97–9; P. von der Osten-Sacken, 'Die Bücher der Tora als Hutte der Gemeinde – Amos 5.26f. in der Damaskusschrift', *ZAW* 91, 1979, 425–35; O. Loretz, '*Šlm* in Am. 5, 22 und das *šlmjm*-Opfer', *UF* 13, 1981, 127–31; Barstad**, 111–18, 118–26.

---

5 [21]I hate, I despise your festivities,
I can no longer smell the odour of your festivals:
[22]When you offer me burnt offerings
. . . ;
I do not appreciate your offerings,
your sacrifices of fattened beasts
I will not even look upon.
[23]Take away from me the racket of your songs,
I do not want to hear the melody of your zithers.
[24]But let the law roll down like water,
justice like an everflowing stream.

²⁵Did you offer me sacrifices and burnt offerings in the
desert,
for forty years, O house of Israel?
²⁶You will have to carry away Sakkuth, your king,
and Kewan, your image (a star!),
the glory of your gods that you have made for yourself.
²⁷Then you shall take them into exile beyond Damascus,
says YHWH whose name is the 'God of hosts'!

[22] After the first line (22aα) something is certainly missing; many
scholars are agreed on that. Otherwise we would have the phrase 'if not
when you offer me burnt offerings', which would contradict the whole sense
of the discourse and destroy the parallelism. The omission must be ancient,
since the majority of the ancient translations confirm MT. So something
should be inserted like 'do not please me' or 'displease me' or another
similar phrase: for the various possibilities cf. Rudolph*. In that case there
would be no question of deleting it. However, for Loretz, perhaps rightly,
the phrase is to be deleted since it seeks to correct the polemical affirmation
originally present in the phrase. So we would have:

'I hate . . . your festivals,
I do not appreciate your offerings.'

'Fattened' is equivalent to our 'of prime quality'. LXX read τῆς ἐπιφανείας
ὑμῶν, i.e. the root rā'āh, see. [23] 'Depart from me': infinitive absolute with
the value of a finite verb, so a correction to hāsīrū (BIIS and others) is
unnecessary. 'Racket': literally 'multitude', 'quantity', but as Rudolph
points out, the context calls for an 'acoustic phenomenon' and not quantity.
'Your . . .': most scholars would prefer to correct to the second person
plural, perhaps so that hāsēr is understood as an imperative (Rudolph*),
but changes of person are frequent in Western Semitic. [24] 'Roll down',
root gālal; Vg read et revelabit, i.e. the root gālāh, as did other translations,
wrongly. 'Everflowing': in the area of Syria and Palestine (like Greece, Italy
and southern Spain) there is a clear distinction between the watercourses
which only carry water during the rainy season, and those that carry it all
the time. A. Weiser* and E. Würthwein, however, suggest another
translation:

But judgment will flow down like water,
justice like an everflowing stream,

thus considering the whole phrase to be an introduction to the announcement of judgment in v. 27. [25] The discourse continues in prose. Loretz
considers the whole section vv. 25–27 secondary, probably rightly so. 'Did

you . . .': *ha-* here is interrogative, not an article, because otherwise it would also be repeated before *minḥah*: but others would prefer to read, 'Certainly you did not offer me . . .', the exclamatory *ha-*, a rare form but one which is attested, Joüon § 161b and accepted by G. Rinaldi*. It is possible that 'in the desert', of uncertain syntax, is a later addition. Vollmer** wants to link vv. 25 and 26, making two rhetorical questions: 'Did you offer me sacrifices and burnt offerings in the desert . . . and did you carry Sikkuth and Kewan?' In this case it is not denied that Israel offered sacrifices in the desert; what is implied is that it demeaned the cult of its God to that of other deities. This text, which is intrinsically clear, will have been understood by a later commentator to refer solely to the idolatrous cult. This is a possibility to take into consideration. **[26]** 'Sakkuth' and 'Kewan', vocalized in the original as Sikkuth and Kiyyun, i.e. with the vowels of *šiqqūṣ*, abomination, a term which appears often for pagan deities, are usually identified with astral Assyro-Babylonian deities (*Šurpu* II, 1800) connected with Saturn and the deity Ninurta, Maag**, 90, Speiser and Rudolph*. LXX read τὴν σκηνὴν τοῦ Μολοχ, i.e. *sukkat* for the first term, and this reading is preferred by Amsler* (*la tente*, thus recently also Isbell) and cf. the article by von der Osten-Sacken for the exegesis along these lines from Qumran, where the *tōrāh* is understood as a 'cabin', a refuge for the community. For the other term Amsler* wants to read *kēn* or *kiyōn*, 'footstool' or 'pedestal'; 'a star' and 'your gods' would then be a gloss. Sellin and Weiser also try to eliminate the astral reference by correcting the text, followed here by Willi-Plein** (cf. there for details, 37f., and also for Assyriological questions, which are rather complex). But apart from the above-mentioned authors there is almost unanimous agreement on the astral character of this passage. 'Star' is a gloss, but it is not to be deleted as many would still prefer (Markert**, 159). E. A. Speiser has in fact made it probable that here we have a rather strange use of the term *ṣelem*: in Babylonian, *ṣalmu* serves to express in astronomical contexts the anthropomorphic representation of a star or a constellation (cf. *AHw* III, 1078, 60),[33] so that the gloss simply seeks to explain the unusual meaning of 'image'. Be this as it may, there remains the difficulty of explaining how in the eighth century BC Amos could attest here the presence of Mesopotamian astral cults, a presence which is not only unsubstantiated but seems utterly improbable (McKay). But a feature which demonstrates the secondary character of these verses is that at the beginning the passage speaks of the worship offered to YHWH, not syncretistic or idolatrous worship, a theme which does not otherwise appear in Amos. However, the theme does appear in Hosea,[34] notoriously in line with Deuteronomy and Dtr, and the expression 'the gods which you have made' belongs to the school, so it seems that we

---

[33]Cf. É. Dhorme, *Les religions de Babylone et d'Assyrie*, Mana 1.2, Paris 1949, 80ff.; W. H. Schmidt**, 189.

[34]Cf. H. W. Wolff, 'Hoseas geistige Heimat', *TLZ* 81, 1956, 83–94 = *GS*, Munich ²1973, 232–50.

should probably follow Schmidt in attributing the passage to this school. M. Cogan seems to differ; he cites the annals of Sargon in which we read: 'I looked on the gods in whom they put their trust as booty of war', a reference to Samaria (for the passage cf. there). But the author does not go more deeply into the problem, and the phrase that he quotes is not conclusive since the reference that he makes is not to the Mesopotamian deities in question.

1. Rudolph* entitles this section 'Not cult, but justice', but as we have seen in other passages (above 4.4f. and 5.4f.), the alternative, apart from being wrong, seems intrinsically absurd, given that in the ancient world, both East and West, a society that was not founded on religion and the cult was inconceivable. This section discusses, rather, the impossibility of a cult which is not matched by a commitment which translates the faith confessed into specific acts. And in fact Rudolph* himself concedes that elsewhere: on p. 209 he actually speaks of 'the attitude of YHWH towards the cult of Israel' and not of the cult per se; he is even more precise on p. 214: 'it is not said that he (the prophet) rejects any form of cult in principle.'

The most obvious parallel to this text, at least as far as vv. 21–24 are concerned, is Isa. 1.10–17. The text does not seem to want to take up the previous vv. 18–20; that was perhaps the intention of the redactors, but it was certainly not that of the prophet, as is shown by the transition from the second person plural (the words of the prophet) to the first person singular (YHWH is speaking). Here, too, the place in which the proclamation was delivered could have been the sanctuary in Bethel.

2. In vv. 21–23 we have an opinion on the cult in the form of an oracle of YHWH himself, formulated in the style of *tōrāh*, prophetic and priestly teaching, which we have already come across in connection with 4.4–5. The difference here is that the *tōrāh* is not sarcastically turned into its opposite but expresses in markedly polemic form what is YHWH's real view of the cultic life of the people, a life which should be honouring him (against Rudolph).[35] The terminology used, as Rudolph* rightly observes, indicates not only hostility but aversion, disgust, feelings which cause hate, repudiation, rejection.

The text begins with an evaluation of the cult in general (v. 21), and then passes on in v. 22 to the sacrifices and the offerings: the sacrifices of fattened animals, i.e. of the best quality, are such that they imply a very substantial renunciation by those who offer them, since they are beasts

[35]For this literary genre cf. the basic study by E. Würthwein, 'Kultpolemik oder Kultbescheid?', in *Studien zur alttestamentlichen Prophetie – FS A. Weiser zum 70. Geburtstag*, Göttingen 1963, 115–31; *Wort und Existenz, Studien zum Alten Testament*, Göttingen 1970, 144–60; this also contains a complete bibliography on the theme of prophecy and the cult down to the beginning of the 1960s.

of high commercial value; we find the contrary instance, of reject animals being offered in sacrifice, much later, in Mal. 1.8ff. Verse 23, however, speaks of music and sacred song. All these offerings are rejected by YHWH; so the song sounds like a racket, though clearly it must have included psalms and other forms of sacred songs. It is also interesting to note with Rudolph* that here, too, as in the other passages of Amos which adopt polemical positions towards the cult, the object of the accusation is not idolatry or syncretism; here the cult seems to be perfectly orthodox. Nor is this a 'purely external cult', as Osty* states, or 'reprehensible cults', as Rinaldi* would have it. The fact is that its practice in the sanctuaries seems to the prophet to be blasphemy when compared with the situations of corruption and injustice existing within the people of God, situations in which the lion's share again goes to those who administer justice in the tribunals (v. 24). Moreover similar phrases are the common heritage of ancient Near Eastern wisdom: Israelite (Prov. 21.3; cf. 15.8; 21.27); Egyptian, cf. the Instruction for King Merikare, line 129 (*ANET*, 417) which says: 'Better is the virtue of the just man than the ox of the wicked' (Wolff*). And if it is permissible to adopt Rudolph*'s conjecture we might suppose that one of the aims of the cult was to confess and expiate the many crimes committed by the people and by the monarchy, which gave it a kind of excuse – an attitude which the prophet firmly rejects. And it is at this point that the 'opinion', the *tōrāh* on the cult, comes to an end.

3. Verse 25 begins an explanatory discourse. However, the most probable explanation of the verse does not seem to me to be that put forward by Vollmer** and indicated above in the discussion of the text: to combine vv. 25 and 26 in one question if possible, deriving the union between syncretistic or idolatrous cults and orthodox worship from the time in the desert; Rudolph* and the majority of scholars, however, rightly suggest that the phrase should be understood not as an impossible reference to a stay in the desert with no sacrifices being offered (an argument often put forward at the beginning of the century),[36] but as an assertion meant to indicate that during the forty years of the stay in the desert it was not in any case possible to offer the rich sacrifices which characterized the time of the prophet, offerings typical of a country civilization: nor was this the problem; fidelity and commitment (already attested, among others, by Jer. 2.1ff.) were enough. The promise could have been fulfilled despite the modest character of the sacrifices, evident proof of the fact that the nub of the question did not lie there. The theory of a time in the desert in which

---

[36]E. Würthwein, art. cit., 115/144 and the bibliography in nn. 1, 2.

there were no sacrifices, which was often argued for in the past in the sphere of Pentateuchal criticism, thus proves to be a 'deplorable equivocation' (Rudolph*): in fact it contrasted too much with a unanimous tradition for an argument of this kind to be logically effective. No audience, regardless of whether the passage goes back to the prophet or whether it should be attributed to a later insertion, could have taken it seriously. Be this as it may, it is not easy to say whether this verse, which like the whole section is certainly secondary, is Deuteronomistic: in his study of the subject Schmidt** does not discuss the verse in his text, but includes it in the Latin-English summary at the end of his article, and on the basis of this mention the theory appears in Wolff*, 262.

4. With v. 26, however, we have a typically Deuteronomistic inter polation, which probably continues in v. 27, as Schmidt has demons-trated. The opening phrase seems 'astonishing' (Rudolph), suggesting that Israel should have to carry in procession the statues of two Meso-potamian astral deities (only Kewan can be identified with some degree of certainty, with Saturn, Barstad** 126), but the explanation of this assertion appears in v. 27: the people will have to go into exile (a practice of the Assyrians and later the Babylonians towards subject peoples and one which was generally known) and here would be confronted with a situation similar to that for which David rebuked Saul in I Sam. 26.19, another late text: to have to offer worship to ('serve') other gods. But in this case the situation would be even more serious: the people would not just have to offer worship to the deities in question generally but to play an active part in the processions carrying the images. Israel organized all those feasts in honour of YHWH, and he responded by handing them over 'into the hands of the competition', as Rudolph* puts it.

'Beyond Damascus': until a few years earlier the enemy *par excellence* of Israel, is an expression which demonstrates clearly that Amos had Assyria in mind, as W. Rudolph* rightly notes against H.-W. Wolff*. The text is quoted in Qumran, CD VII.12–21.[37]

13. The third invective: the 'consumer' society (6.1–8a)

A. Parrot, *Le musée du Louvre et la Bible*, Neuchâtel 1957, 93ff.; O. Eissfeldt, 'Etymologische und archäologische Erklärung alttestamentlicher Wörter', *OA* 5, 1966, (165–76) = *KS* IV, Tübingen 1968, (285–96) 166/285ff.; Willi-Plein**, 39ff.; W. L. Holladay, 'Amos VI 1B', *VT* 22, 1972, 107–10; W. Rudolph**,

[37]For the text cf. E. Lohse, *Die Texte aus Qumran*, Darmstadt [2]1971, 81, and L. Moraldi, *I manoscritti di Qumran*, Turin 1971, 244f.; also H. W. Wolff*, 311f.; P. von der Osten-Sacken, art. cit.

1973, 160; Markert**, 164ff.; Barstad**, 33ff., 42ff., 127–42; U. Dahm, 'Zur Text- and Literarkritik vom Am. 6, 6a', *BN* 31, 1986, 7–10.

---

6 [1]Woe to those who are at ease on Zion,
to those who feel secure on the mountain of Samaria,
the nobility of the firstfruits of the nations,
to whom the house of Israel comes.
[2]Pass over to Kalneh and see,
from there go to Hamath the great,
then go down to Gath of the Philistines.
Are you better than these kingdoms,
were their territories greater than yours?
[3]You who believe that the fatal day is far away,
but bring near a violent end [dominion].
[4]Those who lie upon beds inlaid with ivory,
who stretch themselves upon their couches,
who eat lambs from the flock,
calves from the stall.
[5]Who improvise on the lyre
inventing musical instruments like David,
[6]who drink from bowls of wine,
and anoint themselves with the finest oil,
without noticing that Joseph is going to ruin.
[7]Therefore they will go into exile at the head of the exiles
and the revelry of those who are stretched out shall pass away.
[8a]Oracle of the Lord, God of Hosts.

The title given to this section is taken from J. L. Mays.* **[1]** The mention of 'Zion' in this context has always caused difficulties, even if at a purely formal level 'the parallelism could not be better' (Hammershaimb*): in fact the prophet's preaching is addressed exclusively to the North, as we have seen. For N. H. Snaith*, H.-W. Wolff* and others before them (cf. the latter) this is a later addition, a rereading once the text had been transferred to the South: others (cf. *BHS*) would prefer to correct it to *big^e'ōnām*, 'in their orgy', while according to W. Rudolph* we should read *babbiṣṣaron*, 'in strength'. Here the theory of Snaith and Rudolph would seem better in detail. An attempt at a solution to the difficulties in the last line of the verse has been put forward by Holladay, who suggests reading *t^{e}bū'at leḥem bēt yiśrā'ēl*, 'the harvest, the food/bread of the house of Israel'. The reading suggested by some scholars, *w^{e}kē'lōhīm hem l^{e}bēt yiśrā'el* or *b^{e}bēt yiśrā'ēl*, 'and they are as divinities for the house of Israel', seems overloaded. **[2]** Kalneh: somewhat north of Aleppo, called Kalno in Isa. 10.9. It has nothing to do with the Kalneh of Gen. 10.10, situated in Mesopotamia but not yet identified with certainty.

Hamath is in the construct, an unusual form but here apparently without particular significance, cf. Joüon, § 131n and the commentaries: the place is about half way from the Orontes. The two places were conquered in 738 by Tiglath-Pileser III (cf. *ANET*, 282), but in 720 the latter revolted, was defeated and deported, and its king was tortured and killed (*ANET*, 284f.). Be this as it may, in terms both of style and content the discourse recalls that attributed by Isa. 10.8ff. to the Assyrians (a text which is often considered late), cf. II Kings 18.34//Isa. 36.19, while the theme of the smallness of Israel is typical of the evaluation made by Deuteronomy and Dtr. So it is probable that this text is the product of later re-reading. For many scholars, however, the mention of Gath and the Philistines is the product of another addition: the place does not match the kingdoms already mentioned, nor does it appear on an itinerary from south to north; and it is not mentioned in 1.6–8. **[2]** 'Their . . . your . . .': some scholars invert the suffixes, 'Your . . . their', but the Massoretic reading seems to be the *lectio difficilior*. The text implies 'Woe to those . . .' **[3]** 'Believe . . . far away' root *nādāh*, rare, or should we read *nādad*, 'chase'? 'But': *waw* adversative, the vocalization of which is perhaps to be explained by attraction from the following *a*. 'End'; the root *yāšab* here is usually connected with the Arab *watbat*, 'attack', cf. Wolff* and Rudolph*, but it is probably (Rudolph) better to connect it with *šābat*, 'interrupt'. If we read *yāšab* we also have the verb 'sit on a throne', producing 'dominion'. Finally, other scholars suggest reading *š^enat*, the year of violence, parallel to the *yōm* which precedes it. **[4]** 'From the stall', where they are put to fatten up, a meaning implicit in the Hebrew term.

[5] 'Improvise': thus *KB*³ on the basis of mediaeval Hebrew exegesis, but as Zorell rightly observes, the stress is on the inept, incompetent way of playing (Rinaldi*, 'set to bawling', Wolff* and Rudolph*; 'shout', 'scream'). 'Like David' seems a doubtful expression, all the more so since it interrupts the context (cf. II Chron. 7.6), and would be the only passage in the book which referred explicitly to an ancient hero; moreover, it is missing in LXX. Wolff* and others delete it, while Rudolph* would prefer to read *yeḥaš^ebū* for *ḥaš^ebū*, 'consider themselves like David: perfect singers', also correcting *k^elē* to *m^ekallē šīr*. **[6]** 'Bowls' here is the technical term for libations, with the stress on their great capacity. 'Noticing': root *ḥālāh*. The line is often considered a later comment, but for its probable antiquity see the commentary. So it should not be deleted. **[7]** 'Revelry': LXX read χρεμέτισμος ἵππων ἐξ Ἐφραιμ, 'the neighing of the horses of Ephraim', probably the product of a false reading. 'Who are stretched out': Rinaldi* effectively translates: 'the spineless'. As Eissfeldt demonstrates, outside the Old Testament the term *mirzāh* has the meaning 'associations', whereas here it is not completely clear, even if the context calls for it to be understood in a negative sense. Others translate 'howling'.[38] However, in Jer. 16.5 the term refers rather to a funeral party (as Coote would prefer here, 35f.), an interesting example of the semantic

[38]For this term cf. recently R. Meyer, *Gegensinn und Mehrdeutigkeit in der althebräischen Wort- und Begriffsbildung*, SSAW 120.5, 1979, 8, and VF 11, 1979, 601–12.

ambivalence of a biblical root (cf. also for *tā'ab* in 6.8), but with the stress on the noise. The term has recently been examined by Barstad**, also on the basis of ancient Near Eastern texts from Ugarit to Palmyra. The examination shows (there is plenty of material, but not very precise) that the term denotes associations with a sacral basis, during whose meetings ritual food was consumed, a kind of agape: the term derives from the root *rzḥ*I or *rzḥ*1 II, respectively 'cry out' and 'be united', which explains the plurality of meanings. **[8]** Section aβ is added by many scholars to the end of this discourse where it would fit very well; in 8 it would seem to be a duplicate.

1. Augustine already recognized the organic and well-defined character of this unit (*PL* 34, 96ff.; *CCSL* 32, 128f.); it deals with one of the basic themes of the book: the luxury of the ruling class along with its lack of vigilance and corruption. The passage, originally addressed to the authorities of the northern kingdom ('on the mountain of Samaria'), must have had remarkable success and its vividness does not seem to have diminished over the centuries, as is shown by application of the invective to the inhabitants of Jerusalem (v. 1aα), as we saw when looking at the text ('who stand secure on Zion').

This is the third of three invectives (the formula 'woe to . . .' is to be understood in vv. 3–6) which quotes, probably sarcastically (v. 1), the term which they apply to themselves: 'the nobility of the firstfruits of the nations'). The second part of the description evidently refers to Israel as an elect people, the first to the chosen element within it which the group in question claims to be. Here we have a concept of election which the prophet can only treat sarcastically, since it corresponds so little to reality; later, too, the Deuteronomistic school would let fly in a similar rage against concepts of this kind. To take one's stand on such a concept is tantamount to blindness, politics which amounts to putting one's head in the sand: not to know what is happening outside the walls of Samaria and to trust in their impregnability. We find a not dissimilar situation between 597–96 and 587–86 in Jerusalem, on the evidence of Jeremiah and Ezekiel, but at least Jerusalem was the holy city, a status which Samaria seems never to have had. But external events provided a justification: Jeroboam II certainly succeeded in expanding towards the north-east and his frontiers were approximately those that had existed under David and Solomon; however, the example of the two city states, once powerful and flourishing and now in utter decadence, must have drawn the attention of these nobles to the intrinsic weakness of any small nation in the political game controlled by the great powers Assyria and Egypt. And the prophet attributes this error of judgment in the political field to an erroneous faith and an inadequate theology: faith in itself and in its election, believing that election was some form of right acquired on a political and economic level and therefore guaranteed. Cf. below, 9.10.

2. The mention of the two cities conquered by Tiglath-Pileser III towards 738 and finally subjugated around 720 (cf. on the text) has suggested to some scholars[39] that at least v. 2 should be dated to a time later than that of the prophet, probably in the last quarter of the eighth century, cf. N. H. Snaith* and H.-W. Wolff* (the latter refers to 'disciples of Amos'). But such a theory is not needed to explain the text. First of all we know little of the detailed history of the region at this time, and secondly the discourse may simply refer to the political and economic decadence of the two places without as yet raising the problem of their final fall. These were kingdoms which emerged in circumstances not very different from those of the Davidic empire, and like that empire they were somewhat fragile constructions which could dissolve with equal rapidity under the pressure of internal centrifugal pressures as well as under the stimulus of external attacks. So the prophet gives a warning, and his message seems to be essentially political: 'A favourable situation in the present is no guarantee for the future.' (Rudolph*): it is not enough to be able to ward off the fatal day if, objectively speaking, one is hastening its arrival with blindness and corruption. Living in a favourable period can produce a sense of security and complacency, but the awakening and confrontation with reality will be all the more dramatic. In the first half of the eighth century it was possible, at least for the nobility, to enjoy considerable luxury: inlaid furniture (cf. on 3.15), a high consumption of meat, unthinkable in a period of general undernourishment, a life of ease spent in parties and orgies. The bowls from which these people drink are libation bowls, mentioned for their extravagant size, but the cult is not involved here, as some scholars think; these are either syncretistic orgiastic cults or the profanation of Israelite orthodoxy: re'šīt here is not, as Rudolph rightly notes, the first fruits which went only to YHWH but, we might add, oil that is even better in quality, that of the first pressing.

3. Given that the nobility is in this state, the embodiment of irresponsibility (v. 6c), to such a degree that some scholars describe them as politicians with their heads in the sand, there is no hope that things can improve. Wellhausen once summed up the situation without mincing his words: 'Not to be preoccupied with the ruin of Israel, and not to sense the present or have an intuition of the future, is the most serious charge that can be directed against politicians.' So v. 7 can draw the conclusion, appropriately introduced by 'Therefore'.

[39]In the wake of M. Noth, *OTW*, 261f.; cf. also K. Elliger, 'Hamat', and M. A. Beek, 'Kalne', *BHH* II, 1964, 629 and 922 respectively. Cf. what is said on the text of v. 2.

14. The judgment on the capital (6.8–11)

G. Garbini, 'Note semitiche II', *Ricerche linguistiche* 5, 1962, 179–81; Willi-Plein**, 43ff.; Markert**; 170ff.; M. J. Dahood, 'Amos 6.8 $m^e t\bar{a}$'ēb', *Bibl* 59, 1978, 265f.; G. W. Ahlstrom, 'King Josiah and the DWD of Amos 6.10', *JSS* 26, 1981, 7–9.

---

6 [8]The Lord, YHWH, has sworn by himself,
oracle of YHWH, God of hosts:
'I abhor the pride of Jacob,
I hate his palaces,
and I will deliver up the city and what is in it.'
[9]And if it should happen that ten persons survive in a house, they shall die.
[10]And an uncle or a kinsman will lift him up to carry his bones outside the house; and he will say to him who is still in the inner part of the house, 'Is there still anyone with you?' and he will reply 'No one'. And he will say, 'Silence! The name of YHWH must not be mentioned.'
[11]For behold, YHWH has ordered
the great house to be reduced to fragments,
the small house to pieces.

[8] 'Oracle . . . hosts' seems here, as in 6.7, to be a superfluous addition which weighs down the discourse and makes it top-heavy. 'Abhor': note the use of the root $t\bar{a}$'ab, whereas for a similar discourse 5.10 rightly has $t\bar{a}$'ab. But $t\bar{a}$'ab normally means desire, and is therefore the opposite of what the text means. G. Garbini supposes that the root t'b has two meanings,[40] a phenomenon for which he cites other examples; other scholars think in terms of a deliberate exchange of the two roots to tone down the very heavy character of the root t'b. However, Dahood looks in a different direction: he wants to divide the word into two terms, *mt* and *'b*, the first equivalent to "^{e}met, 'truth', written in apocopated form, i.e. 'in truth', 'certainly', whereas the second is the equivalent of '*ōyēb*, Ugaritic *'ib*, 'enemy', thus producing 'Indeed, in truth, I am an enemy of the pride . . .', but this is a makeshift proposal which does not succeed in explaining the origin of the reading in the text. It does, however, seem possible that this is a euphemism: we would have a parallel here to the way in which in Job 2.9 the root *brk*, 'bless', is used to mean 'curse' (so that this would have to be the translation): 'desire' is written to mean 'abhor'. The only difficultý arises from the fact that in Job the expression 'curse God' could in fact be thought scandalous, hence

---

[40]Cf. also R. Meyer, *Gegensinn* (see n. 38), passim, though he does not cite this passage. There is also a bibliography there.

the need for the euphemism, whereas here any such motivation is lacking. But in no case should we emend to *t'b* what is a *lectio difficilior*, as *BHK*[3] and some commentaries suggest. I have found a similar case in Gen. 24.20 for the root *š'h/š'h*. 'I will deliver up': for this meaning of *sāgar* in the hiphil cf. on 1.6, 9, where we have 'I will deliver up'. **[9]** The beginning of a prose section, probably the explanation of the preceding passage, but later. 'Person': *'ⁿōš* denotes a human being without differentiating between the sexes.

[10] A classical *crux interpretum*. *Dōd* is the 'paternal uncle', so it is not surprising that already in ancient times it was thought that the expression *mᵉsārᵉpō* was another term indicating kinship; however, it is to be associated etymologically (*srp-śrp*) with fire: rabbinic texts listed by V. Maag**, 164, envisage the closest kinsman after the uncle, similarly Syr, while the Karaites, quoted by Zorell, understand the term as being equivalent to 'maternal uncle or aunt'. There is also some agreement in rejecting any reference to the cremation of corpses, a practice not attested in Israel except in the case of plague, so the term 'burner' cannot exist. Another commentator (Snaith*) suggests rather the person in charge of funeral processions. This first attempt as solving the difficulties, which we can call traditional, is paralleled by those scholars who want to correct the text, regarding it as corrupt. A. van Hoonacker and, following him, Osty* and S. Amsler*, suggest reading *wᵉniš°'ārū nodᵉdē mispār*, 'and only a (small) part of the refugees will remain'; however, this proposal is not completely convincing because it does not take much account of what comes next. E. Sellin* would prefer rather to insert *wᵉniš'ar niš'ar* at the beginning with LXX (see below), 'and if some survivors come forward', a phrase which Rudolph* accepts, suggesting the continuation: *wᵉnāsᵉ'ū yᵉdēhem mᵉpannē lāḥūṣ*, 'when those responsible for carrying out the corpses lay hand on them to carry the corpses outside, . . .' A very recent proposal is that put forward by Ahlström: *dōdō* does not refer to a kinsman but to Josiah of the house of David, who in the course of his reform profaned the temples and altars of the north (II Kings 23.15ff.). Such suggestions, none of which is clearly definitive, show the difficulty of the text, if nothing else. And these difficulties are ancient. LXX read: 'And the survivors shall remain inside and their kinsmen shall take them and shall grow weary carrying their bones out of the house. And someone shall say to the person in charge of the house: "Is there still anyone in there with you?" And he will reply, "No one else." And the other will say, "Silence: do not mention the name of the Lord."' By contrast Vg has: 'And his neighbour will take him and will compel him to carry the bones outside and say to anyone who is in the innermost part of the house, "Is there still someone with you?" And he will reply, "It is the end." And (the other) will say: "Be silent, do not recall the name of the Lord."' It would therefore seem less dangerous to follow MT, while keeping in mind its very bad condition. At all events the reference would seem to be to a form of epidemic whose victims are being collected, an epidemic explained as a divine punishment.

[11] Rudolph* would prefer to put this after v. 8, but such an arrangement does not seem necessary.

1. This section too, like the previous one, is directed at the capital of Israel, Samaria: Samaria is told that YHWH will abandon it, that he will depart from it (v. 8), precisely as happens later in Ezek. 10.18, where the prophet sees the divine glory leave Jerusalem at its destruction. But this text presents some noteworthy difficulties. Whereas v. 11 can form the logical conclusion of v. 8 in that the abhorred palaces collapse (as also do the little houses), vv. 9–10 would seem to refer rather to a plague, as almost all commentators but Rudolph* agree (we shall examine his theory later). Now a plague can certainly be the consequence of an enemy invasion – one is described in *I promessi sposi* – and this invasion can be connected with the fact that God has abandoned the place which he had earlier protected: but the collapse of the buildings is not necessarily the consequence of invasion and enemy pillage; it can also be considered the consequence of an earthquake. However, that is not presupposed by vv. 9–10, where people, whether helpers or gravediggers, move freely through houses which clearly have not collapsed. So it would seem quite obvious that at least vv. 9, 10 are the product of one or more later additions, meant to explain v. 8 and its conclusion, v. 11 (which Rudolph, as we saw, therefore wants to connect with it) in an atmosphere of pestilence, a real product of the divine anger. Ahlström makes an interesting proposal, seeking to connect the text (which is deliberately obscure) with the destruction and killings which we can suppose to have taken place during Josiah's reform in 622–21. But the state of the text prevents us from arriving at results which have any more than minimal probability.

2. We have already met the divine oath 'by himself' in 4.2 and we will find it again in 8.7. This is an absolute pledge made by God, who cannot swear by anyone greater than himself. This is a dominant theme in the Old Testament which appears in the New, cf. Heb. 6.13: 'When God made a promise to Abraham, since he had no one greater by whom to swear, he swore by himself . . .' But the theme also appears in rabbinic literature: in the Talmud, bBer. 32a, Ex. 32.13 is explained like this: 'Moses said to the Holy One, blessed be He: "Lord of the universe, you would have sworn by heaven and earth, if you could say as one day heaven and earth will pass away, so too his oath will come to an end; but you swore by your great name, so that your oath too should last to all eternity."' These passages, usefully listed by Rudolph*, are thus an

essential feature of Judaism. And the content of the oath is even briefer: the divine joy is replaced by abhorrence at the pride of Israel. Therefore the only consequence can be that indicated in v. 11, a consequence which is not due to the circumstances or to disgrace, but happens by decree of YHWH.

3. Rudolph* would also prefer to see the consequence of the destruction in vv. 9–10; the house which stands upright would be the exception; a few survivors in the only building remaining upright, and thus a kind of elect remnant, where the figure ten indicates a minimal quantity, as in Gen. 18.32 or Isa. 6.13.[41] So this would be an instance of what Rudolph calls the 'exceptional and unreal case' that someone has succeeded in escaping, hiding himself in the most remote part of the house. So in this case it would be possible to suppose a destruction due to an invading army or even an earthquake. However, this explanation does not seem justified. The situation in v. 10 is clearly that of a plague with bodies piled up among the intact houses; vv. 8, 11, however, speak of a destruction. If nothing else, this is proof of the composite character of our text.

According to Rudolph* the 'silence' imposed by the searchers on one another would show the utter confusion of what is at work: they are afraid that the Lord, invoked and alerted to what has happened, might again intervene in a negative way, so at all events this is a desolate setting of the scene for what is thought would happen if YHWH deserted Samaria.

15. Two appendices (6.12–14)

M. Haran, 'The Rise and Decline of the Empire of Jeroboam ben Joash', *VT* 17, 1967, 266–97; J. A. Soggin, 'Amos VI: 13–14 and I:3 auf dem Hintergrund der Beziehungen zwischen Israel und Damaskus im 9. und 8. Jahrhundert', in *Near Eastern Studies in Honor of W. F. Albright*, Baltimore and London 1971, 433–41; Willi-Plein**, 44; Markert**, 170ff; M. Dahood, 'Can one Plow without Oxen (Amos 5, 12)?', in *The Bible World, Essays . . . C. H. Gordon*, New York 1980, 13–23.

---

6 [12]Do horses run on the rock?
Does one plough the sea with oxen?
But you have turned justice into poison,
the fruit of justice into bitterness.
[13]O you who rejoiced for Lodebar,

[41]H. A. Brongers, 'Die Zehnzahl in der Bibel und in ihrer Umwelt', *Studia . . . Vriezen* (n. 16), 30–45.

who said, 'Have we not by our own strength
conquered Qarnayim?':
Behold, I will raise up against you.
O house of Israel (oracle of YHWH, God of hosts)
a people who shall oppress you from the 'Gate of Hamath'
to the 'Brook of the Arabah'.

[12] 'The sea': the question as it appears in MT and in the ancient
translations (literally: 'Can you plough the earth with oxen?') is manifestly
absurd and robs the wisdom riddle of its point; moreover, the plural of 'oxen'
is suspect in Hebrew because it is so unusual: it is usually a singular collective
(*GesK* § 123). So the phrase is unanimously corrected to read *babbāqār yam*.
However, M. Dahood suggests understanding the preposition *ba-* as a
negative particle, 'without', thus producing an intact MT: 'Can one plough
without oxen?' But the correction also seems to give a text which is better
from the point of view of parallelism. 'Poison': Hebrew *rō'š₂*, a poisonous
plant not otherwise known. The argument is identical to that put forward in
5.7, but with different words. [13] Something has perhaps fallen out at the
beginning of the verse, since it is unusual for Amos to begin with a participle.
But it is impossible to know what to insert, even by way of a conjecture. So I
understand the plural participle to be a reference to a second person plural on
the basis of v. 14: otherwise the third person plural would also be possible, as
Rudolph* suggests. *L^eb̄ō' h^amat* is present-day *lebwe* (coord. 277–397), while
the 'brook' is to be connected in some way with the Dead Sea, cf. II Kings
14.25, which mentions it explicitly: either the *wādī el-aḥsa* in the extreme
south where the *'ārābāh* proper, the depression between the Dead Sea and the
Red Sea, begins, or some tributary of the Jordan immediately north of the
Dead Sea (Amsler), which is improbable. The *wādī el arīš*, the traditional
border between Palestine and Egypt, is to be ruled out. 'Lodebar': MT and
the translations read *l^elō' dābār*, 'for nothing', 'without a motive', but there is
an obvious play on words between the expressions and *lōd^e bār* (elsewhere also
written *lōdābār* and *lō'-d^ebār*), the name of a homonymous place, today
probably *umm ed-dābār* (coord. 247–247). In other words, the conquest of
Lodebar is not an important event, as the name indicates. Qarnayim is
located further inland (coord. 247–249), the present-day *šeiḥ es-sa'ad*. The
reference is evidently to the conquest or reconquest by Jeroboam II in
Transjordan to which the people attached a good deal of importance. [14]
'Oracle . . . hosts' is deleted by some scholars, as in other cases, like 6.7–8,
but others (Rudolph*) would prefer to put it at the end of the verse, where it
would go much better.

The two sections of this appendix are very different in content. The first of
the two asks two rhetorical questions which seem to expect a negative
answer. From this the conclusion drawn is: if the two things indicated are

110

impossible or absurd, how has the people managed to do what it has done, turn right into poison, justice into bitterness? The second question is clearly a popular proverb, which we also find attested in the classical world.

The second section, however, has a clear political content: you rejoice at the victories of Jeroboam II in Transjordan and think that the worst is now past; but the name of the first place is fateful: it is 'nothing', or 'without a motive', while the second, which would suggest power, often connected metaphorically with 'horn', falls under the same verdict.

So the two texts stress the absurdity of the popular attitude. In the second the play on words between 'nothing' or 'without a motive' and the name of the place (an otiose mention, seeing that Qarnayim is further east and therefore includes the territory of Lodebar) is deliberate. Through it the people is to be convinced of the lack of cause for their optimistic attitude: in political terms all seems to be going well, the battle for the liberation of Transjordan would seem to have come to a favourable conclusion and indeed the outrage of which the prophet speaks in 1.3ff. would seem to be avenged. But in reality these are only appearances: the worst is still to come. II Kings 14.25–27 describes the events and mentions a favourable oracle which Jeroboam II is said to have received from the prophet Jonah ben Amittai; v. 14 seems meant to be a negative addition to this oracle,[42] and the Jonah of the narrative proves to be a false prophet, of the kind there were at the time of Jeremiah.

[42]Following the plausible hypothesis of O. Eissfeldt, 'Amos und Jona in volks-tümlicher Uberlieferung', *FS E. Barnikol*, Berlin 1964, 9–13 = *KS* IV, Tübingen 1968 (137–42), 11f., 140, accepted by H. W. Wolff* and W. Rudolph*. Cf. also F. Crüsemann, 'Kritik an Amos im deuteronomistischen Geschichtswerk', *Probleme biblischer Theologie, FS von Rad*, Munich 1971, 57–63.

The Visions of Amos
(7.1–8.3; 9.1–6)

1. First vision: the locusts (7.1–3)

H. Reventlow, *Liturgie und prophetisches Ich*, Gütersloh 1963, 85; W. Brueggemann, 'Amos' Intercessory Formula', *VT* 19, 1969, 385–99; Willi-Plein**, 44ff.; J. M. Ward** 1969, 53ff. (for all four visions).

7 [1]Thus the Lord, YHWH, showed me:
Behold, a swarm of locusts was forming when the late seed began to shoot: this was the week after the royal reaping. [2]And it happened that when it had finished devouring the green of the earth, I said, 'Lord, YHWH, forgive, I beseech you. What can Jacob do? He is so small.'
[3]And YHWH had compassion because of this: 'It will not happen', said YHWH.

[1] 'Showed me' is the technical term for a vision produced from elsewhere. Note the autobiographical style of the account and its prose composition. 'Swarm': *gōbay* denotes the swarm of locusts which is forming and dispersing. 'Was forming': in the Hebrew text the subject seems to be YHWH himself, who is showing the vision, cf. also vv. 4, 7. LXX, however, read ἐπιγονὴ ἀκρίδων ἐρχομένη, 'A series of locusts which came', similarly Vg, without involving YHWH. This presupposes the word *yeṣer* instead of *yōṣēr*, a reading accepted by Amsler* and others. Be this as it may, MT does not say that God creates the locusts; however, he forms the swarm of them and he can dissolve immediately a swarm in the process of forming. At all events an emendation seems unnecessary. For the image cf. Joel 1.4. 'The late seed' (explained at the end of the verse by a gloss which would seem meant for an audience no longer familiar with the practice) could be either of grain or of grass: both look similar when they shoot. The term *leqeš* is a *hapax legomenon* in biblical Hebrew but appears in the 'agricultural' calendar of Gezer, *ANET*, 320: '(2?) Month(s) of seed – (2?) month(s) of late grass.' The destruction of the crop a little before the summer, when there would be no more rain,[1] is obviously fatal for the economy. [2] Note also the use of *mī* as a interjection, cf. *KB*[3], sv. § 7. LXX understands it as a subject:

[1]G. Dalman, *Arbeit und Sitte in Palästina* I, 2, Gütersloh 1928, 411f.

'who will succeed?' a translation which some scholars would also suggest for the Hebrew text; but it is improbable, given that *qwm* is intransitive in the qal. 'The royal reaping' (literally 'reaping of the king') is that of the first fruits, which were particularly valuable. Note the use of the root *gāzaz*, which normally refers to shearing, a meaning which it cannot have because shearing took place after the harvest, at the beginning of the summer. This could have happened because in Hebrew one of the names for the locust, *gāzam*, probably derives from the root *gāzaz*. LXX again had a different reading: καὶ ἰδοὺ βροῦχος εἰς Γωγ ὁ βασίλευς, i.e. an eschatological rendering: for a similar reading in LXX cf. Num. 24.7, where, however, it reads Gog for Agag.

2. Second vision: the fire (7.4–6)

E. Ullendorff, 'Ugaritic Studies within their Semitic and Eastern Mediterranean Setting', *BJRL* 46, 1963–64, (236–49) 239; D. R. Hillers, 'Amos 7, 4 and Ancient Parallels', *CBQ* 26, 1964, 221–5; S. Talmon, 'The Ugaritic Background of Amos VII 4', *Tarbiṣ* 35, 1965–66, 301–3 (Hebrew, English summary). See also the works mentioned in the previous section.

---

7 ⁴Thus YHWH, the Lord, showed me:
Behold, he called forth a judgment by fire [a rain of fire] which devoured the Great Abyss and began to eat up the fields. ⁵I said, 'Lord, cease, I beseech you: what shall Jacob do? He is so small.'
⁶And YHWH had compassion for that reason: 'It shall not happen this time either', said the Lord YHWH.'

[4] A judgment . . .' or 'rain of fire . . .': the first is a literal translation, but it does not give an acceptable sense and in any case contrasts with the verbs in the feminine; so following a conjecture put forward a few years ago it is now usually divided as *lirᵉbīb 'ēš*; the first term is not attested in the singular in Hebrew, but appears in Ugaritic (*WUS*, 2430, 2; *UT*, 2298) for a rain deity (Hillers); for another similar interpretation see the study by Talmon. Note how *tᵉhōm rabbah* has no article, as in Gen. 1.2. 'The fields': for this rendering of *ḥēleq*, normally 'part of, parcel of, participation in, property' cf. Rudolph*. Various authors (e.g. Snaith*) would prefer to render 'the part, the portion (of the Lord)', in other words as a reference to the people of God and its country. This is improbable. The second *ᵃdōnāy YHWH* is an evident repetition of the previous one and is therefore to be deleted. 'To devour': the verb should not be emended (as Weiser* and others would prefer); though it is true that the sequence consecutive imperfect – perfect is irregular (Robinson*), it is also attested in Ugaritic, as Ullendorff indicates. In any case the two verbs '*ākal* must have different connotations: that is the only explanation for the difference and irregularity of the tenses (Rudolph*, to whom I am indebted for the rendering above; for details see there).

In the first two visions Amos appears as an intercessor for his own people. The intercession stops after the second vision, a feature which can hardly be coincidental: the prophet is either convinced of the uselessness of all intercession or perhaps had been explicitly forbidden to engage in it, as in Jer. 7.16; 11.14; 14.11; 15.1; cf. 27.18. In any case we here have a qualifying feature which the two first visions have in common and which distinguishes them from the others; it is clear that in the economy of the narration we are at a point at which a substantial change is still possible: later, however, we have the announcement of irreversible judgment.

The first vision derives from the sphere of natural catastrophes: an individual locust or a small group of them is not dangerous, but a swarm is. Once the swarm had formed, nothing could be done about it with the techniques of the time. Now the swarm was only forming and could still be dispersed. In no way does YHWH 'create' the locusts, as Rudolph* would have it, but he does form the swarm.

The second vision includes mythical material, though it is not clear how much of that there is. The accent is in fact on the fire which is about to devour the fields, another phenomenon which derives from the sphere of natural catastrophes and which does not differ from the previous visitation in its effects. The mention of the 'great abyss' does not therefore seem to belong to the economy of this text. W. Rudolph has put forward an explanation: the expression would refer only to the subterranean water, the exhaustion of which would dry up the springs and therefore the wells. He also has in mind that the Palestinian sirocco, the Arabian *ḥamsīn*, is a dry east wind which, if it blows for long enough, can cause serious damage to the crops and therefore to the economy. But this text speaks only of fire and connects it with a cosmic phenomenon: first it burns the abyss and then it goes on to destroy the crops. It is not possible to say more and this passage remains somewhat obscure.

3. Third vision: the plumb-bob (7.7–9)

B. Landsberger, 'Tin and Lead: The Adventure of Two Vocables', *JNES* 24, 1965, 185–96; G. Brunet, 'La vision de l'étain', *VT* 16, 1966, 387–95; H. H. Schmid, 'Amos. Zur Frage nach der geistigen Heimat des Propheten',

WuD, NF 10, 1969, 85–103; Willi-Plein**, 44ff.; P. R. Ackroyd, 'A Judgment Narrative between Kings and Chronicles?', in G. W. Coats and B. O. Long (eds.), *Canon and Authority*, Philadelphia 1977, 71–87; G. Garbini, *Storia e ideologia nell'Israele antico*, Brescia 1986, 194f.

---

7 [7]Thus he showed me:
Behold, a man was standing right beside a wall built with a plumb line, with a plumb-bob in his hand. [8]And YHWH asked me, 'Amos, what do you see?' I replied, 'A plumb-bob.' And the Lord said to me: 'Behold, I have put a plumb-bob in the midst of my people: I cannot spare them further. [9]The cultic high places of Isaac shall remain desolate, the sanctuaries of Israel shall be destroyed, and against the house of Jeroboam I will rise with the sword.'

[7] An *[a]dōnāy YHWH* such as we find in the other visions has probably fallen out after 'showed' through dittography with the second *[a]dōnāy*; for this term, however, LXX[SA] read 'a man', a reading which many scholars prefer and which I too have adopted. YHWH explains the vision; he neither appears in it nor acts. 'Built with a plumbline', following the Italian Revised Version: the text is uncertain. The first *[a]nāk* (the word is a *hapax legomenon* which appears only in this context) presents difficulties to such a degree that some scholars would replace it with *'eben*, 'a wall of stone'. But this explanation and correction do not appear necessary, especially if we accept Snaith's* theory that the wall is the image of Israel whose uprightness is being checked. 'Plumb-bob . . .' is the most frequent rendering of *[a]nāk*, on the basis of the Akkadian *anāku(m)*, *AHw* 1, 49; this means 'tin', as Landsberger demonstrated in his article (and this is how G. Brunet and C. Hauret* would prefer to render it), but probably also 'lead', as *AHw* indicates. Hebrew has another word for lead, *'ōperet*, but this could be a technical term for the instrument in question. However, W. Rudolph*, preceded by others (cf. ad loc.), notes that the mention of plumb-bob or plumbline is incongruous here; these are in fact instruments for building, not for demolishing (but cf. II Kings 21, 13; Lam. 2.8; Isa. 28.17), and therefore he suggests crowbar or pickaxe. But the text does not refer to demolition but to verification, to checking that the wall is vertical and stable (Mays*); moreover the plumb line is still used in manual demolition, even today. In all instances LXX differs by reading ἀδαμάς, 'steel', and then 'diamond', while Vg at one point has 'clay', and at the other *trulla*, 'builder's trowel', which is also a building instrument. [8] Instead of 'in the midst' some scholars would prefer to correct to *b[e]qīrōt*, 'in the wall', again presupposing the implement is being used for destruction. [9] Note the orthography *isḥaq* for *iṣḥaq*, also attested in the verb *šāḥaq* and *ṣāḥaq*. LXX translates 'ridiculous heights', one of the meanings of the root and therefore

not a proper name, while Σ read 'Jacob'. The parallelism between Isaac and Israel appears only here in the Old Testament and in v. 16 and has not yet been explained satisfactorily; moreover it appears all the stranger because Isaac belongs to the South and lived in the vicinity of the sanctuary of Beersheba. A recent, interesting explanation for the unusual orthography of the name has been proposed by G. Garbini: we are dealing with an ancient, voluntary corruption of the text, aimed at eliminating Isaac, who, together with Abraham, is always connected with the South, from a context which deals with the North; and the name, thus distorted, has deceived LXX and Vg. For P. R. Ackroyd and I. Willi-Plein**, as we shall see on 7.10–17, this verse comes before that section, forming a summary of the prophet's 'subversive discourse'.

1. The interpretation of this text and the possibility of connecting it with the other visions in Amos depend on an exact understanding of its intentions. For those for whom the text presages the destruction of Israel (the implements for which would thus have already been prepared, whether a plumb line, understood in terms of its frequent use as an implement in demolition, or a pickaxe), the presence of YHWH beside or on top of the wall with something of this kind in his hand is sinister. Moreover the meaning of the first two visions would seem obvious to anyone who saw them, and had no need of an explanation; this one, however, had to be explained, all the more since the prophet, on being questioned, seems to concentrate all his attention on the implement in question and not on the rest. Given this interpretation of the problem, that of many scholars, the logical consequence is that God himself is about to demolish the people. But that does not seem to be the most obvious explanation of the text, as we have seen: here, rather, we have YHWH checking the wall, built with the skill of the craft ('built with a plumb line', v. 7b, not by eye), which is a symbolic representation of the people: will it stand firm in an upright position or does it lean or seem unstable, so that it will have to be demolished because it is a danger? Understood in this way the vision loses much of its initially sinister character: after all the wall may pass the text, or leave room for doubt, so that as in the first two visions there is still a chance of averting the catastrophe. But the result of the check is negative: the wall has to be demolished. God can no longer continue to spare it (note the use of 'ābar, 'cross', in the sense of 'pass beyond' and therefore 'spare'); it is leaning and may fall at any moment, so it has to be demolished. So the image seems to presuppose that previous tests have been made, checks which have revealed an increasingly precarious situation, even if only now has the time come for extreme measures. Until now there has been only a

situation of long-term danger; now the danger is imminent and there is a need to act.

2. For those who understand the text as an announcement of the immediate destruction of Israel by means of implements which God holds in his hand, v. 9 is the explanation of the metaphor of the 'wall': it would refer to the various cult places in which Israel had been wont to celebrate its own religious functions. But if we understand the text as a reference to the test in which Israel is found wanting, v. 9 simply shows the consequences of the 'demolition', the judgment, as a sequel to the failure to pass the test. The first element in the parallelism refers to those places which did not possess a temple and which were therefore the sites of cults and lesser devotions; the second refers to the sanctuaries, i.e. to Bethel, Gilgal and Dan. Both the abandonment of the minor sanctuaries and the destruction of the major temples are a clear announcement of the enemy invasion and the exile of at least a part of the inhabitants. And the judgment did not spare even the royal house: Zechariah, son of Jeroboam II, was assassinated in the course of a *coup d'état* (II Kings 15.10). Nor can we exclude the possibility that v. 9 is a Deuteronomistic-type addition, the aim of which seems to have been (Wolff*) to provide a transition to vv. 10ff., which interrupts the series of visions. In other words the text will originally have mentioned Jeroboam II, and then have been extended at a later stage to his house, after the sovereign had died quietly in his bed. Its character as unfulfilled prophecy (at least as far as its first subject was concerned) is clearly a feature in favour of its authenticity.

4. Fourth vision: ripe fruit (8.1–3)

W. Baumgartner, 'Die Etymologie von hebräisch $k^e lub$, Korb', *TZ* 7, 1951, 77f.; B. D. Rahtjen, 'A Critical Note on Amos 8.1–2', *JBL* 83, 1964, 416f.; S. E. Loewenstamm, '*Klwb qyṣ.* A Remark on the Prophetic Vision Amos VIII 1–3', *Tarbiṣ* 34, 1964–65, 319–22 (Hebrew with an English summary); Willi-Plein**, 44ff., 48.

---

8 [1]Thus the Lord YHWH showed me:
Behold a basket of ripe fruit. [2]He asked me, 'What do you see, Amos?' I replied: 'A basket of ripe fruit.' And YHWH said to me: 'Ripeness has come upon my people Israel; I cannot again spare them.' [3]Then the singers of the palace will lament in that day oracle of the Lord, YHWH; a number of bodies; they are cast out everywhere! Silence!

[1–2] 'Ripe fruit': as the 1924 Italian Revised Version already saw, it is possible to reproduce the word play of the original. Instead of 'summer fruit', which is the literal meaning of the Hebrew text (usually thought of as being fresh figs, which cannot be kept or transported well), and 'the end has come upon my people' (word-play between *qayiṣ* and *qēṣ*), one can translate the word-play by means of the idea of ripeness. Others suggest: 'A basket for the harvest . . . the harvest has come', or 'A basket of autumn fruits . . . autumn has come upon my people.' **[3]** 'The singers': read *šārōt* for the *šīrōt* in the text; the context calls for a personal subject; but 'Then the songs of the palace lament', in the sense that the songs of joy become lament, though a prolix and rhetorical expression, is not an impossible one. It is difficult to establish whether *hēkāl* means palace, as I have translated it here, or temple. Temple singers are not attested for this period. Others suggest *šārōt*, princesses.

The end of the verse is difficult. 'They are cast out . . .': the Hebrew has the perfect hiphil with impersonal force. Rudolph* suggests correcting to *hašlēk*, infinitive absolute with finite value, with the same meaning. The final 'Silence!' is like that in 6.10 and presents similar difficulties.

In many ways the fourth vision is similar to the third. Formally we have the same construction, as is shown by the effective table in G. Rinaldi*, 201:

Visions 1 and 2	Visions 3 and 4
Thus he showed me . . .	Thus he showed me . . .
And behold . . .	And behold . . .
	And the Lord said to me . . .
And I said . . . (intercession)	And I said (without intercession) . . .
	And the Lord said . . .
The Lord have mercy . . .	I will not again spare them.

There are also analogies in content: in both we have the element of checking, the result of which is negative, leading to the announcement of judgment. However, there is a difference in the fact that YHWH does not appear in the fourth vision, so we have essentially an audition. But it should be remembered that in the third vision, too, there are two LXX uncials which omit the vision of YHWH, so that it becomes an audition.

The play on words is similar to that in Jer. 1.11–12, where it is between *šāqēd*, 'almond', and the root *šāqad*, 'watch'; this is an untranslatable play on words. In both cases the word-play hinges on the assonance of two terms which are not necessarily connected at an etymological level; a similar case is recorded by Loewenstamm: Alexander the Great, who besieged Tyre in 332 BC, saw in a dream a 'satyr' falling, the interpretation of which was σὴ Τύρος, 'Tyre is yours', evidently this time a presage of victory; for details cf. ad loc.

A term *qs*, usually understood as *qayṣ*, appears in the Gezer calendar, *ANET*, 320, and denotes the 'harvest of summer fruit'. The homophonous *qēṣ* would come to denote the end in an eschatological sense, cf. perhaps already Ezek. 7.2, 6 and later all of apocalyptic. The specific significance of this discourse is explained by the last verse which portrays a funeral lament which has replaced the songs of joy.

5. Fifth vision: YHWH at the altar (9.1–6)

F. Horst, 'Die Doxologien im Amosbuch', *ZAW* 47, 1929, 45–54 = *Gottes Recht*, Munich 1961, 155–66, II. Gese**, 1962, 436ff., E. C. Kingsbury, 'The Prophets and the Council of Yahweh', *JBL* 83, 1964, 279–86; J. M. Ward**, 112ff.; F. Foresti, 'Funzione semantica dei brani participiali di Amos 4, 13; 5, 8 ss.; 9, 5s.', *Bib* 62, 1981, 169–84; W. Berg**, 1974, 25ff.; Willi-Plein**, 55ff.

---

9 [1]I saw the Lord standing beside the altar.
He said to me, 'I will shatter violently the capitals,
the door jambs will tremble
and all will perish in the earthquake.
And what are left of them I shall slay with the sword:
no fugitive shall succeed in fleeing,
no escaper shall succeed in escaping.
[2]Though they penetrate into the underworld,
my hand will take them from there,
though they climb up into heaven
I shall bring them down from there;
[3]though they hide on the summit of Carmel,
I shall discover them and catch them;
though they hide from my eyes at the bottom of the sea,
I shall command the serpent to devour them;
[4]and though they go in procession as prisoners before their enemies,
I shall command the sword to kill them;
I shall set my eyes upon them for evil and not for good.
[5]The Lord, YHWH of hosts,
is the one who touches the earth and makes it tremble
(and all its inhabitants mourn),
so that it all rises up like the Nile
and sinks like the Nile in Egypt.

⁶Who builds his dwelling in the heavens,
and founds his vault upon the earth;
who calls the waters of the sea
and pours them out on the surface of the earth
YHWH is his name!

[1] 'Beside': for this rendering of *'al*, normally 'above' something, cf. Ps. 1.3. Of course it can also be rendered 'on the altar' or 'above the altar', although the normal place to stand is 'beside'. Others would prefer to move 'told me' after 'the door jambs': we shall return to the question below. 'I will shatter violently': the Hebrew text has 'Smite . . .', presumably addressed to the prophet: there is no mention of the presence of an interpreting angel (cf. Zech. 1–6) or of other similar creatures: we would then have a symbolic action by the prophet: he strikes and the earthquake follows. Others would prefer to read *wayyak*, 'he smote', with YHWH as subject, then putting the phrase 'told me' after 'the door jambs' (Weiser*, Rinaldi* and Wolff*); though it is true that this produces a smoother text, in the first four visions vision and word of God follow immediately upon each other. But the construction of this text seems to be substantially different. I accept the proposal by W. Rudolph* for an emendation, suggested for the first time by K. Budde in 1925 and accepted by E. Sellin*; the proposal would seem conclusive even if MT is not nonsense: read *hakkēh 'akkeh*, an infinitive absolute plus the first person of the imperfect, which would have fallen out by haplography. The technical terms of v. 1a are respectively the 'capital', cf. Zeph. 2.14 (ἱλαστήριον of LXX = Hebrew *kappōret* is the product of an obvious mistake in reading the original Hebrew, while Σ and Θ have κιβώριον, literally 'beaker' or 'shell', but a technical term for 'capital', Rudolph*), and the 'door jambs': the part of the pavement on which the doors turn. This is clearly an announcement of the earthquake (a theme which appears several times in Amos), cf. the use of the verb *ra'aš*, which is the technical term for it. It is probable, as Rudolph* notes, that a half-line has fallen out here, describing the general consequences of the phenomenon: therefore he suggests inserting *wᵉyippōl hassippūn*, 'and the ceiling will fall'. 'And all will perish in the earthquake': a difficult phrase where only a conjecture can help. It is often corrected (Osty*) by replacing the imperative in the text with the first person singular of the imperfect: *wᵉ'ebsā'em*, 'I will make it crumble' or 'I will strike it'. But the root *bāsa'* never has this meaning: it always means simply 'break the thread' (a technical term in weaving) and hence, with a derived meaning, 'end life'. So with Maag**, 45, and Rudolph* I read *waᵘbaseaʿ*, also reading *bᵉra'aš* for *bᵉrō'š*, according to an old suggestion by P. Volz, though to say the least this is doubtful. For the explanation of *'aḥᵃrīt* as 'remnant', 'that which goes on', see Gese's article.

[3–4] The last *miššam* is usually corrected by deleting the *mi-*, but note the constant construction through vv. 1b–4 using the expression which, as Rudolph indicated, sometimes means 'there'.

[5] The Nile which rises and falls is here used as an image of the earthquake. This imagery seems problematical, cf. Berg for possible explanations. The only partially relevant one is that the rising and falling of a river is often seen in the Old Testament as being rather sinister: Jer. 46.7f.; Isa. 8.7; and other passages. The origin of the imagery is unknown, just as we do not know its function. It also appears in Amos in 8.8. [6] 'Dwell': Hebrew, 'his steps', but read *'ᵃliyātō* (dittography of the *mem*). The end repeats that of 5.8b, perhaps a sign that the doxologies go together; moreover, this fits well with this context and the reference to the earthquake.

1. The reader will note immediately that the fifth vision is substantially different in form from the other four, though like the majority of scholars I have partly modified MT. The introduction is different; there is no formula according to which YHWH shows something to the prophet; this time he sees immediately. Nor does the Lord ask a question and then go on to introduce an explanation of visions which are not obvious. Rather, the prophet immediately sees YHWH, as I have said, right 'by the side of (or above) the altar' and also hears directly the announcement of judgment and imminent catastrophe. If we read the Massoretic text in its present form the prophet receives the order to perform a symbolic action (in fact, in Reventlow**'s opinion, 48ff., this would not be a real vision but only an injunction to perform the symbolic action in question); and it would be this symbolic action that would give rise to the earthquake, to be followed by other catastrophes in turn. As we have seen, others would prefer to put 'and said' after 'the door jambs', further correcting into 'and he smote', with YHWH as subject. These different evaluations are symptomatic of the difficulties inherent in the text, difficulties which it is virtually impossible to resolve with certainty; and this is another feature which distinguishes this text from the other four visions. For these reasons some scholars (most recently Willi-Plein*) would prefer to detach this vision from those which precede it. In other words, despite some differences the first four visions seem to be more or less a unity, in terms of both form and content, and now appear to have been separated artificially by the insertion of the episode of the encounter with the priest of Bethel (7.10–17); the fifth is substantially different and appears to be separate from the others for quite basic reasons. Another reason for separating this vision from the rest for anyone who accepts the order to strike as being addressed to the prophet, following the Massoretic text, is the fact that it is impossible for

a man to give such a strong blow (Amsler* and Wolff*); however, this is a vision, not a physical experience, and moreover the whole event is a symbolic action which represents something rather than being identical with it, as Rudolph* rightly points out. Also in favour of Rudolph's emendation, which I have adopted, is the fact that in the other proposals the presence of YHWH beside the altar does not have any real function. However the task of the exegete, he again rightly points out, is to explain why this vision is so different from the others, though it should not be isolated from them. And here Rudolph's suggestion also seems convincing: the difference is to be seen in the fact that YHWH is seen inactive, while in the other visions he is either doing something or getting ready to do it. In 9.1, he only makes an announcement, if we accept the emendation to the first person; what he intends to do and what he will do soon, so that the 'brevity of the vision is in fact compensated for by the length of the audition'.

2. The prophet sees YHWH right beside the altar or above it. I prefer the first rendering, which is clearly the most obvious and logical: beside the altar was the place for the celebrant or the head of the cult to be placed; no one is placed above the altar. Nothing is said to identify the sanctuary which is about to crumble away and in which the altar stands. It seems logical that this is a northern sanctuary, possibly Bethel, the only place we know to have been a scene of Amos' ministry. However, for Tg it was the Jerusalem temple: YHWH will have left the cherubim, to approach the altar and threaten King Josiah, a theory which is clearly absurd, even if it has been restated from time to time.[2] But the fact that the prophet was probably thinking of Bethel does not allow us to conclude that he was in the temple at the time of the vision and that here, as in the other visions, we are in the midst of one of the great festivals (according to Kingsbury the autumn festival), as Rudolph* rightly indicates. The vision also presupposes that YHWH is of gigantic stature, so as to be able to touch the capitals of the columns which held up the architraves of the ceiling. This feature appears frequently in Eastern, especially Egyptian, iconography where the king is portrayed, represented in the act of trampling upon conquered enemies or being shown enemy prisoners. This feature could impart an atmosphere of fear to the scene, though it is true that the presence of YHWH beside the altar without any instrument of destruction in his hand and without performing any damaging action (as in the previous visions), where the priest normally stood to offer the sacrifice, or in the act of interceding for the community was quite a reassuring feature. So

[2]There is a list in W. Rudolph*, 24 n. 4.

this would seem to be a vision tending to confirm the people in its faith: that God was present at its side and would keep his ancient promises, his old pledges. But the words of the vision very soon destroy this idyllic prospect and fully confirm what has already been said in the third and fourth visions: the earthquake will make the sanctuary collapse, burying the faithful, and the few survivors have no chance of flight. They will be discovered even if they hide in the least accessible places: the underworld and heaven, Carmel and the bottom of the sea, or hidden in a column of prisoners.

3. The mention of the underworld is a feature of some interest, as Rudolph* rightly notes. In the Old Testament this is usually the place from which God is absent and in which relations with him end. In Ps. 88.6, 11–13 [EVV 5, 10–12] it seems no longer possible to pray or praise God in $\check{s}^{e}$'ol (cf. also Ps. 6.6 [EVV 5]; 115.17; Isa. 38.38).[3] But in the Old Testament itself there is also a doctrine according to which the underworld, too, is subject to the sovereignty of God, and this is a doctrine which in time gained the upper hand: Hos. 13.14; I Sam. 2.6; Ps. 49.16 [EVV 15]; 139.8, and others in addition to this text. Job 14.13 even prays God to hide him in $\check{s}e$'ol until his anger is past. It seems all the more absurd to want to hide from God in heaven, which seems to be his most typical dwelling, not to mention the other places on earth. Even the bottom of the sea is subject to him, so that he can command the sea monsters who have been tamed and enslaved by him (Job 9.13; also 26.13; Ps. 74.13f.; 89.11 [EVV 10]; 104.26; Isa. 51.9; 27.1; Jonah 2.1, 11). Not even looking for camouflage in a column of prisoners will do. All this seems to seek to present a negative parallel to Ps. 139.

4. As after 4.12 and 5.7, Amos also adds a doxology at this point, or repeats a traditional one which serves as a proof text for he had been arguing. It is also possible that these are texts put here by the redactors. In all these cases the doxology seeks to prove that God has done otherwise, to those who might suppose that he did not succeed in doing what he planned. This doxology has a traditional style, but also some special features: e.g. the references to the earthquake. Other variants are the building of his dwelling in the heavens and of the vault (the term $raqi^{ea}$ is not used!) on earth, while the conclusion of the passage is the same as 5.9; perhaps this was originally a single doxology with the same refrain, now adapted by the redactors as a proof text for various contexts.

5. In negative terms we should say of these visions that:

[3]For this last, difficult text see my 'Il Salmo di Ezechia in Isaia 38, 9–20', *BeO* 16, 1974, 177–81.

(a) There is no trace that they are to be connected with the prophet's vocation. This theory of a relation to calling was put forward by Wellhausen and has often been repeated.[4] But two features get in the way of its validity. According to the basic study by N. Habel, in the 'vocation scheme' we find the following more or less developed points: I The divine calling; II the introductory words; III the bestowal of the charge; IV objections, sometimes refuted by the one who is called; V confirmation of the vocation with possibly reassuring words. Now in the visions of Amos there is no form of a call nor any conferring of a charge; moreover, the visions extend over a certain period of time: some months pass between the 'late sowing' (7.1) and the ripe fruits (8.8).

(b) There is nothing to suggest that the visions are to be derived from an ancient liturgy of the Israelite cult, as H. Reventlow**, 53ff. would have it. We saw above that there is no need for the vision, even that of the altar, to have taken place in a temple (above 117).

[4]See my *Introduction to the Old Testament*, 221f., which expresses doubts. For the 'vocation pattern' cf. the important study by N. G. Habel, 'The Form and Significance of the Call Narratives', *ZAW* 77, 1965, 297–323.

INTERLUDE

Report on the Incident at Bethel

(7.10–17)

(*a*) *For the section in general*: J. Pedersen, *Israel. Its Life and Culture* III–IV, London and Copenhagen 1940, 180f.; H. H. Rowley, 'Was Amos a Nabi?', in *FS O. Eissfeldt zum 60. Geburtstag*, Halle 1947, 181–98; E. Würthwein** 1950, 16f.; H. W. Wolff, 'Hoseas geistige Heimat', *TLZ* 81, 1956, (83–90) = *GS*, Munich 1970, (232–50), 90/243 n. 39; G. R. Driver, 'Amos VII 14a', *ExpT* 67, 1955–56, 91f.; J. MacCormack, 'Amos VII 14a', ibid., 318f.; P. R. Ackroyd, 'Amos VII 14a', ibid. 68, 1956–57, 94f.; E. Vogt, 'Waw Explicative in Amos VII 14', ibid., 301; A. Gunneweg, 'Erwägungen zu Amos 7, 14', *ZTK* 57, 1960, 1–16; S. Cohen, 'Amos was a Navi', *HUCA* 32, 1961. 175–8; H. Reventlow**, passim; R. E. Clements, *Prophecy and Covenant*, SBT 13, London 1965, 36f.; N. H. Richardson, 'A Critical Note on Amos 7, 14', *JBL* 85, 1966, 89: Herbert Schmid, '"Nicht Prophet bin ich, noch Prophetensohn", zur Erklärung von Amos 7, 14a', *Judaica* 23, 1967, 68–74; J. M. Ward**, 23ff.; S. Wagner, 'Überlegungen zur Frage nach den Beziehungen des Propheten Amos zum Südreich', *TLZ* 96, 1971, (653–70) 656f.; Willi-Plein**, 46ff.; H. Schult, 'Amos 7, 15a und die Legitimation des Aussenseiters', in *Probleme biblischer Theologie, FS G. von Rad*, Munich 1971, 462–78; G. M. Tucker, 'Prophetic Authenticity. A Form Critical Study of Amos 7, 10–17', *Interp* 27, 1973, 423–34; O. Loretz, 'Die Berufung des Propheten Amos (7, 14–15)', *UF* 6, 1974, 487f.; Z. Zevit, 'A Misunderstanding in Bethel – Amos VII 12–17', *VT* 25, 1975, 782–90; P. R. Ackroyd, 'A Judgement Narrative between Kings and Chronicles? An Approach to Amos 7, 9–17', in G. W. Coats and B. O. Long (eds.), *Canon and Authority*, Philadelphia 1977, 71–87; Y. Hoffmann, 'Did Amos Regard himself as a Nabi'?', *VT* 27, 1977, 209–12; Z. Zevit, 'Expressing Denial in Biblical Hebrew and in Mishnaic Hebrew, and in Amos', *VT* 29, 1979, 505–7; A. J. Bjørndalen, 'Erwägungen zur Zukunft des Amazja und Israels nach der Überlieferung Amos 7, 10–17', in *Werden und Wirken des Alten Testaments, FS C. Westermann*, Göttingen 1980, 236–51; R. R. Wilson, *Prophecy and Society in Ancient Israel*, Philadelphia 1980, 266–70; R. Bach, 'Erwägungen zu Amos 7, 14', in *Die Botschaft und die Boten, FS H. W. Wolff*, Neukirchen 1981, 203–16; G. Pfeifer, 'Die Ausweisung eines lastigen Ausländers, Amos 7, 10–17', *ZAW* 96, 1984, 112–18; M. Weiss*, 102–6, 417–20.

(*b*) *On Amos's profession*: H-J. Stoebe, 'Der Prophet Amos und sein burgerlicher Beruf', *WuD* 5, 1957, 160–81; S. Segert, 'Zur Bedeutung des Wortes *nōqēd*', in *Hebräische Wortforschung*, FS W. Baumgartner, *SVT* 16, 1967, 279–83; L. Zalcman, 'Piercing the Darkness at *bōqēr* (Amos VII 14)', *VT* 30, 1980, 252–5; P. C. Craigie, 'Amos the *nōqēd*', *Studies in Religion* 11 (Waterloo, Ontario 1982), 29–33.

The eight verses in this text present a series of difficulties as well as forming one of the best known sections in the Old Testament. The abundant bibliography is evidence of its difficulties. However, the passage is not difficult at a textual level; indeed it seems in particularly good shape. But we should see if its situation is due to the fact that extraneous factors have been introduced into the text, as H. Schmid (followed and endorsed by H. Schult) has suggested, or whether there are real problems, not textual by nature but historical and exegetical.

7 ¹⁰One day Amaziah, the priest of Bethel, sent a message to Jeroboam (II), king of Israel, in these terms: 'Amos has conspired against you in the midst of the house of Israel; the country can no longer bear all his words.' ¹¹Amos has in fact said: 'Jeroboam will die by the sword and Israel will certainly be exiled from its own land.' ¹²But Amaziah said to Amos, 'Seer, go without delay from the land of Judah and prophesy there to earn your bread. ¹³But do not return to Bethel to prophesy: this is a royal sanctuary, a temple of the kingdom.' ¹⁴But Amos replied to Amaziah: 'I was not a prophet nor did I belong to a group of prophets. I was a breeder of cattle and I prepared sycamores. ¹⁵But YHWH took me from behind the flock, saying to me: "Go and prophesy to my people Israel." ¹⁶And now hear the word of YHWH: You say, do not prophesy against Israel and do not preach against the house of Isaac. ¹⁷Therefore YHWH has spoken thus:
Your wife shall be a harlot in the city,
your sons and your daughters shall fall by the sword,
your land shall be parcelled out by line,
you will die in an unclean land,
and Israel shall similarly go into exile,
far from its land.'

[10] 'Priest': the priest responsible to the king for the running of the sanctuary. [11] According to II Kings 14.29 'Jeroboam . . . slept with his fathers.' So we would have an unfulfilled prophecy, provided that, as Osty* suggests, this is not 'a somewhat forced interpretation of 7.9'; in which case, I would add, this would be the work of the interpolator of the passage. The

accusation of conspiracy was not so absurd at that time, if we think of Elijah and Elisha (II Kings 8–10).

[12] 'Seer': this is not necessarily a derogatory term, as some scholars suggest: it is used positively in II Kings 17.15, a Deuteronomistic passage. 'Go without delay': literally 'Go, flee.' 'Prophesy': literally, 'eat your bread there and prophesy there'. It is also possible that Amos had eaten at the temple table and had been expelled by the priest, hence the sarcastic invitation. **[13]** 'Royal sanctuary' and not 'royal palace', as is indicated by the parallelism.

[14] This is the verse which poses the most difficulties, as I noted in the introduction. There are two main problems:

1. How to translate the verbless sentence: in the present ('I am not . . .') or, as I have done, in the past ('I was not'). The problem is heightened by the fact that it is associated with another question artificially introduced into the text, that of the discussion begun at the end of the last century and still not over, as is evident, as to whether or not the great prophets are to be identified with $n^e b\bar{\imath}'\bar{\imath}m$.[1] It is often argued that the former tended to distance themselves from the latter for various reasons. Now this phrase is a verbless sentence and has an interesting parallel, as we have seen, in Zech. 13.5, which reads $l\bar{o}\ n\bar{a}b\bar{\imath}'\ '\bar{a}n\bar{o}k\bar{\imath}$, $'\bar{\imath}\check{s}\ '\bar{o}b\bar{e}d\ ^{ia}d\bar{a}m\bar{a}h\ '\bar{a}n\bar{o}k\bar{\imath}$, a reply which presupposes that the prophets want to hide their own identity; however, the second part of the line is corrupt (cf. BHK^3 and BHS), so it does not give us much help in clarifying the present context. At all events the text has the second part in the past, whereas the first, which refers to the desire to get lost in the crowd, is obviously to be translated as present. In this case too, given that in translation the verbless sentences take their tense from the context, one could think of the present, all the more so since the imperfect with *waw* consecutive in the following phrase, which usually indicates the past, does not necessarily do so. But it seems that the almost certain past context of the passage is an indication that the past should be read, and this is what LXX and 'A already did: ἤμην, 'I was', followed by Syr; similarly mediaeval Hebrew exegesis, Kimchi and Ibn Ezra (the passages are in Rowley) but not Maimonides. However, Vg already has *non sum*, though Jerome[2] explains in his comment that both forms, *sum* and *eram*, are possible. R. R. Wilson is another one who is doubtful but clearly leans towards a rendering of the phrase in the present. Following the now classic study by Rowley in 1947, many scholars have opted for the past: A. H. J. Gunneweg*, 1960, 1–

[1]Thus E. Sellin* 1929, 254: 'Amos denies that he belongs to the corporation of the $n^e b\bar{\imath}'\bar{\imath}m$, similarly J. Morgenstern, *Amos Studies 1*, Cincinnati 1941, 31: 'It goes without saying that Amos did not consider himself a prophet for nothing.' More recently in a similar vein see still N. H. Snaith*, 1946, 126; G. Rinaldi*, 1952; E. Hammershaimb* 1970. The absurdity of this theory emerges in 2.11, where Amos (or the redactor) makes favourable mention of prophet and Nazirite; 3.7, as we have seen (cf. ad loc.), is a Deuteronomistic-type addition. 'The dispute hardly deserves the attention it has given' (Koch**, 38), even if it keeps getting revived.

16; J. M. Ward**; J. L. Mays, 1969; R. Bach, 1981 and others; among those who at present favour a translation with the present are W. Schottroff** 1979; H. Weippert**, 1985, 2ff.[2]

I am ruling out some suggestions because they are inadequate: (a) *lo'* cannot be understood as an interrogative particle equivalent to *hᵃlō'*: 'Should I not be a prophet because I am . . ?' as G. R. Driver and P. R. Ackroyd would prefer because this contradicts v. 15; (b) it cannot be an emphatic *lamed*, something like *lū'*: 'Certainly I am not a prophet, but I am the son of a prophet . . .', a variant of (a) suggested by Cohen and Zevit.

Thus with Rowley, preceded by many scholars and followed by Wurthwein**, Robinson*, MacCormack, Osty*, Amsler*, J. M. Ward**, Mays*, R. Bach and others, it still seems logical to translate the phrase in the past. Before his vocation Amos was not a prophet but kept cattle and flocks; but when YHWH called him, he left the land and could no longer look after his cattle and his sycamores: now he had really become a prophet, but even if he was sent away, he would certainly not starve because on returning home, even if he could not continue his own ministry (after all, he had been charged with prophesying to Israel, not to Judah), he could always return to his first occupation, an occupation which he could clearly no longer pursue while he was at Bethel. H.-W. Wolff* also recognizes that there are a number of elements in favour of a rendering in the past (312f.), but argues that the discussion does not relate to Amos's past but to his present. But is that statement right? And if it were, would it exclude a rendering of the text in the past? To the priest who forbids him to exercise his ministry Amos retorts with a clear appeal to his own divine vocation, appealing to an authority higher than that of the priest, that authority from which the priest derives his own. So this is the most obvious rendering, once we detach the text from the problem of the relationship of the great prophets to the *nᵉbī'īm*. Moreover the phrase probably means: 'I was not a master nor a disciple of a prophetic association or a prophetic school.'

2. The second problem is that of the profession or occupation of the prophet before his calling. The use of the root *bāqār* suggests an activity connected with raising cattle, while the other word, *bōlēs*, is connected with the cultivation and processing of sycamores.

In the first case, if we can take literally the indication in 1.1 that Amos was a *nōqēd*, a title also given to King Mesha of Moab (II Kings 3.4), Amos will have been a cattle breeder, information confirmed by Tg, and not a herdsman or shepherd, as '*A, Σ, Θ*, Vg (*armentarius*) and Syr would have it. This occupation presupposes a fixed residence: cattle do not migrate if they do not have to, unlike sheep and goats. LXX also read αἰπόλος, goatherd, a mistake probably deriving from the reading of v. 15 (Rudolph*): the other Greek translations already mentioned have a similar term, βουκόλος,

[2]PL 25, 1077.

probably in an attempt to harmonize v. 14b with v. 15a. Amos would then appear to belong in the superior category of a breeder: a cattle breeder can also have sheep or goats but a sheep farmer cannot have cattle. For sycamores (trees which incidentally, as Jerome already noted, do not grow in Tekoa because of the altitude, so that exploiting them presupposes going to a lower altitude), Jerome speaks (PL 25, 1076f.) of *vellicans sycomorus*: other versions are offered by the old translations. Here we have an operation which involves making an incision into the cortex of the fruit before it is ripe to bring out the juices which would otherwise ferment and make it taste bitter. This provides modest food for humans and in particular fodder for animals during the dry season. Rudolph* rightly notes that Amos did not necessarily incise the fruit himself but owned the plants with which the operation could be done and from which he derived the fodder for his cattle.

[15] This seems to contrast with the previous verse and also with 1.1; it in fact speaks of the shepherd who follows a flock of sheep and goats, the meaning which *ṣō'n* always has in biblical Hebrew. But the expression appears with slight variants for David in II Sam. 7.8[3] and in this text could be an addition; that is, according to the theory of O. Loretz, who wants to delete it for stichometric reasons. Moreover in that case the tense of the phrase could at a pinch be used to date Amos's reply in the past (v. 14); this is the argument Loretz used. But the question is more complex and I shall return to it in the commentary. It is enough to anticipate here that as the theme appears to be literary, the expression used can be proverbial, without having any historical significance.

[16] 'Preach against': root *nātap* 'pour out'; 'words' is understood but we have to 'pour out', supply it. For the orthography *yiśḥāq* cf. on vv. 9, 17. 'Shall be a harlot': there are two possibilities, the first that she will be raped by the conquerors to outrage her noble husband, and the second that she will have to follow her husband into exile, there earning her livelihood in a precarious way. The two possibilities are not mutually exclusive. 'Similarly': takes up the theme of v. 11.

1. This text seems to be the only one with biographical content that we find in Amos. In fact, as follows unequivocally from the studies by Schult 1971 and Ackroyd 1977, the pericope cannot be given the biographical value that so many scholars want to attach to it, as it is characterized by the motive of the call of a humble person to a high office (Saul, David, and outside Israel, Sargon I and others). It stands out clearly, moreover, from the remaining material (cf. the studies by Tucker and Ackroyd) in being composed as a prose narrative, with the

[3]This is probably a pre-Deuteronomistic oracle, cf. T. Veijola, *Die ewige Dynastie*, Helsinki 1975, 78.

exception of the oracle in v. 17. It is not possible to establish whether it is a fragment of an original biography of the prophet, at any rate anonymous in the present state of our knowledge, or another work, perhaps an apologia by the prophet to justify his departure and therefore the renunciation of his mission. Most scholars think it improbable that it is a biography. At any rate it seems to have been inserted between the third and fourth vision by the redactors, who saw in the announcement of v. 11a a reference to 7.9b, that is, if the theory put forward by Ackroyd and Willi-Plein that v. 9 is really the beginning of our section, containing in amplified form the seditious phrases that Amaziah reports, does prove valid.

It does not seem easy to evaluate this text in a historical setting. It clearly sets out to relate the episode which made it impossible for Amos to stay in the north any longer and which therefore marked the end of his mission; in fact the text states that in Israel in general and in Bethel in particular there was no longer a place for him after the events described. And since we know nothing of any possible continuation of his ministry in the South (it would be improbable if we consider that Amos's specific mission was to preach to the North), it seems evident that it marks the end of Amos's ministry *tout court*. It also seems evident, after what has been said, that Amos and not Amaziah, as some would prefer, is the true protagonist of the episode (against H. -W. Wolff*).

As has been said, the episode seems to presuppose that the prophet has already been exercising his ministry for some time. The threat to the king may therefore have been one of the culminating points of his preaching. We hear virtually nothing of this elsewhere, except generally in 7.9. It should also be noted how the episode is not related by Amos in the first person but by others in the third, so it would seem clear that the redactors were aware that other hands were at work here, as has been indicated. So in any case the aim of the narrative is to motivate the interruption of the prophet's mission and his return home; and since a need of this kind evidently arose after his return to Judah, it is obvious that it arose there and not elsewhere. At the same time the narrative seeks to declare that even when the prophet is prevented from fulfilling his mission, the word he announced remains valid, a feature which also appears in the story of Micaiah ben Imlah (I Kings 22.10–38, cf. esp. vv. 26ff., or in that of Jeremiah, chs. 37f.).

2. The narrative falls naturally into two sections:

(*a*) The first, vv. 11–12, refers to the denunciation of Amaziah the priest to the king with an accusation, essentially, of subversion. As I indicated in the textual-critical section, the accusation is far from improbable if we suppose that the cases of Elijah and Elisha (II Kings

8ff.) were a precedent; moreover, as is well known, the latter is also mentioned in Hos. 1.4. And this was a *coup d'état* which put on the throne that dynasty of Jehu to which Jeroboam II belonged. The oracle of Amos, 'Jeroboam will perish by the sword', could be interpreted in this precise sense: the foreign policy of the king had in fact evolved, as we saw elsewhere, against a background of military victories and the recapture of much territory (cf. 6.13), so that his death in battle appears all the less improbable. In such a situation, an announcement of this kind could refer only to a *coup d'état*, hence the accusation of subversion. That Jeroboam then in fact died in his bed would seem, rather, to support the truth of the note: a prophecy which was manifestly unfulfilled does not serve for an invented story, where everything has to run smoothly.[4] The exile announced to the people, however, could not appear a real danger, given its manifest absurdity in the political conditions of the time. It is also to be noted, as Rudolph indicated, that the narrative is completely silent about the prophet's attacks on the national sanctuaries; this was probably considered much less serious and at the limit of what was permissible – if, that is, it was in fact a serious offence.

And Amaziah who, as Rudolph* has justly observed, is a court official responsible for an institution which is headed directly by the palace, feels in this capacity the obligation to denounce to the competent authority anything illegal or even only suspect that happens within his sphere: for all the extra-territorial privileges which the sanctuaries enjoyed in antiquity, in the East and in the West, the sanctuary of Bethel, like the temple of Jerusalem in Judah, depended directly on the jurisdiction of the king, the supreme patron of the cult, as appears clearly in what Amaziah says.[5]

Otherwise, the passage seems strangely incomplete. It is not said how many times Amos preached in Bethel and if he also preached elsewhere in Israel. The second possibility seems more likely, as is shown by the passage 3.9ff., and as also appears from his invectives against the dishonest practices in the courts: these last also seem to presuppose a knowledge of the complex material which it would be difficult for the prophet to obtain except through public complaints and private conversations. Nor is it said what kind of action the king had ordered to be taken in the face of potential sedition. In other words, the question arises whether the meeting of Amaziah with Amos was the result of a royal order which Amaziah was merely carrying out or whether it was

---

[4]Cf. L. Rost, 'Die Gerichtshoheit am Heiligtum', in *Archäologie und Altes Testament*, FS K. Galling, Tübingen 1970, (225–31) 228.
[5]E. Jenni, *Die politischen Voraussagen der Propheten*, ATANT 29, Zurich 1956, 38ff.

an initiative taken by the priest on his own account, in the expectation that he would be supported by the palace (thus Osty and Weiser). Yet other scholars even think that Amaziah acted on his own initiative before receiving an order from the king because he was secretly sympathetic to the prophet, out of respect for his charisma, or because he was really playing a double game, just maintaining the appearance of the zealous and strict official. But all this seems very improbable. The logic of the discourse suggests that the former of the two alternatives is the valid one. Since it is not possible to accept that the priest wanted to act against the will of the king, it is clear that he acted in accordance with the orders he had received: to remove the prophet from the sanctuary and to silence his preaching in that way. Only thus does the note make sense.

(*b*) The second section describes the encounter proper. Despite the dialogue character, which is not without some rhetorical elements, as I shall note shortly, there is no reason not to consider the essential elements of the story historically likely. One thing is certain: the priest Amaziah addresses Amos in a sarcastic tone, clearly speaking down to him. So this is not a simple, kind piece of advice: 'It is better for you to leave . . .', far less a quiet confidential talk about something that could get out of hand; and certainly not a particularly gentle warning, to help the prophet avoid condemnation to imprisonment and perhaps even to death. As G. A. Smith* 1908, [2]1928, saw clearly and Rudolph* has recently pointed out, 'we see rather the indignant irony of a royal official who knows that he has behind him all the authority of the state, facing a foreign starveling', 255; while G. Rinaldi* expresses a similar view: 'The "priest" in the complex thus has something of the commissary of police about him, firm but very courteous, the one who is removing the undesirable individual.' There are many resemblances here to the modern deportation order.

But despite all his sarcasm Amaziah recognizes that Amos is a prophet, even if he demands, not without a degree of logic, that his ministry be exercised in his own country and not in Israel. In Judah it will be easy for him to earn his bread because his prophecies against Israel and its king will be very welcome. He does not have the right to speak in Israel, particularly in the sanctuary of Bethel.

3. Amos's response is given in three verbless sentences with all the problems that they pose for chronological determination. In them the prophet says: (*a*) first of all that originally, before his vocation, he was not a prophet but reared animals, independent of external factors to the point of having his own fodder during the dry season, derived from sycamore fruit which he treated. (*b*) That he had never belonged to a

prophetic school as either a master or a pupil. He does not seem to have broken with his former occupation even if now he could no longer exercise it, contrary to what is so often said, because of the distance. In any case he could go back to his own profession when he wanted to. So it was not economic factors which turned him to prophecy (and both Amaziah's injunction and Amos's reply imply that there were plenty of people who turned to prophecy for such reasons!). Rather, YHWH had called him, as is specifically said in v. 15. This is a text which, as we have seen, poses a number of problems and which at least one scholar wants to describe as an explanatory addition. But the situation seems much more complex: this is a very widespread literary theme, that of the 'call of the shepherd or farmer' (there is a list in Schult's study, from David to our own times). And this theme 'legitimates' someone who originally did not have the requisites for exercising a particular function. That also explains the difference between the occupation practised by Amos (bringing up cattle) and the mention of the flock, a term which the Old Testament always uses only for smaller animals, sheep and goats.

So Amos's explanation is followed by the announcement of judgment: Amaziah wanted to prevent the prophet from exercising his own function and vilified him; therefore he will be prevented from exercising his own functions and be vilified. Moreover his attempt has been vain: the people will go into exile just the same! However, we do not hear a word about the fate of the king. So the character of retribution has been rightly noted by Rudolph; in reality Amaziah has outraged and ostracized not only Amaziah but YHWH himself, as Wolff* observes.

We find similar instances in the book of Jeremiah: the priest Pashhur in 20.3–6; the 'false' prophet Hananiah in 28.13ff.; King Jehoiakim in 36.31. We hear nothing of the fate of Amaziah, nor do we know whether and how Amos reacted to the expulsion order. Nor, as we have seen, do we hear anything of the continuation of his ministry in Judah. For theories about the later fate of Amaziah see Bjørndalen's study.

The 'Words of Amos of Tekoa' II
(8.4–14; 9.7–10)

1. Against the dishonest traders (8.4–8)

Cf. on 2.6–16. Also Willi-Plein**, 49ff.; J. L. Sicre**, 112–16; Markert**, 180ff.

---

8 [4]Hear this, you who trample upon the poor
and destroy the poor of the country,
[5] saying, 'When will the new moon be over,
that we may buy grain,
the sabbath, that we may offer wheat for sale?
That we may make the ephah small,
and the shekel heavy,
tamper with the scales so that they weigh wrongly?
[6] So that we may buy the wretched for a coin
the poor for a pair of shoes?
So that we may sell the refuse of the wheat?'
[7] But YHWH has sworn by the Pride of Jacob:
'Surely I will never forget any of their actions.'
[8] Shall not for a reason like this
the land tremble
(so that everyone who dwells on it is in mourning)
and all of it rise like the Nile,
and fall like the Nile of Egypt?

---

[4] 'Trample': for the problem of the relationship between the roots *šā'ap* and *šwp* cf. on 2.7. 'Destroy': or 'remove from the midst': for the contracted form instead of the normal *lᵉhašbīt* cf. *GesK* § 53q. In a context like this the *lamed* often does not denote the final clause, but in conjunction with a copulative *waw* denotes 'in the form of', 'so that', cf. Rudolph*, who rightly has: 'Who . . .' **[5]** The 'new moon' and the 'sabbath' are both pre-exilic festivals, cf. the commentary. Note the observance of the festivals, formally correct, accompanied by prevarication, an argument which Amos often pursues in connection with his criticism of the cult, cf. above 4.4ff.; 5.5ff. 'Offer for sale' is the meaning that the root *pātaḥ* sometimes assumes in commercial contexts, often in fact 'put up for auction'. Tg has a different text: 'When the intercalary month comes'[1] (thus to have another month), 'when they see the day of jubilee' (and debts are remitted, whereas the price of grain soars, since there is no sowing for a year). This is an obvious re-reading. Note that the first two half-lines speak of operations which are permissible, if honest, and the last three of operations which are always forbidden because they are dishonest; however, all are considered equally wrong by the text. [6] For the first two lines cf. on 2.6. But there are important differences, notwithstanding the analogies in form and context: there we have an accusation which the prophet makes on the basis of facts, whereas here we have a plan by dishonest merchants to reduce the poor to slavery. There are doubts as to where the third line should be put in the context: Robinson*, Weiser*, Rinaldi* and Wolff* would prefer to put it immediately after v. 5a, Rudolph wants to put it at the beginning of v. 6, i e after the speech in v. 5; others, e.g. Snaith*, see in its present position evidence that the first two half-lines are merely an interpolation from 2.6. [7] The oath of YHWH is therefore by himself, even if the expression is not clear because it is not attested elsewhere. [8] The sections aβ–b are almost identical to 9.5aγ–b; with 8b, 9.5 and with LXX, Syr and Tg I read *kayᵉ'ōr* (*BHK*³ and *BHS*). The form *nšqh* in the Kethib is a manifest error: 'is irrigated' makes no sense here; with Q I read *nišqᵉ'ah*, the same root as 9.5, which has *šaqᵉ'ah*. The first verb 'will overflow' is a gloss from elsewhere, no longer understood because it has been wrongly transmitted, and is therefore to be deleted. For Willi-Plein** the verse belongs to the next section.

1. This fragment is yet another piece of 'social' invective by the prophet. This time it is addressed to dishonest traders. One of their main characteristics appears to be greed: they cannot wait for festivities to be over in order to resume their business. A second is dishonesty: false scales, weights and measures to their advantage, thus cheating the purchaser.[2] In the first of these two cases, on the borderline of what is permissible, these merchants, infuriated because 'religion' ruins their business, seem to see religion as something against which, as Rudolph* observes, they do not dare protest openly, for fear of ruining their reputation, and also because the observance of the prohibition must

[1]The Hebrew calendar, which is lunar, adds an intercalary month in the bisextile years, doubling the twelfth month, that of Adar, and thus synchronizing the lunar month with the solar month. Cf. G. A. Barrois, 'Chronology, Metrology, etc.' *IB* 1, 1952, (142–64) 152f. So in the periphrastic rereading of Tg the presence of a bisextile year offers one more month of business!

[2]R. B. Y. Scott, 'Weights and Measures of the Bible', *BA* 22, 1959, 22–29; K. Galling (ed.), *BRL*, ²1977, 205, 93f.

have been very strong. So we are in the same area as in 4.4ff.; 5.4ff.; 5.21.ff

2. This text seems to be one of the earliest pieces of evidence for the observance of the sabbath, a problem with which we cannot deal here. The fact that it is certainly pre-exilic allows us to see beyond the boundary which is so often hard to cross, the exile in 587/86–539/38. One thing seems certain: that already when the sabbath was being observed, and production stopped every seventh day, it was the object of marked opposition, even if some information suggests that its observance was much less strict than in the post-exilic period. The mention of the new moon is also interesting;[3] this is a feast that is no longer attested in the post-exilic period, but it is mentioned in I Sam. 20.5ff.; II Kings 4.23; Ps. 81.4 [EVV 3] (where it appears in parallelism with *kese'*, 'full moon'); and Isa. 1.13 in addition to our text, while in Hos. 5.7 we have a text over which there are some uncertainties. In Ezek. 45.17 (cf. 46.13), the prince must offer a special sacrifice on that day. However, we know nothing of the festivities in question and their ideological and ritual content: the name, *hōdeš*, suggests the root *hādaš*, 'renew', so it probably celebrated the renewal of the month; it seems that it was a day of rest similar to the sabbath, or at least a day on which it was unlawful to sell things.

3. Scales, weights and measures of capacity falsified to give the greatest advantage to the seller and to harm the buyer are an ancient abuse. The scales are of the steelyard type with an arm and moving weight on one side and a pan hanging from the other, while at the centre of gravity is the hook by which it is suspended. Shifting the equilibrium gives the advantage mentioned. Measures of weight could either be filed or changed in such a way that they indicated less, while those of capacity could be given a double base, which in practice was invisible. To sell bad merchandise as good ('rejects', at best useful as fodder or feed) is also an ancient practice, while v. 6, if it is authentic, seems to imply an active trade in slaves, fuelled by insolvent debtors, who were sold, again for small debts.

4. There is discussion as to whether v. 8 announces an imminent earthquake or one that has already happened. The latter theory seems more probable: in fact the text seems meant to account for the catastrophe, and to explain the cause and the ethical reasons, understanding it as a divine judgment according to rules of retribution

[3]Cf. A. Caquot, 'Remarques sur la fête de la "Neoménie" dans l'ancien Israël', *RHR* 158, 1960, 1–18, and recently W. W. Hallo, 'New Moons and Sabbaths: a Case Study in the Contrastive Approach', *HUCA* 48, 1977, 1–18. All the information is collected in R. de Vaux, *Ancient Israel*, London 1971, Part V, ch. 15.

attested throughout the Old Testament. The problem whether this text can be attributed to Amos remains open.

2. The solar eclipse (8.9–10)

Willi-Plein**, 55ff.; Markert**, 186–9; Weiss**, 188f.

---

8 [9]And on that day it will come about, oracle of the Lord YHWH,
that I will make the sun 'set' at midday,
that I will darken the earth in broad daylight.
[10] I will transform your feasts into mourning,
and all your songs into lamentation;
I will bring sackcloth upon all your loins
and baldness on every head.
I will make it like mourning for an only son,
and the end of it shall be like a bitter day.

[9] Note the use of 'set' to describe the eclipse. 'In broad daylight', literally 'in day of light'. [10] 'An only son': for this rendering (literally 'the only') cf. KB^3 sv.

The revision of this passage and other passages in the book seems intended to recall 5.18, where there is a mention of the 'day of YHWH', which will be 'darkness and not light', an announcement the mechanism of which they seek to explain: this will be a solar eclipse. However, that the phenomenon has this character is not generally accepted: G. Rinaldi* rejects it, though he accepts that the prophet (as we shall see shortly) could have experienced at least two eclipses. Rather, he sees this as material by nature belonging to the various eschatological literary genres, in the categories of which the sign is expressed. On the other hand it is difficult to deny that the eclipse is the phenomenon that the text most immediately brings to mind. Amos may have experienced two eclipses, one that of 15 June 763, of which he was certainly a witness, noted by the Assyrian lists of eponyms.[4] This would fit perfectly with the chronological horizon of the prophet, to such a degree that Robinson* favours this explanation, though Snaith* appears doubtful. Another eclipse took place on 9 February 784, i.e. about twenty years

---

[4]Noth, *OTW*, 272f.; E. Thiele, *The Mysterious Numbers of the Hebrew Kings*, Grand Rapids 1965, 93, 218 (table); I have had no access to [3]1985.

earlier; we do not know whether the prophet was aware of having seen this. Moreover the problem remains whether these eclipses, attested for Mesopotamia, will also have been visible in Palestine, and if so, to what degree. But there are difficulties in accepting that Amos is referring to a particular eclipse: for example it means accepting that this is a *vaticinium ex eventu* and not a real prophecy, something which would have to be demonstrated or at least made probable (as, moreover, Wolff* rightly tries to do); it also seems to contrast with the eschatological tone of the passage. For these reasons W. Rudolph* and J. L. Mays* are doubtful of such attempts. At all events the eclipse as a 'warning sign of the end' (A. Weiser) also appears elsewhere in the prophets, cf. at least Joel 4.15 [EVV 3.15].

The sequence of events described: mourning, laments, wearing sackcloth, shaving the head, are features which are well known from the ancient cult of the dead (cf. Jer. 16.6), a cult which was later forbidden (cf. Deut. 14.1; Lev. 19.27; 21.5). However, they were hard to kill off, as Tobit 2.6 still shows. At all events the prohibition is not (yet?) known to our author, a feature in favour of an early date. The context suggests that the rite celebrated the death of the sun, a phenomenon connected with an eclipse, and that would explain the prohibition against practising it. The mourning announced will be terrible: like that observed for the death of an only son.

3. Hunger and thirst for the word of God (8.11–12)

Willi-Plein*, 50f.; Markert**, 189–97.

---

8 ¹¹ Behold the days are coming, oracle of the Lord YHWH,
when I will send a famine on the land:
not a famine of bread nor thirst for water,
but of hearing the words of YHWH.
¹² They shall wander from one sea to the other,
they shall go from the north to the east
to seek the word of YHWH, but without finding it.

[11] 'I will send': note the hiphil, which is rare but not unknown (cf. Ex. 8.17) for the sending of plagues (Rudolph*). 'Nor thirst for water': some scholars (Maag**, Rudolph* and perhaps Robinson*) suggest that this should be deleted because it artificially introduces a parallelism which the text does not require. 'The words': LXX, Vg and Syr read the singular, which many prefer. L. Markert**, 189ff., would like to consider all v. 11b as

a spiritualizing-type addition; the original announcement was of a famine which is here reinterpreted as a famine of the word of God. Similarly for 12b. **[12]** The *atnach* should probably be put under *yᵉšōtᵉtū*, but even if we leave it in its present position, the meaning of the phrase is correct.

This time the text does not speak of 'in those days' but of days to come: days which, as Rudolph* well puts it, will be of 'spiritual penury'. According to some scholars the text, if it can be attributed to the earliest part of the book, presupposes the expulsion of Amos from the North and therefore would derive from the disciples whom Amos left there (though we hear nothing about them); once Amos had gone away, who would now proclaim the word of God? The term translated 'hunger' can also denote 'famine'. As Pedersen indicates,[5] the presupposition of the whole discourse is that the word of God announced by the prophet is as indispensable to the people as food and water.

The geographical indications are at least strange: 'from one sea to the other' clearly means from the Mediterranean to the Dead Sea, the latter a sea with which the North had little or nothing to do; 'from the north to the east' is not to be corrected because it is the *lectio difficilior*. It probably indicates something similar; the text does not say 'from the north to the south' because Judah was in the south, and was a country which also lived by the same divine word.

Thus the word of God will become a rare product, to be sought everywhere because it is precious, but in vain, cf. I Sam. 3.1ff. and especially Deut. 8.3. In other words, it will no longer be possible to ask questions of God by ordinary means. This is an image known in at least one Near Eastern treaty, that of Sefire[6], 1–A, line 24, as a curse; here we read that 'seven daughters' (but the term is uncertain) will seek a husband in vain without finding him.

However, more than fifty years ago B. Duhm[7] saw the text as originally the announcement of a famine, similar to I Kings 17.1ff., then spiritualized into an announcement of a famine of the word of God; this theory has been taken up again, as we have seen, by L. Markert**, and would give a basically different structure to this passage. Note again how the expression 'hear the words of YHWH', which some scholars

[5]J. Pedersen, *Israel. Its Life and Culture III–IV*, Copenhagen 1940, 121.
[6]*KAI*, 222, and J. Fitzmyer, *The Aramaic Inscriptions of Sefire*, BiblOr 19, Rome 1967, ad loc.; cf. also J. C. L. Gibson, *Textbook of Syrian Semitic Inscriptions* II, Oxford 1975, 18ff., for this difficult text which is connected with the present one by M. Weinfeld, *Deuteronomy and the Deuteronomic School*, Oxford 1972, 195 n. 5. For an interesting and probably definitive solution see now A. Lemaire, 'Sfire I A 24 et l'araméen *št*', *Hen* 3, 1981, 161–70.
[7]B. Duhm, 'Anmerkungen zu den Zwölf Propheten, *ZAW* 31, 1911, (1–43) 16f.

would prefer to read as 'word', brings us close to the time of Jeremiah (cf. Jer. 36.11; 37.2; 43.1) so that theologically we would have to do more with Dtr than with Amos. Markert** would also like to connect this passage with the following passage, vv. 13–14; this is possible, but not necessary, as we shall see shortly. The temptation to connect the passage with the immediately pre-exilic period or even with the exile of 587/6 is great, though the features in favour of this are not decisive.

4. The end of the idolaters (8.13–14)

Willi-Plein**, 51f.; Markert**, 189f.; H. M. Barstad**, 1984, 143–201.

---

8 [13]In that day shall faint for thirst
the beautiful virgins and the young men
[14] who swear by *'ašmat* of Samaria,
who say, 'Behold your god, Dan,
Long live the "Power", Beer Sheba.'
They shall fall never to rise again.

[14] *'ašmat*: this can certainly be translated 'for the crime of . . .', but even then it is a euphemism for some kind of deity, probably with a similar sounding name. This is evidently the *'ašīmāh* mentioned in II Kings 17.30, and the term has been vocalized as if it were in the construct, when in fact this is the archaic termination in *-t*. According to the text of Kings the cult would have been introduced into the territory of Israel by the inhabitants of Hamath, settled by the Assyrians after the deportation of the Israelite population, but this kind of comment is not necessarily correct, given the late Deuteronomistic context. From the Elephantine papyri we know of the cult of a deity called *'ašīm bēt'el*, which has the air of being identical with this one. On the other hand the name could also be Aramaic: *'šm*, with a prosthetic *aleph*, 'name',[8] so that the deity could well be the 'Name of Samaria'. So a correction to *'ašerat* would seem irrelevant, despite the theories of Maag** and others.

'The "Power"': LXX has ὁ θεός, the indication of a tradition which saw the term as denoting a deity, even if it could not be identified. The Hebrew term *derek* is normally rendered 'way', i.e. the pilgrimage to the sanctuary of

[8]That was already suggested by M. -J. Lagrange, review of E. Sachau, *Aramäische Papyrus und Ostraka aus . . . Elephantine . . .*, Leipzig 1911, in *RB* 21, 1912, (127–37) 135 n. 1, who has been followed by many others. A. Vincent, *La religion des judéo-araméens d'Eléphantine*, Paris 1937, 655 (and cf. the analytical index), does not accept the suggestion but for reasons (that there is no evidence of *šem* with a prosthetic *aleph*) which have now been overcome.

Beer Sheba (Weiser*), but in Ugaritic *drkt* denotes power (*WUS*, 792; *UT*, 702).[9] So this is obviously the name or the honorific title of another deity. An emendation to *dōdᵉkā* (confusion between *res* and *dalet*), the title of a deity, 'your darling' (thus Snaith*, Robinson*, Osty*, Hammershaimb* and Markert**) is therefore inadvisable.[10]

This passage seems to be connected to the previous one by the theme of hunger. But in the previous passage, as we have seen, this theme is at least secondary and perhaps even to be deleted, whereas here it is central and indeed real. Moreover v. 13, 'in that day', here relates to v. 9 (cf. 5.18ff.). So it seems appropriate, against Markert**, to treat the two passages as distinct entities, combined by the redactors simply because of formal affinities like the mention of thirst. It has long been recognized that v. 13 is a parallel to 5.2; in 8.10 we have the common theme of lament (Rudolph*). This explains well why the 'beautiful virgins' are mentioned, unusually, apart from the 'young men'. The reader of this text cannot avoid the impression that it is an attempt to explain 5.2: 'the virgin Israel . . . fallen' has fallen because of thirst; then the thirst is changed into thirst for the word of God, thus giving the whole passage a theological tone.

There is a marked tendency among scholars not to attribute v. 14 to Amos: the prophet in fact speaks only of the cult in the sanctuaries and never mentions syncretistic or pagan cults. The deities listed here (and the list recalls that in II Kings 23.6ff.) cannot easily be identified, given that they are called by euphemisms or epithets, cf. the notes on the text for the details known to us. The term 'Samaria' (of whose cult we know nothing) could be used here as in Hos. 8.5: here 'the calf of Samaria' is in fact the golden bull of the Bethel sanctuary (I Kings 12.18–32). This theory is confirmed by the mention of the sanctuary of Dan, for which we have evidence of a similar cult. However, if this is 'the Name', we have a different deity and a less gross interpretation of the phenomenon, in that it avoids the confusion between the bull and the deity who rested on it as upon a pedestal (cf. moreover the ark of Jerusalem, which was a real divine throne). 'As YHWH lives' or 'by the life of YHWH' is an expression which very soon became part of the Israelite cult: here it still belongs to the Canaanite cult, cf. *hy 'lyn b'l*, an invocation with a very similar form, addressed to Baʿal.

[9]The problem has been discussed by M. J. Dahood, 'Ugaritic DRKT and Biblical Derek', *TS* 15, 1954, 627–31; his solution is accepted by E. Jacob, *Ras Shamra et l'Ancien Testament*, Neuchâtel 1960, 60 and S. Amsler*.

[10]For details cf. J. J. Stamm, 'Der Name des Königs David', in *Congress Volume: Oxford 1959*, SVT 7, 1960, 165–83; id., *Beiträge zur hebräische und altorientalischen Namenkunde*, OBO 30, Freiburg 1980, 25–43; and Barstad**, who offers a thorough analysis of the problem.

5. The election of Israel and the others (9.7–10)

J. M. Ward**, 1968, 72ff.; J. Vollmer**, 1971, 33–7; Willi-Plein*, 55f.; Markert**, 97–207.

---

9 [7]Are you not like the Nubians to me,
O Israelites? (Oracle of YHWH)
Did I not bring up Israel from the land of Egypt,
And the Philistines from Crete
and the Aramaeans from Kir?
[8] Behold, the eyes of the Lord God
are upon the sinful kingdom,
and I will destroy it from the surface of the earth;
except that I shall not destroy utterly
the house of Jacob (oracle of YHWH).
[9] For lo, I stand giving the order
to shake the house of Israel among all the peoples,
as one shakes a sieve,
but nothing falls to the ground:
[10] All the sinners of my people shall die by the sword
who say 'Evil shall not overtake or meet us.'

Again as in 5.1–2 the text adopts the metre of the lament, the *qīnāh*, 3 + 2. [7] 'Nubians': classical Ethiopia, present-day Sudan, whose inhabitants stand out by their dark skin without being black; they were proverbial, cf. Jer. 13.23. 'Crete' is usually identified with the biblical Caphtor, already attested in Ugaritic, cf. *WUS*, 1134; *UT*, 1291; others think in terms of the Aegean world generally; Σ, Vg, Tg and Syr have 'Cappadocia', i.e. a region in Asia Minor (a theory which is not to be excluded *a priori*), while *'A* and Θ simply transcribe the Hebrew term. For Kir cf. on 1.5; we know nothing for certain about this: Vg and Tg have Cyrene, Θ τοῖχος, wall, LXX βόθρος, 'ditch'. To what point we have ancient traditions which are trustworthy is hard to say. [8] 'The eyes of the Lord': some scholars would prefer to read 'my eyes', thus maintaining the first person of the context with YHWH as subject; however, changes of person are by no means rare in Western Semitic. 'Utterly': note how the negation precedes the coupling of absolute infinitive and finite verb, *GesK* § 113v, a feature which strengthens the declaration (Wolff*; Rudolph*). [9] 'Shake': for the impersonal niphal cf. *GesK* § 121a–b. 'Among all the peoples', perhaps an addition after 587/86. 'Nothing': *s⁽ᵉ⁾rōr* is an unknown term, rendered variously by the ancient translations: LXX has σύντριμμα, 'fragment'; Syr *d⁽ᵉ⁾qīq*, 'the smallest'. 'A, Vg and Tg, however, have 'pebble', cf. similarly the meaning in II Sam. 17.13. However, in that text as in the present one the stress is evidently not on the material which passes into the sieve and remains in it, but on the fact that nothing manages to fall. The image is obviously taken from sieving the grain after threshing (Rinaldi*), cf. Ecclus. 27.4: 'When a sieve is shaken, the impurities remain . . .', in the sense that they remain behind whereas the good material goes through (Snaith*). This image seems better than that of the sieving of sand; in that case the sieve is fixed and the sieving is done by throwing the sand against it. **[10]** Note the value of $b^{e'}ad$, which in this context is positive (Rudolph*).

1. This scene, too, seems to presuppose, as at other times, a debate between the prophet and his audience, probably the people met to worship in the sanctuary. As in 3.2, the people relies on its consciousness of its own election and thinks that thanks to that and to the status which it confers, no evil can happen to it (v. 10). To this certainty which the prophet unmasks as being false he now opposes a new doctrine: if in 3.2 the election is connected with a greater responsibility, here it is dissociated from all privileges over against the other people. So the other nations also have a history of salvation, even if they are unaware of it and Israel does not recognize it: their migrations, too, are to be seen in the context of the saving plan of God. This is the response that Amos makes to the objections of the assembly. Because there are objections. The rhetorical questions do not expect an affirmative reply. But as Vollmer** rightly notes, this is a completely absurd argument as far as the people are concerned. The reality is that not one of the phrases of the discourse seems comprehensible to the people, given the premises. Nor is this some form of degradation which the people has undergone because of its transgressions, as Sellin* 1929 would suppose: the question here is a basic one; here is a clash between two fundamental views of the same matter which are quite different.

It would seem evident that the oracle proper ends with v. 7; so much so that some authors (Weiser*, Amsler*) would prefer to consider the rest of the passage as a collection of more or less independent texts. However, it seems more probable that we should think in terms of amplifications due to comments, to rereadings, or to adaptations in other periods, for example during the exile of Judah in Babylonia.

The mention of the inhabitants of Nubia is not made for ethnic or even racial reasons; these are not a people that was considered inferior (a theory which is often repeated even today) but one which was far away and different: the God of Israel is just as concerned with remoter and more different people (and a sense of this distance and difference already appears in Homer, *Od.* 1, 23, where the 'Ethiopians' are ἔσχατοι ἀνδρῶν, Rudolph*) as he is with those closest to Israel, the Aramaeans and the Philistines. But strangely Amos chooses two enemies, one traditional and one of a few decades standing, and not for example the Phoenicians, with whom Israel had notable ethnic and linguistic affinities and with whom relationships had been almost always good. The parallel with the exodus from Egypt, a basic element of any confession of faith in Israel and therefore of any religious teaching, must therefore have sounded particularly scandalous.

2. The additions first of all produce an invective against the 'sinful kingdom'. This reference can be understood only as being to the kingdom of Israel, as the article shows, and not to any kingdom which is sinful, a theory which has been put forward by some exegetes from Calvin on (E. Sellin*, T. H. Robinson*, S. Amsler* and others). Nor does it seem possible to affirm with V. Maag**, 250, that Amos simply wants to stress Judah indirectly at the expense of Israel, a feature which would anticipate the positions of the Deuteronomist and the Chronicler. It is simply about the kingdom of Israel and that is enough. It is more difficult to say whether the phrase is intended to refer to particular features, for example those which Amos condemned in his preaching (an argument which is put forward by a number of scholars) or whether this is a form of global condemnation of the northern kingdom, typical of the Deuteronomist and later of the Chronicler, so that this text would have to be connected with the former of these two schools of history writing. W. Rudolph* rejects this second possibility and sees the invective as a condemnation for specific transgressions committed by the people. But that presupposes what it is meant to prove, or at least make probable, namely the authenticity of vv. 8ff. And it is precisely this which, for chronological reasons, appears all the more doubtful: only in 734, cf. II Kings 15.29ff., was a part of Israel, the northern part, led into exile by Tiglath-Pileser III and a reference to an event of this kind seems all the more plausible. So we must ask whether the reference is not directly to Israel and to Judah, now considered a single nation in the face of the catastrophe of the exile, as E. Osty* suggests. However, this would make the date of the text even later.

Another possibility is that indicated by H.-W. Wolff*, that v. 8a is a title to what follows: that would explain the use of the third person in place of the first.

One addition to the addition is the mention of the 'elect remnant' in v. 3b, a concept which does not seem to go with the subsequent image of the sieve in v. 9; this in fact continues and illustrates the thesis of v. 8a: the fact that 'nothing falls to the ground' can only signify the totality of the catastrophe. The image is clear; all the bad elements, whether of grain in the ear which is winnowed, or of flour which is sieved by the

144

baker, remain in the sieve: and even if they are not thrown away, they remain bad elements, at best good for use as fodder. So the reference to the remnant would seem secondary and seeks to mitigate the original harshness of the discourse; it seems to reflect the point of view of someone who has already escaped the disaster, considers his own group the elect and derives his own legitimation from there. One can think only of those who returned from exile after 539 BC. And if this explanation is right, then the expression 'among all the peoples' is not a late addition but a specific reference to the real purpose of the addition.

EPILOGUE

The Restoration of the House of David
(9.11–15)

J. Pedersen, *Israel. Its Life and Culture* III–IV, London and Copenhagen 1940, 548; T. C. Vriezen, 'Prophecy and Eschatology', *SVT* 1, 1953, (198–229) 205f.; V. Maag**, 60f.; W. Vischer, 'La prophétie d'Emanuel', *ETR* 29.3, 1954, 54; E. Rohland, *Die Bedeutung der Erwählungstraditionen Israels für die Eschatologie der alttestamentlichen Propheten*, Diss. Theol. Heidelberg 1956; K. Galling, 'Die Ausrufung des Namens als Rechtsakt in Israel', *TLZ* 81, 1956, 65–70; G. von Rad, *Old Testament Theology* II, 138.; H. Reventlow**, 90–110; R. Fey, *Amos und Jesaja*, WMANT 12, Neukirchen 1963, 54–6; S. Herrmann, *Die prophetischen Heilserwartungen im Alten Testament*, BWANT 85, Stuttgart 1965, 125ff.; J. Scharbert, *Die Propheten Israels bis 700 v.C*, Cologne 1965, 130ff.; T. C. Vriezen, *An Outline of Old Testament Theology*, Oxford 1958, 358; H. D. Preuss, *Jahweglaube und Zukunftserwartung*, BWANT 92, Stuttgart 1978, 138–41; D. Kellermann, 'Der Amosschluss als Stimme deuteronomistischer Heilshoffnung', *EvTh* 23, 1969, 169–83; S. Wagner**, 661ff.; Willi-Plein**, 57; K. Seybold, *Das davidische Königtum im Zeugnis der Propheten*, FRLANT 107, Göttingen 1972, 17–19, 60–7; N. H. Richardson, 'SKT (Am 9, 11) "Booth" or "Succoth"?', *JBL* 92, 1973, 373–81; M. Weiss, 'These Days and the Days to Come according to Amos 9, 13', *ErIs* 14, 1978, 69–73 (in Hebrew, with an English summary); P. Weimar, 'Der Schluss des Amos-Buches', *BN* 16, 1981, 60–100.

---

9 [11]In that day I will raise up the unsteady booth of David, and repair its breaches and rebuild its ruins, and restore it as it was in the days of old; [12]that they may inherit what remains of Edom and all the nations over whom my name has been called, oracle of YHWH who does this.

[13] Behold the times are coming, oracle of YHWH, when the ploughman shall follow the reaper and the treader of grapes the sower. The mountains will drip must and all the hills will be bedewed with it. [14]Then I will transform for the better the fate of my people Israel; they will rebuild the desolate cities and inhabit them; plant vines and drink their wine; plant fruit trees and eat their fruit. [15]And I will plant them upon their land, and

they shall never again be deported from the land that I have given them, says YHWH your God.

[11] The expression *sukkat dāwīd* is unusual, even if we find a similar phrase in Isa. 16.5 (probably an inauthentic passage):[1] *bᵉ'ōhēl dawīd*, 'in the tent of David', where there will be a 'government which loves the law'. Stylistically the expression is similar to others like *bēt* or *'īr dāwīd*, or *gēza'yišay* (Isa. 11.1), and other analogous phrases. The strange character of the expression has led to solutions being found which would result in different translations from the traditional one: thus Richardson wanted to read *sukkōt dāwīd*, the name of the place of the same name in Transjordan, identified with *tell deir 'alla* (coord. 209–178), which is mentioned several times in the story of the patriarchs and the settlement (cf. especially Judg. 8.5ff.).[2] This place will be restored to Israel in the context of a Hebrew reconquest of the Transjordan, a region which was part of the empire of David and Solomon but was then lost. The varying fortunes of the Israelite presence in the region cannot be discussed here. But Sukkoth is never mentioned in connection with David, nor does it have anything to do with Edom, but only with Ammon. So this theory does not seem to rest on a solid basis and it would be better to drop it, keeping to the traditional version. 'Unsteady', literally 'falling', is one of the key terms of the discourse. The problem has been raised as to the tense of the translation: does it refer to the time of the author (thus Pedersen, in part Rinaldi*, Dhorme*, Osty*, Scharbert, Preuss, von Rad and Rudolph*, cf. *GesK* § 116d)? Or should we follow the grammars of Joüon, § 121i, and Meyer, § 104, and understand it in line with the tense of the context, i.e. as a future, with the participle not as a predicate? Robinson*, Amsler*[3] and, in part, Rinaldi* opt for the future. Certainly this second argument seems to be more probable: so the booth is unsteady at a future time and it is then that it will be restored: hence the more obvious reference would be to the years 597/6–587/6 or even to the exilic period.

[12] LXX read ὅπως ἐκζητήσωσιν οἱ κατάλοιποι τῶν ἀνθρώπων, in other words the Hebrew *lᵉma'an yidrᵉšu šᵉ'rīt 'ādām*, with *'et YHWH* as object (cf. Acts 15.16f. which in fact adds τὸν Κυρίον). The last word is the result of a confusion of vowels in a consonantal text, while in the first case we have a confusion between *yod* and *dalet*. 'To invoke the name of someone over someone or something' is an affirmation of sovereignty, as Galling indicates. The reference would therefore seem to be to those territories which were under Israelite sovereignty at the time of David and Solomon

---

[1]Cf. my *Introduction to the Old Testament*, 263.
[2]Cf. my *Judges*, OTL 1981, ad loc.
[3]The former with a wrong reference to *GesK*, the latter with a wrong reference to O. Grether, *Hebräische Grammatik für den akademischen Unterricht*, Munich ²1955; cf. also H. Bergstrasser, *Hebräische Grammatik* II, Leipzig 1929, 68f., 13.

(cf. Num. 24.15–18). But the phrase is also Deuteronomistic, albeit only in connection with the central sanctuary, and does not seem to be used in political contexts.[4]

The negative mention of Edom could well be understood in the context of the polemic following the attack by this people during the invasion of Nebuchadnezzar II and the siege laid to Jerusalem (cf. Obadiah and Jer. 49.7ff.); but this dating does not seem necessary but only possible, if we consider the varying fortunes of relations between Israel and Judah and Edom during the first half of the first millennium BC. [13] Cf. n.a in *BHS*. [14] Play on words between *šūb šᵉbūt*, 'turn in the opposite direction',[5] and *šub šᵉbīt*, 'bring back prisoners',[5] probably a deliberate cryptic reference to the repatriation of the exiles. [15] 'Your God' is not to be deleted, as by LXX, or otherwise corrected: it refers to the prophet himself (Rudolph*).

The greatest difficulty in this text, as we have seen from the textual notes, lies in establishing the exact period to which the participle *hannōpelet* of v. 11 refers; and on the solution of this problem also depends the solution of the problem of the authenticity of this passage. Anyone who argues for the authenticity of the passage is for obvious reasons forced to connect the participle with the situation of the house of David at the time of the prophet, and those taking this view have included scholars of considerable reputation, like Alt in his Leipzig lectures in 1950–51 (quoted by S. Wagner) and G. von Rad somewhat later. The Davidic kingdom is ironically or sadly called an 'unsteady booth' (an expression which recalls one used for Jerusalem, a 'booth in a field of cucumbers', Isa. 1.8), full of holes; this would therefore be a series of references to the fact that after the schism which led to the break-up of the empire of David and Solomon only the part which was weaker in economic and political terms remained under the house of David, and a promise that the Davidic kingdom will be restored and reintegrated in its ancient glory (Scharbert, Fey). Isaiah 11.1ff. seems to say the same sort of thing (Vriezen), but here too the problem connected with authenticity is similar. At all events, it is evident to anyone who accepts the authenticity of this text that a promise of this kind would evoke special reactions in the post-exilic period, lending itself very well to rereading and reinterpretation, thus explaining two additions: v. 12 (Maag** and Rohland) and vv. 14–15 (Rohland). But in this view there

[4]Cf. M. Weinfeld, *Deuteronomy and the Deuteronomic School*, Oxford 1972, 36 n. 21, 193, 325, 327.

[5]The classical study of this argument is E. Baumann, 'SWB SBWT – Eine exegetische Untersuchung', *ZAW* 47, 1929, 17–44; cf. also W. L. Holladay, *The root šûbh in the Old Testament*, Leiden 1958, 110–14, and J. A. Soggin, 'ŠWB, šûb, Zurückkehren', *THAT* II, 1976, (884–91) 886f.

would not seem to be enough reasons to deny the authenticity of the text. In fact Maag** points out how in contrast to so many exilic and post-exilic texts there is no reference to sin and its expiation, no reference to the return of those who have been scattered, and no mention of the Messiah and how moreover the political side is suppressed. Seybold's position, 17ff., seems to be similar; he states that the features used in arguing for a late date are largely inadequate. So (p. 64) he sees the text as a new criticism of the ambitions of Jeroboam II, who would have aspired to the restoration of the Davidic empire. Rudolph*, too, argues that the mention of the 'booth' indicates that the house of David, though shaky, still exists and functions; thus, the oracle would be a kind of confirmation of Nathan's oracle in II Sam. 7.[6]

But as we have already seen in connection with the participle, it does not seem possible to consider the passage contemporaneous with Amos: it must clearly be regarded as a future reference, just as the whole of the context is future. In other words we have here a problem similar to that in 7.14, with a similar solution. For Kellermann the whole passage would be Deuteronomistic: v. 9 is a gloss, vv. 11–12, 14–15 are an announcement of salvation after the judgment, and therefore after 587/86, whereas v. 13 is even later, with a marked eschatological hope. This, moreover, was already the theory of Herrmann, Robinson* and Weiser*, while Fosbroke* would want to say that the birth of such a faith was possible only thanks to the ministry and preaching of Amos. Moreover 'in that day' is usually a reference to the day of YHWH, which Amos 5.8 called darkness and not light: how could it now be contradicted in such a blatant way? The grammatical and syntactical features, and indeed the content, thus favour a late date. This view is also taken by I. Willi-Plein**, who suggests the time of Cyrus and Deutero-Isaiah.

Depending on whether or not the text is attributed to Amos, its assignation to one or another literary genre changes. For Preuss, who considers the text authentic, the passage is one of the few oracles of salvation in Amos, or at least one of those which do not announce the total end of the people (cf. 4.5ff.; 5.4–6, 14–15) and which are therefore an exhortation to conversion. Von Rad, who is also in favour of authenticity, as we have seen, sees the passage as evidence of the pro-

[6]A recent attempt at arguing for the authenticity of this text is that by S. Yeivin, 'The Divided Kingdom', Chapter VII of *The World History of the Jewish People*, Vol. IV.1, edited by A. Malamat, Jerusalem 1979, (126–78) 164f.; the text is said to be an 'invitation to rebellion against the king and his powers' to whom Amos put forward as an alternative 'the restoration of all Israel under the Davidic dynasty'; thus the anger of the organized ruling powers would be very understandable. Yeivin does not mention the objections made to its authenticity.

Judahite tendency of Amos, while Rinaldi* would prefer to date it between 722 and 587/86.

The visions in vv. 13–15 belong to a well-known literary genre, what we might call popular eschatology, with tones which are at the same time both realistic and idyllic. In 13–14 we have a hope which clearly recalls Hos. 2.20–25; Isa. 11.6–9; 30.35; Joel 4.18 [EVV 3;18]; Isa. 2.24//Micah 4.1–4; Zech. 8 (Osty* and others), a hope which, we might add, is not attested in early times. The use of *šūb šᵉbūt*, which indicates the rehabilitation of the condemned, the complete reversal of the situation (cf. Hos. 6.11; Zeph. 2.7; Job 42.10), suggests judgment that has taken place rather than judgment to come.

With the final restoration of the house of David in the future (so that this passage ends with having a clearly messianic tone) remarkable material well-being also comes about, as we have seen; as Weiss indicates, in contrast to the picture in later eschatology, nature will not be changed; it will be blessed by God and made fertile by the constant work of man. However, this work will no longer be under the curse of crops destroyed by external enemies (cf. Lev. 26.3ff.; Joel 4.18 [EVV 3.18]). This, as we know from Zechariah, was the hope that the prophets held forth in the immediate post-exilic period, for the time once the Jerusalem temple had been rebuilt. But these are considerations with which the message of Amos clearly has little or nothing to do.